THEORY AND PRACTICE IN HISTORICAL STUDY: A REPORT OF THE COMMITTEE ON HISTORIOGRAPHY

SOCIAL SCIENCE RESEARCH COUNCIL
230 PARK AVENUE · NEW YORK 17

THEORY AND PRACTICE IN HISTORICAL STUDY: A REPORT OF THE COMMITTEE ON HISTORIOGRAPHY

SOCIAL SCIENCE RESEARCH COUNCIL
230 PARK AVENUE · NEW YORK 17

D
13
.S6
1946

THEORY AND PRACTICE IN
HISTORICAL STUDY : A REPORT
OF THE COMMITTEE ON
HISTORIOGRAPHY

SOCIAL SCIENCE RESEARCH COUNCIL

The Social Science Research Council was organized in 1923 and formally incorporated in 1924. Its members are chosen from seven associated professional societies in the social sciences and from related disciplines. It is the purpose of the Council to plan and promote research in the social fields.

ASSOCIATED ORGANIZATIONS

American Anthropological Association

American Economic Association

American Historical Association

American Political Science Association

American Psychological Association

American Sociological Society

American Statistical Association

The Committee On Historiography

CHARLES A. BEARD
                      New Milford, Connecticut

SHEPARD B. CLOUGH
                      Columbia University

THOMAS C. COCHRAN
                      New York University

LOUIS GOTTSCHALK
                      University of Chicago

JEANNETTE P. NICHOLS
                      Swarthmore, Pennsylvania

RICHARD H. SHRYOCK
                      University of Pennsylvania

ALFRED VAGTS
                      Institute for Advanced Study

MERLE CURTI, *Chairman*
                      University of Wisconsin

FOREWORD

By MERLE CURTI

THE POINT of departure for the present volume was the memorandum, "Current Research in American History," prepared for the Social Science Research Council by Professor Roy F. Nichols. This memorandum provided the basis for a discussion of "Trends in Research in American History" at a conference held on November 8, 1942, at the New York office of the Social Science Research Council. At this meeting a group of historians and the members of the Committee on Problems and Policy of the Council considered some of the relations between historical studies and other fields in the social science area. The historians included Charles A. Beard, Crane Brinton, Merle Curti, Paul W. Gates, Louis Gottschalk, John A. Krout, Roy F. Nichols, Arthur M. Schlesinger and Richard H. Shryock. In view of the nature and importance of the problems considered at this conference, the Committee on Problems and Policy asked a smaller group of historians to explore further some of the issues raised at the November conference. This smaller group was subsequently constituted as the Committee on Historiography of the Social Science Research Council.

The Committee on Historiography, as a result of several conferences and an extensive correspondence, decided that it might best fulfil its obligations to the Council and to the historical profession by preparing a manual designed to help clarify thought about history and to aid historians in teaching and writing it. The committee encountered a great many problems in its labors. Many modifications of our plans were necessary from time to time.

The first part of the present volume was prepared by Mr. Beard at the request of the committee. In this essay the grounds for a reconsideration of historiography are set forth. Long before Mr. Beard was asked by the

Council to take part in the November, 1942 Conference and to serve on the Committee on Historiography, he had, of course, given serious consideration to the matters discussed in the introductory essay. The members of the committee on the whole adhere to the main tenets of the essay. The material and the ideas in it, whatever contributions the other members of the committee made in the discussions, must largely be credited to Mr. Beard.

The committee believed that a survey of some of the major influences, especially movements of thought, which have affected the study and writing of American history in the last three quarters of a century, would illustrate some of the issues raised in the introductory essay and help clarify thought about the nature of historical interpretation. Professor John Herman Randall, Jr. of Columbia University agreed to prepare such an essay in collaboration with Professor George Haines, IV of Connecticut College. This essay is the second chapter in the manual.

Hoping still further to clarify the nature of historical thought, the committee gave much consideration to the problem of "causality" in historical writing. It decided to include a case study of the treatment of "causality" in specific historical works. Professor Howard K. Beale of the University of North Carolina has prepared an analysis of the handling of "causal" factors in writings about the Civil War. This essay is the third chapter in the volume.

The committee assumed that every branch of knowledge presents or rests upon a number of propositions accepted by persons competent in such fields as valid in themselves and for application. It further assumed that advances in any given field of knowledge are made by devising hypotheses for further appraisal, exploration, testing, correction, and generalization. Being in agreement on the foregoing, the committee then sought to discover what propositions in historiography, if any, could be accepted by the members of the committee as valid, as useful for the advancement of learning, and as worthy of submission to the judgment of historians in general. After a great deal of discussion and preliminary work, Mr. Beard was requested, as a matter of procedure, to prepare a brief list of tentative propositions for consideration. This he consented to do. The committee discussed, criticized, and modified the original propositions. This list was then submitted to the members of the Social Science Research Council and to seventy historians, chiefly in the several fields of American history. These scholars were requested to indicate which of the propositions they could agree to, as they stood; which ones they could accept, with minor modifications; and which ones they felt compelled to reject entirely.

Two months after the Propositions had been thus submitted, replies from thirty-five historians had been received. Of these fifteen did not seem to be opposed in any fundamental ways to the thought in the Propositions, although many took exception to the style and diction. Twelve were willing to accept several of the propositions, subject to modifications in style. Eight apparently rejected the propositions altogether or were so critical of them that they could in no sense fairly be said to be in even partial agreement. Many historians wrote lengthy comments. All these were interesting and many were very useful. The committee believes that this substantial body of comments is itself a significant document. It takes this opportunity to thank again the historians and other scholars who gave the benefit of their counsel.

In revising the propositions the committee took into account criticisms, both in detail and in general, wherever this was possible. In many instances, however, critical comments so canceled each other that it was impossible to make any substantial use of them. In addition to simplification of diction and expression, certain other changes were made, principally for the purpose of emphasizing the positive implications of the original propositions. In the work of revision Professor Cochran and Professor Gottschalk were especially helpful. Professor Gottschalk also consented to define some of the basic terms that had been used in the propositions. His definitions, modified in the light of comments and criticisms from fellow-committee members, precede the Propositions, which constitute Chapter V of the handbook.

From the very start terminology posed difficult problems for the committee. It was decided to attempt definitions of some of the most commonly used terms in relation to actual usages of these terms in representative historical writings, in relation to epistemological problems, and in relation to the other social studies. Professor Sidney Hook of New York University agreed to prepare such a glossary; and Mrs. Wallace K. Ferguson searched through a sample of writings on American history in an effort to determine exactly how a selected body of terms had been used. Mr. Beard, in a statement preceding Mr. Hook's definitions, explains how and why the original plan of the committee was modified. This statement, together with Mr. Hook's definitions, for which he alone is responsible, comprise Chapter IV of the report.

Finally, the committee decided that a selective list of articles and books on historiography and the philosophy of history would be useful. Mr. Ronald Thompson of the University of Chicago prepared the list, which concludes the report.

The committee makes no claim to having "settled" any of the issues with which it has dealt. It does believe, however, that it has contributed to a fuller understanding of certain methodological problems in the writing of history. It hopes that its report will prove helpful to graduate students of history, to lay writers of history, and to the profession itself.

CONTENTS

FOREWORD
  By MERLE CURTI vii

Chapter I
GROUNDS FOR A RECONSIDERATION OF HISTORIOGRAPHY 1
  By CHARLES A. BEARD

Chapter II
CONTROLLING ASSUMPTIONS IN THE PRACTICE OF AMERICAN
HISTORIANS 15
  By JOHN HERMAN RANDALL, JR., AND GEORGE HAINES, IV

Chapter III
WHAT HISTORIANS HAVE SAID ABOUT THE CAUSES OF THE
CIVIL WAR 53
  By HOWARD K. BEALE

Chapter IV
PROBLEMS OF TERMINOLOGY IN HISTORICAL WRITING 103
  1—Note on the Need for Greater Precision in the Use of Historical Terms. *By* CHARLES A. BEARD
  2—Illustrations. *By* SIDNEY HOOK

Chapter V
PROPOSITIONS 131

Chapter VI
SELECTIVE READING LIST ON HISTORIOGRAPHY AND THE PHILOSOPHY OF HISTORY 141
  By RONALD THOMPSON

CHAPTER I

GROUNDS FOR A RECONSIDERATION OF HISTORIOGRAPHY

By CHARLES A. BEARD

IF A DESIRE to advance learning or increase precision of knowledge requires any justification, practical as well as theoretical grounds may be put forward to warrant a plea for a reconsideration of historiography —the business of studying, thinking about, and writing about history. Practical persons—academic and lay—concerned primarily with public or private affairs and absorbed in "the instant need of things," are, to be sure, likely to question at once the truth or relevance of this contention. By such "practitioners" history is often, if not commonly, regarded as a kind of old almanac or as an ancient, if sometimes amusing, chronicle, without utility or pertinence in framing and executing policies for the conduct of affairs, public or private.

When leaders in politics, business, labor, agriculture, or other activities deemed "practical," set about forming programs for action they seldom, if ever, think of devoting long weeks and months to the study of history as possibly germane to their procedure. On the contrary, when in the presence of a problem to be handled, they are inclined to employ their impressions derived from current experiences in such affairs; and, if supplements are regarded as desirable, to make use of treatises on law, economics, government, and foreign affairs, or other special works presumably directed to practical ends. To practitioners in general the idea of having recourse to history in a search for firm guidance to effective action would therefore seem to be a waste of time if not absurd.

Yet in the speeches and declarations made by articulate persons among practitioners—economists, reformers, politicians, business men, labor leaders, for instance—and in the newspapers and journals published for their information and satisfaction appeals to "history" occur with striking frequency. The word flows with ease from the pens of publicists, editors, columnists, and other writers for the general public; it crops up in the periods of orators, radio commentators, and special pleaders engaged in advancing practical interests, or for that matter advocating impractical, even dangerous, delusions. History is indeed often treated as the court of last resort by such instructors of the public when they are impressed by the need of "proving" the validity of their propositions, dogmas, and assertions. Men and women who could not demonstrate the simplest proposition in mathematics, chemistry, or physics, or pass a high school examination in history feel perfectly competent to demonstrate the soundness of any public or private policy they espouse by making reference to history, or at least feel competent enough to use history in efforts to support that soundness.

Among the phrases which appear in the speeches and writings of or for practitioners, the following are so common as to be clichés:

All history proves.
The lesson of history is plain.
History demonstrates.
History shows.
History teaches.
History affirms.
History confirms.
History repeats itself.
History makes it clear.
An understanding of history settles the question.
All that belongs to ancient history.
If history is taken as our guide.
The verdict of history has been pronounced in our favor.
His place in history is secure.
The verdict of history is against any such folly.
The truth of history corroborates.
History admits no such contention.
Let us turn to history and see.
The history of that matter is definitely closed.
All history up to the present has been the history of class struggles.
American history must be taught in the schools.

The appeals of publicists to history in short form are frequently supplemented by efforts on their part to "historicize" long arguments for one cause or another; that is, to make what purports to be more or less elaborate statements of historical facts, real or alleged, in a resolve to sustain in this fashion the invincibility of their assertions and contentions.

Although there is no way of measuring the influence of historicizations on public opinion, the immense circulation they attain seems to indicate that laborious students of history probably have less influence in national life than men of science had, let us say, in the New England of Cotton Mather. Great applause is given to works which purport to be authenticated by references to history but in fact bear about the same relation to historical knowledge that astrology bears to astronomy.

Thus recent and current experiences present to workers in historiography a dilemma pertaining to the nature and uses of their work. History is treated as having little or no relation to the conduct of practical affairs and yet is constantly employed in efforts to validate the gravest policies, proposals, contentions, and dogmas advanced for adoption in respect of domestic and foreign affairs. Either historians have failed in giving precision, limitations, and social significance to their work or, by their writings, have lent countenance to the idea that almost any pressing public question can be indefeasibly answered by citations or illustrations selected from historical writings. History can scarcely be at the same time a useless old almanac and the ultimate source of knowledge and "laws" for demonstrating the invincible validity of policies proposed or already in practice.

Here then is a contradiction in contemporary thought which involves nothing less than the fundamentals of historiography in relation to practical affairs of the gravest import. On this ground alone a call for the reconsideration of historiography appears to have ample justification wholly apart from the love of knowledge in itself or the advancement of learning for its own sake.

Reasons involving a still wider reach of philosophic understanding, and yet with a bearing on practical affairs, also justify such a reconsideration. The Western world has long been at a crisis in thought and learning, as well as in practice—the most widespread and tumultuous crisis of the kind since the beginning of recorded history. This is a contention which scarcely needs a supporting argument. The state of things human around the globe demonstrates the soundness of the proposition. If it be urged that the calamities from which mankind suffers are really due to "economic maladjustments," it can hardly be denied that these maladjustments have occurred *in* history-as-actuality[1] and have, in some measure at least, grown out of defects in practical knowledge of history and out of incapacity for thinking about ways and means of preventing them or overcoming them. And if we are to mitigate or overcome them, effective intellectual operations of some kind must precede or accompany effective action in respect of

---

[1] Owing to the loose uses of the term "history" it is necessary in the interest of precision to make preliminary definitions of terms. Otherwise confusion may be confounded. In these pages history-as-actuality means all that has been felt, thought, imagined, said, and done by human beings as such and in relation to one another and to their environment since the beginning of mankind's operations on this planet. *Written-history* is a systematic or fragmentary narration or account purporting to deal with all or part of this history-as-actuality. *History-as-record* consists of the documents and memorials pertaining to history-as-actuality on which written-history is or should be based. Of course for recent history, a writer may use in part his own experiences and observations and oral statements by his contemporaries which he has heard and remembered or written down. Unless these distinctions are made clear by the context they should be explicitly set forth whenever the word "history" is used.

them, unless forsooth action is to be taken thoughtlessly, on impulsive opinions alone.

Since this crisis in thought has occurred *in* and is an aspect of history-as-actuality, then in the nature of things efforts to deal with it in terms of the realities out of which it came involve knowledge of and interpretations of this history. In every attempt to "explain" how we have come into the present state of things, recourse is had, even by persons wholly uneducated, to events, ideas, interests, and personalities of history-as-actuality recent in time. All public policies and personal designs framed with a view to bringing about an ideal or better state of things either present interpretations of history-as-actuality or are based on assumptions, explicit or tacit, respecting the nature of that actuality, past, present, and in the process of becoming. Broad and sweeping as this generalization appears, it is, I believe, incontrovertible and presents one of the supreme intellectual challenges of our time.

Even in times called "normal" similar reliances on interpretations of history-as-actuality occur. Such times are in fact only "epochs" or "stages" of history, general or local or regional. They are epochs characterized by peace or relative peace, in which economy is fairly prosperous or stable, and governments, besides being stable, are less active than in wartime and intervene less in what is called "the natural course" of private affairs—the economic and other undertakings of individuals and concerns.

The idea of "the natural (or normal) course" in human affairs is itself an interpretation of history. By its very terms it implies that such a course is as predominant or general in history as processes are in physical nature and that if broken or interrupted it will or can be recovered or restored, as physical nature tends to overcome aberrations or eccentricities. It assumes furthermore that such a course in human affairs is natural, without inquiring whether *all* nature is taken into account, and that other courses are unnatural, without wondering how and why a part or period of history can be "natural," that is, nature-like, and another part or period can be "unnatural." Here is a dualism in history which arbitrarily breaks the interrelations of events, ideas, interests, and personalities known to exist in history-as-actuality. In addition, it raises one of the most fundamental of historical questions: Does history repeat itself, so that the state of affairs prevailing in some past epoch—as distinguished from merely analogous or similar conditions—will be or may be restored or recovered?

Under the sway of the idea of the normal or the natural—an idea essentially historical—public and private policies are frequently based on the assumption that there will be a return to former conditions or that given actions can bring it about. Statesmen assume that if they act in a particular manner or refrain from action, the return they desire will occur in history to come. Directors of private economic affairs likewise make their calculations on the assumption that the course of history in the past has in fact disclosed, or has permitted, such exact returns, and that the future course—a continuation of the past and present flow—will be or may be made in conformity to expectations. It has been said, even with justification, that military men generally base the beginning of every new war on the experiences of the last war rather than on an exploration of the new potentials or on Napoleon's maxim of "act and then see" (on s'engage et alors on voit).

It appears, therefore, that the idea of history which bulks large in discourses and writings of practitioners and their spokesmen enters also into the daily calculations for action in "normal" as well as "critical" times. Hence, all branches of learning that deal with practice come into any comprehensive consideration of history-as-actuality, and of the nature and uses of written-history.

Indeed all the humanistic sciences—that is, organized bodies of knowledge and thought pertaining to human affairs—including historiography and the social sciences, whether concerned with theory or practice, are a part of history-as-actuality and rest upon assumptions respecting the nature of that history.[2] It is true that workers and writers in these sciences —economics, politics, sociology, anthropology, psychology, ethics, esthetics, etc.—may show little interest in history as such, may indeed claim to discard written-history as irrelevant or useless. Yet all the data of all these humanistic sciences are selected from the data of human experience in time and space, the actuality called history; and the humanistic sciences certainly consist of abstractions drawn from knowledge of phases of human life as lived in history—particular phases such as economic, political, esthetic, or ethical interests and activities—and in turn these sciences become aspects of history-as-actuality.

Great thinkers in the humanistic sciences employ abstractions drawn from knowledge of history-as-actuality and thus covering less than the totality of human life in its time-span. In analyzing, selecting, and organizing their data, they make these abstractions serve their purposes as constructs or fictions[3] based on emphasized particularities, or phases, of

---

[2] Such assumptions, for example, presuppose that things will continue very much as they are, that some former state of affairs will be more or less restored, or that one or more of certain current tendencies will become dominant through change. In any case here appears a theory of a continuum of some kind, a rejection of the idea that history-as-actuality is a senseless chaos of unrelated events, and a penchant for the old or the new which enters into the selection and ordering of "facts" and "dicta" for presentation as economics, sociology, political science, etc.

[3] "*Fictio* means, in the first place, an activity of *fingere,* that is to say, of constructing, forming, giving shape, elaborating, presenting, artistically fashioning; conceiving, thinking, imagining, assuming, planning, devising, inventing. Secondly, it refers to the

history-as-actuality. By making use of such constructs or fictions they advance their respective sciences.

For example, Adam Smith was deeply impressed by the existence of moral sentiments in history. He wrote a book on the subject. Yet when he came to formulating his influential work on *The Wealth of Nations*, he put moral sentiments aside and created the abstraction known as "the economic man" to guide him in his study and writing. In adopting this fiction, Smith evidently assumed that moral sentiments and other manifestations of human history could be taken for granted, would remain more or less constant or at all events would not vitiate the correctness of his economic reasoning and conclusions. He drew upon knowledge of history-as-actuality and his observations of history in the making around him for the data he employed, for information respecting the policies he deplored or approved, and for illustrations of the policies he condemned or advocated. His work was an expression of history-as-actuality and of thought about it in his own age, and his powerful polemic entered into the shaping of history.

The fiction of the economic man was highly useful for many purposes in examining and predicting the behavior of human beings in relation to the production and distribution of wealth. It is still highly useful. Without it we should know a great deal less than we do about the nature of human affairs and we should not be as well equipped to deal with many situations of life, large and small.

But as Adam Smith proceeded he almost became a victim of his own fiction. When he confronted the issue of justifying his emphasis on the economic man and explaining how it came about that general good resulted from the avid pursuit of material interests by acquisitive individuals, Smith lamely referred to the "invisible hand," to some mysterious providence which turns individual greed into collective beneficence. Here he introduced something besides the economic man and sought to escape the moral question that he himself had raised. Here, in effect, he made a fundamental interpretation respecting the nature of all history-as-actuality in which economic men operate.

"The political man"—likewise an abstraction from history—is an overarching fiction employed by political scientists and is useful to them in forming categories, framing maxims and axioms, and attempting predictions respecting political behavior. It also rests upon assumptions concerning the nature of history-as-actuality, the changing contexture or relation-

---

product of these activities, the fictional assumption, fabrication, creation, the imagined case." Students and practitioners in law and natural science openly make use of fictions. In law "an act of God" is a convenient fiction. For natural science, the infinite extension of space and the infinite divisibility of matter are fictions. Indeed matter itself is a fiction. Hans Vaihinger, *The Philosophy of 'As if'* (New York, 1924), 81.

ships in which political behavior arises, takes forms, and changes. Like economics, political science draws upon knowledge of history recent or distant for its data for classification, deduction, and illustration. The ancillary abstractions or fictions of political science, such as democracy, aristocracy, monarchy, dictatorship, and oligarchy, if stripped of the concreteness of historical content, are in truth meaningless and useless to common sense and for practice. As Croce has said of philosophy, so it may be said of political science that, "pursued for its own sake and outside historical knowledge, [it] is only to be found as a profession among others by which man earns his living, and as such is worth little because it has been removed from its live source whence it arose and in which it can renew itself."[4]

It is generally agreed that the axioms and arguments of the one powerful work on political science produced in the United States, *The Federalist*, are anchored in studies of history and directed to concrete ends. Its authors are often disingenuous, if not worse, in pleading their case. They emphasize and they conceal; such indeed is the habit of human beings seeking to inform, persuade, and inspire to action. But they never depart so far from concreteness as to disappear in the fogginess of abstractions devoid of historical content. Besides, *The Federalist* has one quality generally lacking in academic political writings. It has style, that is, the ringing verve of realistic thought directed toward the end of action in fulfilment of a great purpose openly avowed. It is a polemic, of course, but that does not necessarily detract from its science. Nearly all the influential writings in political philosophy or political theory, so called, are polemics directed to ends.

Useful as a fiction or abstraction, like the economic man or the political man, is or may be for limited and practical purposes, it becomes harmful, as Havelock Ellis has said, "when we regard it as hypothesis and therefore possibly true." Certainly great harm was done when writers of small caliber treated the fiction of the economic man as possibly true or as wholly and positively true and shut their eyes and minds to other aspects of history. In another way, Adam Smith himself did harm when, instead of facing boldly the question of the general good, he resorted to a mystical effusion—"the invisible hand."

The crowning weakness of Smith's work lay in his assumptions concerning the nature of all history-as-actuality and historical thought; in his failure to reckon with other aspects of history, with the creative and unique as well as routine activities of mankind, with the impacts of other than economic propensities upon the operations of the economic man. It was in fact the introduction of historical economics and the resort to the study of the history of specific economic activities, toward the end of the

[4] Benedetto Croce, *History as the Story of Liberty* (London, 1941), 138-139.

nineteenth century, that disclosed to those who had eyes to see and minds to grasp the limitations and unrealities of the Smithian creed which had then been driven into absurd extremities.

Since all the humanistic sciences, such as economics and politics, are based on abstractions from knowledge of history-as-actuality, that is, are selective emphases on particular aspects of history, they can be in no respect independent, free-moving sciences. The degree of truth in them, the degree of their correspondence to reality, depends not merely on their logic or cogency of statement but also on the extent to which they cover the relevant and necessary facts in the case. In other words, to ascertain the degree of truth in them, it is imperative to check them against comprehensive knowledge of the actuality of history. Furthermore in seeking to discover the long-term validity of any among these sciences, we must take into the reckoning changes in human societies before that science was formulated, the circumstances in which it was formulated and by whom, changes since its formulation, and the probabilities discernible in recent historical tendencies. Certainly this process of checking abstractions against comprehensive knowledge of history is as necessary in the interest of truth-seeking as checking the conflicting schools to be found within any humanistic science against one another or resorting to a logical analysis of their discrepancies. Indeed such checking against historical knowledge seems to be the chief intellectual operation likely to increase the degree of truth in any of the sciences.

This checking of abstractions in the humanistic sciences against knowledge of history is analogous to the procedure followed in physical sciences —verification by observation of physical performances. The analogy is, of course, far from exact; it is indeed purely figurative in nature, for the observer of human affairs can only "see" the past through the media of documents and memorials. He cannot observe it directly. He may recall memories of events and personalities belonging to his own past but they are at best extremely limited and fragmentary. It is mainly by the use of constructive and informed imagination in the interpretation and exposition of documents and memorials that he is able to describe with any degree of exactness the outstanding features of any situation or age beyond his own past, and even then he is limited by the number and nature of the documents and survivals available to him. If this is discouraging to those who expect the exactness of physics and chemistry in the humanistic sciences, nevertheless the fact remains that for validity any humanistic science must be checked against comprehensive knowledge of history-as-actuality when truth-seeking is pressed toward the limits of the possible.

In some ways history itself, as actuality, passes judgment on the validity of propositions in the humanistic sciences. If, for example, Adam Smith's economics is to be taken as describing what is or will be, as distinguished from a plea for what "ought to be," history has already passed judgments on it. The public policies which he recommended as calculated to increase the wealth of nations were extensively adopted by Great Britain near the middle of the nineteenth century; and this adoption, to his enthusiastic disciples, seemed to herald universal triumph. But in fact, whatever the shortcomings of our present historical knowledge, there is a consensus of competence on the following proposition: Smith's system was not so extensively applied in other countries as in Great Britain and marked tendencies in public policies during the past fifty years, even in Great Britain, have been against, rather than in favor, of the Smithian system. History-as-actuality may be described as cruel and senseless, but, whatever it is, it has passed and is passing judgments on Smith's economics as predicted practice up to the present; and if the spirit of natural science is to prevail in the humanistic sciences this judgment, however deplorable, must be accepted as a historical verdict.

The desirability of resorting to knowledge of history as a check on humanistic sciences is reinforced by the fact that, while they all depend on history for data and ideas, they are, in a large sense, anti-historical. Most, if not all of them, purport to describe "what is" and perhaps "what will be," despite human aspirations and distempers. Except for what may be called historical sociology, they usually make abstractions from a brief or limited span of years, even when they draw, as did the authors of *The Federalist*, upon the writings of antiquity for illustrations. They are concerned primarily with repetitions, routines, constants *in* history-as-actuality. When they use the vague phrase "other things being equal" in attempting to support the validity of their abstractions, they are in effect seeking to escape history, to evade the historical changes which may and probably will invalidate their propositions.

On the other hand, historians are especially concerned, doubtless too much, with the uniqueness of events and personalities, with what is growing and becoming, with changes and creations. Owing to the very nature of history-as-actuality, historians, if true to their subject matter, are bound to exercise this concern. The political scientists, if cautious, may with due propriety and for convenience speak of the regimes of Caesar, Cromwell, and Napoleon as dictatorships, but the historian, adhering to the records, points out dissimilarities among them, the uniqueness of each in the circumstances of its origin and functioning and in its intrinsic character.

Accordingly, to treat any humanistic science as living and scientific and to look upon history as a kind of old almanac compiled by and for curious creatures called historians is to disregard relevant facts in the total case and to give a false security and assurance to that alleged science. To divorce any humanistic science from history is to introduce confusion into the intellectual processes by which we acquire knowledge of human affairs; by which we are enabled to evolve workable statements or formulas that represent the utmost truth attainable to us and that promise to be serviceable in the wiser and better ordering of human affairs.

Nor is the cause of utmost and serviceable truth well served by resorting to the use of analogies drawn from the natural sciences, such as a biological analogy, "the cross-fertilization of related sciences." As analogy of this kind is merely a bit of rhetoric utterly inconceivable in real terms. "Cross-fertilization," like many other words, such as "social forces," falls into the category of figurative expressions, which, as Dubois-Reymond has pointed out, "one uses when the idea is not clear enough to be directly formulated."

Workers in the several humanistic sciences may undoubtedly learn from one another and should endeavor to do so. But history is not just "one" of the related humanistic sciences. History-as-actuality, with which historians are bound by their very office to be concerned, includes all the humanistic sciences and all the data upon which they draw for formulas, axioms, proofs, demonstration, and illustrations; and it is against knowledge of this comprehensive history that the abstractions of the humanistic sciences are to be checked for validity.

The economist, the political scientist, or sociologist may say in reply: "I have read a lot of history and I find in it many features of an old almanac and very little help in enlarging my knowledge of economics or politics or sociology or in checking my abstractions." Anyone well acquainted with historical writings must admit that there is some justice in the complaint as well as some injustice. It is here that the primary distinction must be re-emphasized. History-as-actuality is one thing; written-history purporting to describe all or part of history-as-actuality is still another thing.

For the purpose of truth-seeking in the humanistic sciences this distinction must be clearly and severely maintained in our thinking; for, when the word history is used, especially by laymen, *written* history is usually meant, that is, a kind of book or books written by some person or persons, in a time and place, about history-as-actuality in general or some phases or "periods" of that actuality. And, to speak frankly, a large part, if not all, of the written history, even the best of it, falls far below the highest conceivable level of intellectual performance. It is at this point that the supreme problem of the business before us arises and the obligation of historians to examine their assumptions, procedures, and results appears in full force.

This is not to say that historians have been less intelligent and effective in producing true and workable statements than their colleagues in the other humanistic sciences. To prove such a proposition one way or the other would be a task in historical operations that is probably beyond human powers. But it seems correct to assert that Brooks and Henry Adams, for example, who worked primarily in history, demonstrated a comprehension of events taking place around them between 1870 and 1914 and made predictions as to the probable course of American and world affairs which justify a judgment that they displayed a higher degree of understanding than did most of their colleagues working in economics, sociology, law, or politics. With startling emphasis history-as-actuality since 1900 has verified many of their predictions.[5]

It would be idle, however, to dwell long upon the intellectual merits or demerits of past performances in historiography or any of the humanistic sciences, although we may undoubtedly learn from the analysis and study of such performances. The task before historians, if they are thoughtful rather than fretful, may be put in homely terms: "What do we do now and how?"

Or to break the general question down into subsidiary questions:

Just what intellectual operations does the historian perform in studying and writing history?

What does he think he is doing in performing these operations?

According to what axioms, maxims, assumptions, and methods does he proceed?

For what reason, if any discernible reason, are particular aspects of history chosen for emphasis and other aspects excluded?

Why, for instance, are many ideas, interests, institutions and activities usually excluded from general history and why in particular are one half of the human race—women—except a few queens and courtesans, so completely ignored, even in histories purporting to be "general" or "cultural" in nature?

How can a larger degree of comprehensiveness and exactness be achieved in historical writing?

How can a consensus of competence be secured on the formulas of procedure in historical study and writing best calculated to attain the ends of greater comprehensiveness, exactitude, and utility for theory and practice in the world of thought and action?

In what ways may the abstractions, formulas, and categories of the other humanistic sciences be used to broaden and give precision to historical studies in themselves and as auxiliaries to those other sciences?

By what actions may the most effective cooperation be attained among the parties to this common cause?

The "problem" indicated by these questions is no doubt highly compli-

[5] Charles A. Beard, Introduction to Brooks Adams, *The Law of Civilization and Decay* (New York, 1943).

cated, and the Committee on Historiography, after long discussion, decided that neither the time nor the resources at its disposal would permit it to attempt a comprehensive treatment of the theme. Upon due consideration the committee came to the conclusion that in the circumstances it should simply direct its attention to the formulation of a program relevant to the problem and offer suggestions for further procedure.

In this program the following elements appear: (1) a series of fundamental propositions on the nature and limits of historiography; (2) a discussion of various frames of reference or schemes of thought which have been employed as operating fictions or controlling conceptions in the writing of history in the United States; (3) an illustration of the ways in which frames of reference have been employed by historians in dealing with a selected theme of American history, namely, the Civil War and Reconstruction; (4) a glossary dealing with a few, but primary, terms used in historiography, with a view to concentrating attention on the nature and limitations of such terms; and (5) a bibliography of selected works on historiography, which should be helpful to students who wish to have some idea of what they are doing when they are examining the documents of history, determining the authenticity of records, selecting facts, ordering facts, drawing inferences, exercising the art of constructive imagination, and writing history.

CHAPTER II

CONTROLLING ASSUMPTIONS IN
THE PRACTICE OF AMERICAN
HISTORIANS

By JOHN HERMAN RANDALL, JR.
and
GEORGE HAINES, IV

"HISTORICAL INVESTIGATION," says Santayana, "has for its aim to fix the order and character of events throughout past time in all places. The task is frankly superhuman, because no block of real existence, with its infinitesimal detail, can be recorded, nor if somehow recorded could it be dominated by the mind; and to carry on a survey of this social continuum *ad infinitum* would multiply the difficulty. The task might also be called infrahuman, because the sort of omniscience which such complete historical science would achieve would merely furnish materials for intelligence: it would be inferior to intelligence itself. . . . An attempt to rehearse the inner life of everybody that has ever lived would be no rational endeavour. Instead of lifting the historian above the world and making him the most consummate of creatures, it would flatten his mind out into a passive after-image of diffuse existence, with all its horrible blindness, strain, and monotony. Reason is not come to repeat the universe but to fulfil it. Besides, a complete survey of events would perforce register all changes that have taken place in matter since time began, the fields of geology, astronomy, palaeontology, and archaeology being all, in a sense, included in history. Such learning would dissolve thought in a vertigo, if it had not already perished of boredom. . . . The profit of studying history lies in something else than in a dead knowledge of what happens to have happened."[1]

In view of the situation Santayana thus graphically depicts, it is clear that, as Proposition VI states, "Every written history, particularly that covering any considerable area of time and space, is a selection of facts made by some person or persons and is ordered or organized under the influence of some scheme of reference, interest, or emphasis—avowed or unavowed—in the thought of the author or authors."[2] This means that the historian must employ some principle of selection: he must choose what he

[1] George Santayana, "History," *Reason in Science* (New York, 1906), 51-53.
[2] See below, 135.

will include as significant for his history. In writing the history of the United States, he must decide what is "basic" for that history. Even though he permit himself four lengthy volumes to set forth *The Rise of American Civilization*, and can hence afford a broader base, he cannot escape the need for a principle of selection.

Moreover, if seventeen years elapse between the two written histories, the principle of selection employed in the later one will probably differ appreciably from the principle that served for the earlier. This will be not only because in the interval the historian has found out more "facts," and has a greater store from which to choose those that are really "basic" for a much shorter work. It will be due fully as much to the circumstance that he has grown in the stature of his wisdom. He has come to understand the world and its ways and the pattern of human experience with more maturity and insight, perhaps; at least he now understands it differently. And he understands it differently in large part because there is now something different to understand. The history-that-has-happened during those seventeen years—the history as "actuality"—has not stood still. That history, like all the histories-that-happen, has been progressive and cumulative. In 1944 the United States is not what it was in 1927. Hence the historian, facing the problem of selecting those facts in the American past that seem "basic" for 1944, will not be able to make just the same selection that he made in 1927.

Thus the history the historian will write, and the principle of selection he will employ, will be undergoing continual change. For the meaning and the significance of the past is continually changing with the occurrence of fresh events. Of course, what *did* happen, as brute events, does not change with further events. But, as we have seen, the historian is not and cannot be concerned with all that did happen. He is and must be concerned with those particular events that did happen which turn out to be "basic" for his history. He is not concerned with the entire past, with all its infinitesimal detail; he is concerned only with the "basic" or significant past. And it is precisely this "basic" past, this meaning and significance of the past, that is continually changing, that is cumulative and progressive. Writing the history of the United States, the historian uses what is basic and significant in that history-that-happened for 1927, or for 1944, as the principle that will control his selection of material. What is significant in American history he will understand in one way in 1927, and in a somewhat different way in 1944. For the historian's understanding of the significant past, like that past itself, is progressive and cumulative.

There is really nothing mysterious about this obvious fact that men's understanding of what is significant in their history changes with the lapse of time. For all understanding is in terms of causes and consequences. Now, our understanding of causes naturally changes and deepens as we find out more about the operation of causes; and equally naturally, our understanding of consequences changes with the working out of further consequences in the history-that-happens itself.

In the first place, the understanding of causes changes as we manage to extend and build up our sciences of man's social behavior. When we are content to explain what groups of men do by attributing their actions to the guiding hand of Providence, we will, like the early New England historians, write histories of the operation of God's will, and we will select facts that illustrate it. Or, like Bancroft, we will record "the movement of the divine power which gives unity to the universe, and order and connection to events." When we have come to understand the mysterious ways in which God performs His wonders as the working out of the God-given genius for politics of the Teutonic race, we will, like H. B. Adams, trace the "origin" of the New England town-meeting to the primitive German mark. When we have read John Stuart Mill's *Logic,* and absorbed his Baconian conception of the nature of science, we will eschew all guiding hypotheses and indefatigably collect "facts," hopefully trusting that somehow good, in the form of some "synthesis" that will make it all clear, will be the final goal of all this ill. We will be strictly "scientific" and "critical" historians, like those great pioneers who won respect for "history" as an academic discipline in the seminars set up during the eighteen-eighties at Johns Hopkins, Columbia, and elsewhere. When we have seen a great light, and been converted to the gospel of St. Marx, we will write histories like those of Simons, Gustavus Myers, or Lewis Corey. When we have learned from James Harvey Robinson that the historian must master all the social sciences, and have read—or at least abstracted —all the books in that wide field, we will understand the past in terms of all the different hypotheses of all the social sciences, and will, like Harry Elmer Barnes, adopt a "multiple causation" theory as our principle of selection. Our understanding of the causes of what has happened will change in these ways with our changing—and, we trust, increasingly adequate—schemes of scientific explanation.

Secondly, the understanding of consequences, and hence of the "significance" of past events, changes with further history-that-happens— with what comes to pass in the world of events as a result of the possibilities inherent in what has happened. Thus World War I was understood in one way as leading to the adoption of the Covenant of the League of Nations. It was understood in another way as the Russian Revolution worked itself out, and began to appear as a much more significant consequence of the war than the abortive effort at an international organization. The war took on a still further significance with the rise of the Fascist and Nazi regimes, and with the resumption of German expansion. It is now beginning to look like the first stage in the Russian domination of Europe.

Or take the matter of American participation in that struggle. Ten years ago, the entry of America into World War I was understood as the result of British propaganda and the machinations of munition-makers. It was hard to believe that Americans had been so stupid as to think they were really "making the world safe for democracy"; reputable historians preferred less simple-minded and more diabolical explanations. The years since 1939 have changed profoundly our understanding of American participation in World War I. After Pearl Harbor, it was seen as the first and unsuccessful attempt to curb German aggression and establish a military alliance to guarantee the status quo. With the resumption of Russian and British power politics, our participation in that earlier war may well come to be seen in still another light.

New consequences flowing from past events change the significance of the past, of what has happened. Events which before had been overlooked, because they did not seem "basic" for anything that followed, now come to be selected as highly significant; other events that used to seem "basic" recede into the limbo of mere details. In this sense, a history-that-happens is not and in the nature of the case cannot be fully understood by the actors in it. They can not realize the "significance" or consequences of what they are doing, since they cannot foresee the future. We understand that history only when it has become a part of our own past; and if it continues to have consequences, our children will understand it still differently. In this sense, the historian, as Hegel proclaimed, is like the owl of Minerva, who takes his flight only when the shades of night are gathering, and the returns are all in. The significance of any history-that-happens is not completely grasped until all its consequences have been discerned. The "meaning" of any historical fact is what it does, how it continues to behave and operate, what consequences follow from it.

For example, at a historic moment Winston Churchill said: "With the fall of Singapore we are beginning to realize the meaning of Pearl Harbor." Note the word "beginning." For the "meaning," that is, the cumulative consequences of that specific event, were not completed when Churchill was speaking. They have not been completed yet. They depend on how things will turn out in the future.

In this sense, we understand any history-that-has-happened in terms of the future: our principle for selecting what is basic in that history involves a reference to its predicted outcome. Our "emphasis" will be determined by what we find going on in the present. But what we find there is not yet fully worked out. Rather, the present suggests what will eventuate in times to come. Thus we understand what is basic in a history in terms of what we call some "dynamic element" in the present, some "present tendency" directed toward the future. The present is full of such tendencies: it suggests many different possible futures, according as different tendencies now at work prove controlling. The historian selects one of these possible futures as "just around the corner," and uses it as a principle by which to select what is basic among the multitude of facts at his disposal.

For example, our papers are today full of attempts to understand what has been happening, the recent history of the different phases of the war. Most of this discussion inevitably turns out to be a prediction of what is going to happen: we cannot understand what has happened without reference to a projected future. Thus we cannot understand the Administration's foreign policy—toward the French, toward the Italians, toward Spain, toward Poland—we cannot understand what is "basic" in its history, without trying to predict how it is going to turn out. As we say, we are now beginning to see its significance, as we find out what it has already led to.

The historian must thus choose among the various possibilities of the present that tendency, that predicted future, which he judges to be dynamic or controlling. He chooses as his principle of selection the "real pattern of events," what is "being realized," what is "working itself out." Now, since the future is not foreseeable in detail—though many elements in it can be predicted, and all human action is based on such predictions of what will happen if other things occur—the historian's choice of a principle of selection necessarily involves a certain choice of allegiance, an act of faith in one kind of future rather than another. Thus, to take the growth of science as the basic factor in the intellectual history of modern times, means that we judge it to be of most significance today. "The future lies with it," we say, meaning we are for it. No devout Catholic, for instance, would choose that factor as basic. For him, the future will be different, and consequently he will have a different understanding of the past. In the same way, to take the growth of group control of technology as the principle for selecting what is basic in our economic past, is to express an allegiance. It is to make the problem of establishing such control central in the present. In terms of that principle of selection, the dominance of laissez faire during the nineteenth century will be understood as a "stage" in the reconstruction of the earlier medieval group controls. No "rugged individualist" would choose that focus: in his history he would select a different past.

But to say that a principle of selection is "chosen" does not mean that such choices are arbitrary. Men do not arbitrarily "choose" their allegiances and faiths, even when they are converts. Their faiths are rather forced upon them. Grace, we are told, is prevenient, and it is God who sends faith. The history-that-happens itself generates the faiths and allegiances that furnish the principles for selecting what is important in understanding it. Men do not "choose" arbitrarily to be Catholics—or rugged individualists—any more than they "choose" not to be. Some men indeed have their faiths and allegiances forced upon them by "facts," by knowledge; though presumably for none is this wholly the case. For such men, facts do force the selection of the controlling tendencies, the implicit ends, in the present, in terms of which they can understand the past. For such men, knowledge does declare what has to be done: the furtherance of science, the socialized control of industry, the achievement of international organization.

This is especially true when they are in responsible positions, and have to act to get something done. Thus Mr. Hoover, though a rugged individualist, was compelled by facts to go further than any of his predecessors in setting up group controls. This practical knowledge of what has to be done, like the technical knowledge of how to do it, is relatively free from the "arbitrariness" and irresponsible "relativism"—the "subjective relativism"—of so-called "theoretical knowledge," which is not knowledge at all, but a mere "having of ideas," mere "ideology." In terms of these ends that have to be achieved, these goals forced on us by facts, men understand the present and the past, using these ends as principles for selecting what is basic in the histories they write.

Indeed, there are so many facts and so many patterns of relation discernible in the history of anything, and it is so impossible to include them all, that any selection will remain "arbitrary" and "subjective" unless it is dictated by some necessary choice or problem generated in that history itself. Only by realizing that these are the fundamental problems and choices today, or that they were fundamental in some past period, can we hope to understand or write the history of anything "objectively." Only thus we can understand objectively, for example, the history of the Romantic era. It is notoriously difficult to find any common traits or common pattern in that movement. But we can find the common *problems* in terms of which we can understand its history. As Jacques Barzun writes, "Clearly, the one thing that unifies men in a given age is not their individual philosophies, but the dominant problem that these philosophies are designed to solve. In the romantic period this problem was to create a new world on the ruins of the old"[3]—to criticize the inadequate synthesis of the eighteenth century, and to reconstruct a more adequate one.

The historian must make a selection. From the infinite variety of relatednesses that past events disclose, he must select what is basic for his particular history. If that selection is not to be merely what is important *for him*, if it is not to be "subjective" and "arbitrary," it must have an "objective" emphasis or focus in something to be done, something he sees

---

[3] Jacques Barzun, *Romanticism and the Modern Ego* (Boston, 1943), 21, 22.

forced on men. The history of what is basic *for that problem*—of the conditions that generated it, the resources men had to draw upon, how they dealt with it—will then be perfectly "objective," in a sense in which no mere recording of arbitrarily selected "facts" could ever be. This is the "objective relativism" that is characteristic of all types of knowledge. Knowledge can be "objective" only *for* some determinate context; it is always a knowledge of the relations essential for that context. In historical knowledge, the context is always that of a problem faced by men, of the causes of that problem, the means for its solution, and the course actually adopted. In that context, the relation of cause and consequence, of means and end, will thus be quite "objective."

This objective relativism of the principles of selection and interpretation necessary to the historian's enterprise is set forth briefly in certain of the propositions laid down in this handbook.[4] It has been here elaborated with a little more detail. It is the aim of this essay to illustrate it in terms of the principles of selection and interpretation actually employed by certain of the major American historians of the last two generations. We shall pay special attention to the assumptions controlling the work of those "scientific" and "objective" founders of the profession in this country who claimed to make no assumptions and to have no principles of selection. We shall endeavor to set forth what assumptions they actually adopted, what problems they faced that led them to their principles, and why they made the choices they did.

II

Critical and scientific historical investigation, associated with instruction on a graduate level, began in the United States with the inauguration in 1876 in the newly-founded Johns Hopkins University of study in "History and Politics," and the setting up of an historical seminar under Herbert Baxter Adams. Four years later John W. Burgess founded the School of Political Science at Columbia, which came to rival Adams' seminar in providing training for professional historians. Michigan, Cornell, and Wisconsin, as well as Harvard and Pennsylvania, soon developed able graduate instruction in historical research.

These university scholars were of course not the first American historians to employ critical methods. Many a local historian, as far back as the eighteenth century, had displayed an ability to use sources critically, a zeal for "objectivity," and a range of concerns far wider than the rather narrowly political concentration of the new academic scholars.[5] Bancroft, who took

---
[4] See below, 134*f*.
[5] See Richard H. Shryock, "American Historiography: A Critical Analysis and a Program," *American Philosophical Society Proceedings*, 87 (1943), 35-46; also Michael Kraus, *A History of American History* (New York, 1937).

his degree at Göttingen under Heeren in 1820, brought back to America an enthusiasm for the painstaking methods of the new German school of historical scholarship, of whose giants Heeren was so accomplished a forerunner. By the 'sixties the trickle of pilgrims to the sources of German learning had already swelled to a respectable stream. The year 1857 saw three German-trained scholars, Henry Torrey, Francis Lieber, and Andrew D. White, installed in chairs of history at Harvard, Columbia, and Michigan respectively—though according to J. Franklin Jameson as late as 1880 there were only eleven professors of history in the United States.[6]

The significance of Adams and Burgess does not lie primarily in the methods they had learnt across the seas and now ably taught their American students. It lies rather in the fact that they were establishing a new learned profession. They were introducing a new university discipline on an educational scene just groping, rather self-consciously, to provide itself with postgraduate professional training. The new graduate schools were painfully aware that they had yet to prove their worth in terms of the rigorous standards of their German models. The social studies in particular were on their mettle to justify their pretensions to rank as critical disciplines employing an exacting "scientific" method. And none was under greater compulsion than history to vindicate its new claim to a serious place among the circle of research sciences the emerging American universities were beginning to cultivate.

It is the great achievement of those scholars who began teaching history in American universities after 1880 that in the course of a single generation they completely succeeded in this basic aim. By 1910 the historical profession was firmly entrenched in institutions of higher learning. It was universally recognized as a research discipline as rigorous and exacting—if not quite so exact in its conclusions—as any university study not mathematical in its methods. Its ablest practitioners had won reputations equal to those of their European counterparts; its organized seminars offered a training that did not suffer in comparison with that of Europe. Perhaps most remarkable of all, the practice of historical writing had been transformed from the literary avocation it had been in nineteenth-century America into a highly professionalized discipline. If the academic scholars did not actually monopolize the field of historiography, they had come to dictate its aims and standards. Even the general educated public, though it still preferred the more readable works of the popularizers and journalists, felt guiltily it was getting its history second-hand, and was delighted to discover a work it could enjoy by a real scholar and "authority."

[6] W. Stull Holt, Ed. *Historical Scholarship in the United States, 1876-1901* (Baltimore, 1938), 8.

This professionalization and institutionalization of the practice of history in America we are apt to take as a matter of course. Actually, however, it has been the major factor controlling the way the American historian has regarded his work for the last two generations; it has dictated his methods and his aims and concerns. It is hardly too much to say that for twenty-five years after 1880 the central problems faced by the historian in America were institutional, involved in vindicating the standing of his profession in the learned world. Thus, in an age enormously impressed by the achievements of natural science, and convinced that even literature and the arts must be studied with "scientific methods," the historian too had to be "scientific" at all costs. Because men still construed the aim of science as the sheer discovery and direct reading of the structure of things, this meant that the historian had to be "objective." Since there was as yet little explicit appreciation of the role of hypothesis and theory in scientific procedure, it meant he must try to establish above all as many "facts" as possible. The only hypotheses he could afford to permit himself were those his German and English models accepted, like the Teutonic origin of English and American political institutions, or the colonial character of the colonies. Since his models were concerned with the problems of legal and constitutional origins, he too must prove his weapons on that aspect of the American past. After all, was he not trying to establish himself in a school of political science?

These pioneer critical historians had explicit principles of selection and definite schemes of understanding the past, as well as plenty of class and individual biases reflecting their background. But those principles and schemes were very largely determined by the problems of establishing a profession, which dictated the approved political subject-matter and the respectable European ways of understanding it. Historians were hardly free to make central the new economic problems already insistently emerging in American life. Their own institutional problem left them little liberty to employ the new ways of understanding that generation was working out—new conceptions of the very nature and method of science, a wealth of new knowledge about man and human society, new philosophies and new ways of looking at human affairs.

After 1900 the historians' position was pretty secure. In this newfound confidence it was possible to go on to question the limitations to which the pioneer historians had perforce submitted. The decade of the nineteen-hundreds began to hear the demand to focus on other problems, to include other aspects of the past, economic, intellectual, religious and cultural. Men of ranging mind, inspired by the new sciences of man to which a great series of pioneer thinkers were just giving a characteristic American stamp, began to use their hypotheses as heuristic principles in historical investigation.

But the profession had now itself become stabilized and institutionalized; it had developed traditions of selection and method to which its practitioners had grown intensely loyal. When shortly after 1910 men like Becker, Thorndike, Turner, Robinson, and Beard proposed to cultivate these new interests and to employ these new tools, their programs might have been welcomed—as indeed they were by the nonprofessionals—as a promising extension of horizons. But most of the professionals took this natural expansion of history as an attack on all they stood for. What might have been a shift of interest springing from the steady growth of knowledge and the emergence of new problems became instead a controversy. Historians argued heatedly about the "proper" field and concern of "history." They debated the extent to which the historian should be permitted to use ideas and hypotheses as principles of interpretation. Was it compatible with the scientific standing of the profession to explore what light might be thrown on the familiar outlines of political history by such newcomers as "sectionalism" or the "economic factor"?

Traditionalists were forced to formulate their own assumptions with some care; for the first time "scientific" history became really conscious of its presuppositions. Their critics were naturally led in turn to make exaggerated claims for the ideas and methods they found illuminating: "the new history" or "economic determinism" would give the final answer to all the historian's problems. Before they could go on to show what their programs could accomplish, they had to argue interminably for their right as "historians" to do so. There was now an established profession that had to be converted to any new departure. Thus in another but still controlling sense, the central problems of even the more heretical historians remained institutional and professional. Whatever new ideas or approaches gave promise of illuminating the past had to be first adjusted to the requirements of the profession. Thus socialists might employ the Marxian theory fruitfully to bring to light fully documented "facts." But what they wrote could hardly be reckoned as "history": they frankly had an axe to grind.

The geographical determinism and the sectional hypothesis of Turner, which seemed radical enough when first advanced in 1893, were sufficiently in line with the tradition, and were developed with enough skill and judgment, to enable them to pass muster. It is significant of the state of American historical thought that his "frontier theory" could stand for several decades as the major principle for interpreting the American past, and could exert such influence on the younger Beard and on Parrington.[7] That a theory of such limited scope[8] could have enjoyed the controlling

[7] *Cf.* Charles A. Beard, *An Economic Interpretation of the Constitution of the United States* (New York, 1913), 5*f*.

[8] *Cf.* Charles A. Beard, "The Frontier in American History," *New Republic* 97-98 (1938-39), 359-362. "Turner overemphasized, in my opinion, the influence of frontier

vogue it did makes clear how eager American historians were becoming to seize upon and generalize any fruitful idea presented with the proper professional credentials.

By the nineteen-twenties the critics of the traditionalists had won their fight: they were free to write the kind of history they wanted, economic interpretations, social and cultural history, intellectual history. The monumental works of Parrington and Beard appeared; Schlesinger and Fox started their series. Under pressure of the economic problems of the 'thirties, even writings with a strong Marxian tinge were admitted as "history." Most important of all, the profession now felt so secure that its leaders could begin to challenge the very conception of "science" on which "scientific" history had based its triumphs. Instead of self-consciously asserting the claim that their knowledge is as "scientific" as the next man's, they could now take it for granted that their knowledge is genuine knowledge, and go on to inquire precisely what kind of knowledge historical knowledge actually is.

With its head start of several generations, Continental history had achieved that degree of professional self-confidence by the eighteen-eighties, and had already produced a great literature of self-examination and criticism. Venturesome Americans now began to explore this literature—not always, to be sure, with full awareness of its theoretical presuppositions, or of its foundation in general philosophical theories and epistemologies which they would probably not be prepared to accept. A few pioneers, like Becker and Lynn Thorndike, had indeed dared to raise such issues at the time of the earlier controversies around 1910, and had done so in terms of more American philosophies. The profession had then been hardly ripe for such questions. But now more general searching of heart and debate ensued. Once more theoretical issues were filtered through the screen of professional and institutional interests.

III

These salient facts of the institutional development of the historical profession in the United States have been emphasized, because they provide the framework indispensable for understanding the assumptions and principles of selection American historians have actually employed. They were controlling for the pioneer "scientific" historians who claimed to make no assumptions. With few exceptions, our historians have not only not been very critically aware of their own presuppositions. They have had little independent interest in the philosophical currents or the winds

---

economy on the growth of the democratic idea, on the formation of national policies and on constitutional interpretation. . . .

"The freehold frontier did have a lot of influence on American development, but how much and what kind is still an open question for me. That it does not 'explain' American development I am firmly convinced" (361).

of doctrine that have swept the American scene. When they have absorbed and expressed current attitudes, it has been largely without deliberate intent. The pioneers, carefully trained by their German teachers to eschew any "philosophy of history"—an ever-present temptation and snare in the German situation—found every interest of professional respectability reinforcing this scientific caution. It is rather remarkable that the long line of historical students exposed to the intellectual ferments of the German universities should have carried over so little of the philosophies they there heard expounded; a political thinker like Burgess stands out as a striking exception. It is still more remarkable, in view of the stirring developments in the social sciences in our country during the last two or three generations, that historians, again with outstanding exceptions like Robinson, should have been so slow to reflect these more homely intellectual issues so vigorously debated by the other students of man.

The great idea of evolution did indeed find many repercussions among the historians.[9] Yet even here it is hard to point to any historian before Robinson who made it really central in his work. John Fiske was as widely known for his popularization of the Spencerian version of evolution as for his later historical writing. His humanistic and religious reformulation of Spencer, so influential on the liberal theology of the last generation, is a landmark in America thought.[10] Yet it is difficult to discover much influence of his distinctive Spencerian views on his dramatic historical narratives. Of all American historians Henry Adams had the greatest interest in general ideas. His long search for "the law of history" began with the idea of evolution; in the 'seventies he prefaced his course on medieval history at Harvard with a study of primitive society. Then, unable to reconcile Grant's administration with a belief in cosmic progress, he became the leading philosophical heretic against the reigning religion of evolution. Yet his admirable political history antedated his most distinctive theoretical views, which have themselves remained without effect on historical writing. The great debate between "religion" and "science" did indeed stimulate some notable historical works, like those of Draper, White, Lea, and Robinson. But the abundant American materials bearing on this issue have only begun to be exploited in the less heated atmosphere of our own generation.

Of course, those who have written American history without concern for the standards of the professional guild have never attempted to conceal their own assumptions and principles of selection. The earliest New England historians, like the Mathers, were convinced that events in the Holy

[9] *Cf.* Merle Curti, *The Growth of American Thought* (New York, 1943), 568*f.*
[10] *Cf.* Herbert W. Schneider, "The Influence of Darwin and Spencer on American Philosophical Theology," *Journal of the History of Ideas*, 6 (1945), 5, 10; Richard Hofstadter, *Social Darwinism in American Thought, 1860-1915* (New York, 1944).

Commonwealth revealed the guiding hand of Providence. They wrote in praise of God and Massachusetts, and their histories were designed to magnify both for their strong interest in each other. This Providential view persisted in the years of national self-glorification that followed the establishment of the Republic, though it was no longer the epic of Massachusetts, but the epic of America, that men now celebrated in their nationalistic histories. "God winnowed the nations of Europe and reserved this continent for his chosen people."

But when George Bancroft began his thrilling story in 1834, God had become a humanized and moralized Unitarian Deity whose main concern was to work out in America the culmination of secular political liberty. Bancroft can hardly be said to have brought back from Germany any one of those precisely elaborated philosophies of the *Zeitgeist* in which that generation of German thinkers were reformulating the doctrine of Providence. Göttingen, the university of the Prince Regent's province of Hanover, would hardly predispose a man toward the Hegelian glorification of the Prussian State. But Bancroft certainly did absorb the reigning theological idea of the immanence of God in the world and in human affairs, which made the whole of history the working out of a divine plan.

More significant, however, than the continuation of this Providential view in secularized and political form was Bancroft's conviction that God spoke with the voice of Jacksonian Democracy. The Divine Plan might have employed as its chosen instruments those brave refugees from tyranny and oppression who colonized the land; it might have culminated in the unique achievement of the Founding Fathers who brought forth the Constitution. But it now worked through a party program of organized democracy on which hung the world's hope of happiness. Richard Hildreth, Bancroft's chief rival as a nationalistic glorifier, viewed the American past rather with the eyes of an anti-Jeffersonian Federalist. Acceptance of the Providential view in no wise precluded a strong partisan bias: God was obviously on the side of sound politics.

In the next generation the terminology had changed. Providence was now dressed up as Evolution. But that inspiring idea, now happily enshrined in the very heart of the new science, still spoke in much the same accents of manifest destiny. Between the vaguely idealistic religious optimism of Bancroft and the vaguely religious evolutionary optimism of John Fiske, the difference is slight; each equally could glorify the heroes of the American past. But the horizons are now broader. Where Bancroft traced the epic of liberty in America from its Puritan sources, Fiske expanded it into an epic of the English-speaking peoples, an epic that began in the German forests, came down in unbroken continuity through the constitutional achievements of the British nation, and culminated in the complete working out of the spirit of 1688 in the

American Revolution and the Constitution. Fiske does indeed strike a new note. His Spencerian evolution now definitely chooses the middle class as its instrument, and it is by their valiant efforts that the torch of liberty is handed on.

IV

It was against such a background of popular national feeling and self-esteem, reinforced by whatever rationalization of the guiding hand of God was in vogue, that the new professional historians had to vindicate their claim to scientific impartiality and academic standing. They faced two alternatives. They could radically transmute history into a sociological and evolutionary science, drawing their inspiration from Comte, Quételet and Marx, and from the sociology of Spencer and Tylor. The hope of formulating "the laws of history," in the ultimate interest of predicting the future, has fascinated a certain strain of American historians, from Buckle's disciple Draper down. The classic instance is found in Brooks and Henry Adams, who drew on thermodynamics to combat the prevailing gospel of biological "progress." In our own day a science of history has been sketched with much more sophistication by Teggart.

The other alternative was not to transform history into something else, but to investigate and write "history" itself by means of "scientific" methods. It was at this point that their German training and model proved decisive for American professional historians. Ranke and his expert disciples taught them how to be "scientific" without ceasing to be historical.[11] This meant not only the critical use of contemporary documents, henceforth established as the cornerstone of the historian's technique. To be "scientific" meant also to divest oneself of the "prejudices of the present," indeed, to eschew all attempts at generalization or interpretation, and to set forth "facts," to record "exactly what happened" *wie es eigentlich gewesen ist*. It meant to take toward the historical "facts" the same objective and detached attitude of mind with which the scientist was supposed to regard natural phenomena.

Now, those scholars who during the 'thirties and 'forties were setting the course of German historical methods had made their own appeal to "facts" for somewhat different reasons, and in a rather different atmosphere, from the Americans of the 'eighties. They too were inspired by the professional aim of establishing history as a *Geisteswissenschaft* in the learned world. But they were also living in a generation facing grave political and constitutional questions. They were above all concerned with combating the French Revolutionary ideas of natural rights and natural law by an

---

[11] *Cf.* Carl Becker, "Some Aspects of the Influence of Social Problems and Ideas upon the Study and Writing of History," *American Sociological Society Publications*, reprinted in *American Journal of Sociology*, 18 (1912-13), 641-675; esp. 657*ff*.

appeal to traditional German institutions. In seeking the "facts" of the German past they were in search of those political forms that might be gradually developed in the present, in contrast to all abstract speculations and universal principles. They were turning to German experience and German tradition and historic German rights—to "facts" as against "vain speculations." Hence even Ranke found his aim of objectivity in no conflict with the prevailing notion of a dominant *Zeitgeist*, and he could entertain enthusiasm for the development of the Prussian *Geist* from Luther to the Hohenzollerns.

In the German historians, objectivity and the appeal to facts were thus an instrument of German nationalism as well as of professional prestige, and throughout the century they could consequently both extend their critical and "scientific" methods and become increasingly nationalistic at one and the same time. For the Americans, "scientific" history was rather an escape from the prevalent exploitation of nationalistic prejudices into the exalted company of the pure scientists. For them, "facts" were not the revelation of a normative tradition of historic rights; they were not, as for Ranke, the exemplification of those great ideas whose conflict constitutes the meaning of history. Facts had become detached from any hypothesis or interpretation. Their chief claim to "scientific" importance was that they were beyond peradventure of doubt "so." In an extreme case, McMaster, "facts" were whatever happened to appear in the public press.[12] In general, "facts" were the single element in the historian's subject-matter that were indubitably "scientific." His techniques in laboriously establishing them were the one part of his procedure that could claim to be a "scientific method." Generalizations and "syntheses" could be admitted only if they forced themselves as the direct deliverance of "facts."

This view, of course, involved the unquestioned acceptance of a definite philosophy of science and scientific method. It was the philosophy stamped on that generation by John Stuart Mill, whose *Logic* (1843) still served as the Bible of scientific method. Deriving his own ideas from Francis Bacon rather than from actual scientific procedure, Mill consciously rejected any "anticipation" of nature in the scientist's work. In his view, the scientist does not elaborate an hypothesis which he proceeds to test by comparing its consequences with relevant facts, selected for their bearing on that hypothesis. Rather, he arranges a large number of "facts" in tables in the hope that the Canons of Induction will enable him to see in those facts the connections that are there. The facts must be gathered first; the generalization will then emerge from their comparison. This "inductive" method was applied to history in the *Introduction to the Study of History*

[12] *Cf.* Shryock, "American Historiography," 43.

by Langlois and Seignobos, which H. B. Adams recommends as the best handbook for the historian. The analytic determination of the facts must precede any raising of the question of "synthesis."

This way of escaping all speculation, prejudice, and one-sidedness appealed strongly to the scientific historians. First you gathered all the available "facts"—presumably entered on index cards. Only then could you go on to undertake a "synthesis." Burgess well states this procedure:

> The University professor . . . must *construct* history out of the chaos of original historic atoms. . . .
>
> We seek to teach the student, first, how to get hold of a historic fact, how to distinguish fact from fiction, how to divest it as far as possible of coloring or exaggeration. We send him, therefore, to the most original sources attainable for his primary information. If there be more than one original source upon the same fact, we teach him to set these in comparison or contrast. . . . We undertake . . . to teach the student to set the facts which he has thus attained in their chronological order, to the further end of setting them in their order as cause and effect. And we seek to make him clearly comprehend and continually feel that the latter procedure is the one most delicate and critical which the historical student is called upon to undertake, in that he is continually tempted to account that which is mere antecedent and consequent as being cause and effect. . . .
>
> After the facts have been determined and the causal *nexus* established we endeavor to teach the student to look for the *institutions and ideas* which have been developed through the sequence of events in the civilization of an age or people.[13]

In the light of any present day analysis of scientific methods, it can only be said that if this is indeed the proper procedure in historical investigation, history is the only field of knowledge in which such a pure inductive method without hypotheses or guiding principles obtains. Yet in the eighteen-eighties this seemed the very essence of scientific procedure.

Into the set of assumptions that governed the work of the new professional historians there thus went the conviction, reinforced by the reigning "inductive" theory of scientific method, that any principle of interpretation would lead away from "facts" to speculation, and eventually to a "philosophy of history." This devotion to "the fact," combined with the strong professional sense of having painfully staked out a "field" of their own, now under attack, is perhaps most revealingly expressed in a paper by George Burton Adams, written in 1909 when critical voices were already making themselves heard.[14] Adams distinguishes between the "scientific"

---

[13] John W. Burgess, "The Methods of Historical Study and Research in Columbia College," *Methods of Teaching and Studying History,* ed. G. Stanley Hall (2nd ed., Boston, 1885), 218-220.

[14] George Burton Adams, "History and the Philosophy of History," *American Historical Review,* 14 (1909), 221-236.

study of history, and the science or philosophy of history which seeks "laws."

It is one thing to raise the question, Is human action dominated by law, and can we by discovering those laws construct a science of history, in the sense in which there exists a science of chemistry? It is quite a different thing to ask, Can methods of investigation which are strictly scientific be applied to the study of the past action of the race in such a way as to give our knowledge of what happened greater certainty? The school of Ranke has never endeavored to go beyond this last question, but their answer to it has been a clear and, I believe, an indisputable affirmative. The actual result has been a science of investigation, and a method of training the future historian, which it is not too much to say, have taken complete possession of the world of historical scholarship. At any rate it is true that all technically trained historians for more than fifty years have been trained according to these ideas and they have all found it exceedingly difficult to free themselves from the fundamental principle of their school that the first duty of the historian is to ascertain as nearly as possible and to record exactly what happened.[15]

Adams goes on to complain of the "attacks" made upon such scientific history by parvenus encroaching upon its "field," who dare to use principles of interpretation, and actually want conclusions from its "facts."

During the last four decades of that century, and especially during its last quarter, there arose a variety of new interests, new groups of scholars formed themselves, new points of view were occupied, new methods were loudly proclaimed, new sciences were born and named, all concerned with the same facts of the past which it is our business to study. So closely are these new interests related to us, and to one another, in the common body of materials which we must all use, that we are tempted to call them offshoots of history. . . . but the statement . . . would be neither historically nor logically correct. Certainly their attitude towards traditional history has not been that of dutiful children towards a parent. So uniformly and severely critical have they been of the methods and purposes of the political historian, if we may use that term as a means of differentiation for the historian by name and profession, that we may almost regard their rise as an attack upon our position, systematic and concerted, and from various points at once. This is hardly the literal truth and yet it behooves us to understand clearly that after three-quarters of a century of practically undisputed possession of our great field of study, during which the achievements of the political historian have won the admiration and applause of the world, our right to the field is now called in question, our methods, our results and our ideals are assailed, and we are being thrown upon the defensive at many points.[16]

Adams lists five principal lines of "attack." There is political science: "in many of its members the tendency is strong to assume that the chief

[15] *Ibid.*, 223.
[16] *Ibid.*, 224.

end to be served by the historian is to furnish material for their science." There is the geographers' "movement," "somewhat more aggressive in spirit." There is the drive to give economic explanations: "We do not count the economic historian proper among those who would drive us from the field." But "there is a great difference between economic history and that which calls itself the economic interpretation of history." Finally, there are sociology and social psychology. All five have for their main endeavor "to construct a science or a philosophy of history."[17]

"Are we passing from an age of investigation to an age of speculation?" Adams asks. "There are I think on all sides, in many ways, signs that this may very possibly be the case."

For more than fifty years the historian has had possession of the field and has deemed it his sufficient mission to determine what the fact was, including the immediate conditions which gave it shape. Now he finds himself confronted with numerous groups of aggressive and confident workers in the same field who ask not what was the fact—many of them seem to be comparatively little interested in that—but their constant question is what is the ultimate explanation of history, or, more modestly, what are the forces which determine human events and according to what laws do they act?[18]

Adams can only exhort the scientific historian to preserve the faith:

What should the historian do in view of the threatened invasion of his domain by ideals and methods not quite his own? ... To those whose methods of work are fixed. ... I have one word of comfort. It is this. All science which is true science must rest upon the proved and correlated fact. ... At the very beginning of all conquest of the unknown lies the fact, established and classified, to the fullest extent possible at the moment.[19]

V

This devotion to "the fact," to objectivity and to Mill's theory of induction, did not actually prevent the early "scientific" professional historians from making certain important assumptions which exerted a controlling influence on their work. First, they had a definite principle of selection: "history" was for them not only political history, it was, in its technical and scientific phases, legal and constitutional history, with a strong emphasis on the development of local institutions. Secondly, they were greatly impressed by the persisting continuity of political institutions, and traced the "germ" of the later developments of American liberty and order back through English forms to the primitive German forests. Both H. B. Adams and Burgess were as deeply committed to this Teutonic origin hypothesis as more popular writers like Fiske. Thirdly, and bound

[17] *Ibid.*, 226.
[18] *Ibid.*, 229.
[19] *Ibid.*, 235-236.

up with this principle of continuity, they were addicted to the "comparative method," with all its dubious assumptions about a unilinear evolutionary development. In view of these three controlling presuppositions alone, it is difficult to take seriously protests like those of G. B. Adams against the use of other and more adequate hypotheses.

All three of these major assumptions the Americans took over in professional emulation of their German teachers and of the English models that so impressed them. But the first, their concentration on political development, was for them, too, closely bound up with the characteristic problems faced in the mid-nineteenth century. Over the library of the historical seminar at Johns Hopkins was inscribed the motto from Freeman: "History is past politics; politics is present history." But Adams himself, like Burgess, interpreted this to mean the kind of constitutional and legal history practiced by Bluntschli and his other teachers at Heidelberg, and by Stubbs and Maine in England. "I have no ambition to be known as a Professor of American History," he wrote President Gilman. "I do not object to the phrase 'Institutional History,' for that describes very happily the nature of my university work in class and seminary." Burgess, whose controlling interest was to develop American political science on the German model, likewise made institutional development the center of his attention in history. "This I might term the ultimate object of our entire method of historical instruction. With us history is the chief preparation for the student of the legal and political sciences."[20]

Ultimately, both the Germans and the Englishmen whom these Americans were following were selecting from the past what would throw light on the pressing problems of nineteenth-century constitutional development with which they were themselves vitally concerned. Adams' teacher Bluntschli, under whom he completed a course and took his degree in historical and political science in 1876, and who, we are told, exercised the strongest influence on his growing mind,[21] was a leader among the German liberals. For him history was always the handmaid of politics. His interest in the development of local institutions of self-government was focused on expanding them into a liberal federal constitution for a united Germany. Stubbs, Maitland and Maine were likewise facing very practical problems of legal and constitutional adjustment. In America, too, for the generation of Adams and Burgess, living in the aftermath of the Civil War, the political unification and consolidation of more local communities still seemed the central American problem. The historical profession, in fact, came into existence, in this country as earlier in Germany, as an integral part of the first serious training in political science. Its founders cultivated "past politics" in this institutional sense precisely because

[20] Burgess, "The Methods of Historical Study and Research in Columbia College," *op. cit.*, 220.
[21] John M. Vincent, *Herbert B. Adams, Tributes of Friends* (Baltimore, 1902), 39.

such "political" problems were those of which they were most acutely aware.

Even as late as 1910 Becker could write: "Since the importance of intellectual and religious development has been comparatively slight, apparently at least, historians, in abandoning the purely political point of view, have limited themselves for the most part to exhibiting the influence of economic and social conditions upon political history. For this purpose, American history presented exceptional opportunities, especially in respect of the Colonial period and the period from 1815 to 1860."[22] When economic factors were introduced, they were brought in, as in Beard's early work, not as themselves central, but for the light they could throw on institutional changes. Thus Burgess' student Osgood, who developed such institutional history most completely, and who was for his time unusually sensitive to the importance of its economic conditions, in 1898 defended the older political emphasis: "The political and constitutional side of the subject, it seems to me, should be given the first place, because it is only through law and political institutions that social forces become in a large sense operative. The directions which these forces take are also largely determined by the political framework within which they act."[23]

During the depression of the 'thirties many Americans came to feel that it was economic rather than political problems that were of primary importance. With the situation Becker described in 1910, just before the full swing to the economic interpretation of politics set in, we have only to compare a book like Louis M. Hacker's *Triumph of American Capitalism*, in which political events appear as the symptoms of fundamental economic changes, to realize the complete shift of incidence. And though interest in American intellectual history, awakened by Tyler, had been growing steadily since Parrington's impressive work—Becker's remark sounds curiously remote today—it took the great ideological conflicts so sharply raised during the last decade to give us histories of American thought like those by Ralph H. Gabriel, Merle Curti, and R. B. Perry.

How the crucial problems later shifted to economics and to ideas is clear enough. What is harder to realize is that the pioneer "scientific" historians were equally concerned with what they saw as the crucial problems of their own day, and that it was these problems that determined their selection of "political" material in the past. Just what that selection was, and the professional influences that played upon him, H. B. Adams has himself set down in a revealing passage.

The idea of studying American Institutional and American Economic History, upon co-operative principles, beginning with local institutions, and extending ultimately to national institutions, developed gradually from an interest in

---

[22] Carl Becker, "Some Aspects . . ." *American Journal of Sociology*, 18 (1912-13), 653.
[23] Cited in D. R. Fox, *Herbert Levi Osgood* (New York, 1924), 86.

municipal history, first awakened in the Seminary of Prof. Erdmannsdoerffer at the University of Heidelberg, where, in 1875, while reading the *Gesta Friderici Imperatoris*, by Otto of Freising, seminary discussion turned upon the Communes of Lombardy and the question of the Roman or Germanic origin of city government in medieval Italy. This awakened interest, quickened by the reading of Carl Hegel, Arnold, Von Maurer, Fustel de Coulanges, was ultimately directed toward England and New England by a suggestion upon the last page of Sir Henry Maine's *Village Communities*, where, quoting Palfrey's *History of New England* (II, 13, 14) and certain remarks in the *Nation* (No. 273) upon the passage by Professor William F. Allen of the University of Wisconsin, Sir Henry calls attention to the survival of Village Communities in America. This suggestive idea, verified in all essential details with reference to Nantucket, Plymouth Plantations, Cape Ann, Salem, and the oldest towns in New England, has been extended gradually to a co-operative study of American local institutions in all the older States and throughout the Northwest, where, in Wisconsin, Professor Allen, the original pioneer, had joined in the work, supported by his Seminary of advanced students.[24]

Here we see clearly how the selective interests developed by Germans and Englishmen to bring their medieval past to bear on their contemporary problems were turned by Adams to American political concerns. After his return to the United States Adams is said never to have opened his German notebooks.[25] He trusted his students to apply critical methods to American materials; from the beginning he encouraged Turner's interests. Unlike Burgess, he did not insist that they complete their real education in Germany. It is interesting that the original impetus to colonial history, in which the "scientific" historians did their most impressive work, came from that sturdy enthusiast for the Northwest, William Allen of Wisconsin, where Turner also carried on the war against the dominance of the historians of the seaboard.

In the 'seventies and 'eighties the two other major assumptions of the "scientific" historians, the Teutonic "germ" theory of political institutions and the comparative method, went hand in hand in this country. Both were vigorously advocated and taught by H. B. Adams and Burgess alike. During the 'nineties, however, their students pushed both into the background; and even the comparative method, which lasted the longer, is little heard of after 1900. Adams' able pupil, C. M. Andrews, as early as 1893, while still defending a qualified comparative method, summarizes the evidence against the Teutonic theory, in what is probably the most

[24] H. B. Adams, "Co-operation in University Work," *Johns Hopkins University Studies in History and Political Science*, 1 (Baltimore, 1883), 80, 81. In a briefer account in *Contributions to American Educational History*, No. 1 (Washington, Bureau of Education, 1887), 173, Adams mentions also "the Harvard School of Anglo-Saxon law," referring to a volume of studies by Henry Adams' students, *Essays in Anglo-Saxon Law* (Boston, 1876).
[25] Albion W. Small, *Origins of Sociology* (Chicago, 1924), 328 note.

competent early discussion. He had criticized Adams' Teutonism severely as far back as 1883, as had Osgood also.

The Teutonic theory originated amongst the leaders of the German national revival, Grimm, Eichhorn, and Savigny. Carried to England by Palgrave and Kemble, it was there used to fan the self-esteem of the "Anglo-Saxon race," not only by popular writers like Charles Kingsley, but by historians like Freeman, and was even adopted by the more cautious Stubbs and Green. But with Americans of the eighteen-eighties it hardly bore the same "racial" stamp, though it lent itself to a scholarly version of American political superiority.[26] By them it was accepted, together with the comparative method, primarily as part of the body of evolutionary ideas they found their teachers applying to social development. It was the continuity of political institutions, and the cultural heritage the colonies received from England, rather than any "racial" theory, that impressed them as being in line with evolutionary thought. The biological continuity was incidental, and the term "race" was very loosely used, even in a man like Moses Coit Tyler. Adams is revealing:

> The science of Biology no longer favors the theory of spontaneous generation. Wherever organic life occurs, there must have been some seed for that life. History should not be content with describing effects when it can explain causes. It is just as improbable that free local institutions should spring up without a germ along American shores as that English wheat should have grown here without planting. Town institutions were propagated in New England by old English and Germanic ideas brought over by Pilgrims and Puritans.[27]

The biological analogy is significant; but even more significant is Adams' real point, the cultural continuity with England. This does not prevent him from going on: "Thus, English historians, Green, Freeman, and Stubbs, recognize their fatherland. The origin of the English Constitution, as Montesquieu long ago declared, is found in the forests of Germany."[28]

More important and lasting was the comparative method, which came not only with the authority of the philologists and the legal historians, but also bearing all the promise of the new evolutionary anthropology of Tylor and Spencer. As Andrews explained in 1893, "The philologists were its sponsors, Grimm and Maurer used it in Germany, Kemble brought it to England, and Sir Henry Maine applied it and extended it from a local to a universal method."[29]

---

[26] See Edward Norman Saveth, "Race and Nationalism in American Historiography: the late Nineteenth Century," *Political Science Quarterly*, 54 (1939), 421-441.
[27] H. B. Adams, "Germanic Origins of New England Towns," *Johns Hopkins University Studies in History and Political Science*, 1 (Baltimore, 1883), 8.
[28] *Ibid.*, 10.
[29] Charles M. Andrews, "Some Recent Aspects of Institutional Study," *Yale Review*, (1892-93), 384.

As the study of anthropology continues, it becomes apparent that the people of this earth are not to each other as though they were inhabitants of different planets; that following the general lines of historical advancement, these people have developed from tribal life to political life in much the same manner; that the stages in their growth have had, from the necessities of the case, certain points of similarity, in consequence of which certain principles of development can be established; which, it is inherently probable, will apply to all peoples when they have reached a similar stage in social and political growth. We must, therefore, compare not anything and everything, but only that evidence which, so far as it can be determined, belongs to corresponding periods in the life of a people, and which alone we have an historical right to compare.[30]

The assumptions involved in the comparative method are here clearly stated. Everywhere society was supposed to have followed the same fixed line of development, and to have passed through the same "stages," from a primitive communism and promiscuity to the "higher" forms of present-day Western civilization. Illustrations of this unilinear pattern could hence be drawn from anywhere, and, torn out of context, fitted into the neat scheme. Little attention was paid to the means whereby these changes were effected; they came "by evolution." Burgess states the essence of the method as applied to institutional development:

What we most insist upon, however, is a critical comparison of the sequence of facts in the history of different states or peoples at a like period in the development of their civilizations. If this be done with patience, care, and judgment, the student who possesses a moderate degree of true logic will soon learn to distinguish, to some extent at least, antecedent and consequent from cause and effect.[31]

By 1893 Andrews is already qualifying the comparative method, in the light of the criticisms of Fustel de Coulanges, Seebohm, and Vinogradoff— who were at the same time the major instruments in effecting the overthrow of the Teutonic theory.

Every people [says the comparative method] of whom we have sufficient knowledge to determine the fact, has passed or is passing through certain stages of institutional and social development. . . . But all people will not develop wholly alike; everywhere will there be seen local and racial divergencies from any common type. Inherent ethnological traits, climate, geographical location, adjacency to certain forms of animal life, completeness of commercial relations, attrition of nations and many other influences, will bring about marked social and political peculiarities, out of which has sprung that peculiar people's contribution to the civilization of the world.[32]

And he goes on to ask that historians correct "the natural tendency of the

[30] *Ibid.*, 385.
[31] Burgess, "The Methods of Historical Study and Research in Columbia College," *op. cit.*, 220.
[32] *Op. cit.*, 388, 389.

older method to conceive of all phases of social, economic, and political life as merely evolutions of something which has gone before. For there is at present a too general willingness to eliminate the influence of extraneous factors, and an unwillingness to allow for direct personal or legislative interference in originating or altering a phase of institutional life."[33]

The Teutonic germ theory was a developmental hypothesis, the comparative method was a procedural postulate. Both have been long since abandoned. More significantly, from the point of view of the claims of the "scientific" historians, neither could remotely be said to have been implicit in "the facts" they were actually used to "anticipate." Each had been developed in Europe as a tool to deal with certain problems; both were applied in America to a quite different set of problems. More broadly, they were both part of that body of ideas by which nineteenth-century thinkers supposed they were applying "the principles of the evolutionary philosophy" to social development. As the latest fashion in scientific theory, they were eminently suited to establish the historical profession on a basis of intellectual respectability. And in the long list of scholarly monographs that began to appear at Johns Hopkins and Columbia, among the best of which was the *Introduction to the Local Constitutional History of the United States* (1889) by Adams' student, George Elliott Howard, they proved their value as leading principles of historical investigation. That they were superseded by more adequate and fruitful hypotheses in the next generation goes only to show that like any heuristic principle they led to the discovery of facts which forced their own modification. They were instruments by which that evolutionary generation sought to understand the past of the problems that concerned it. In the light of their many virtues, there is irony in the fact that the one function they clearly did not and could not serve was that of depicting the past *wie es eigentlich gewesen.*

An excellent summary of almost all the ideas that dominated the first decades of critical, "objective" and "scientific" history—that is, of its assumptions and presuppositions here analyzed—is to be found in the list of "Fundamental Principles of American History" which Albert Bushnell Hart wished "to leave sharply defined in the minds of the students."

  1. *No* nation has a *history disconnected* from that of the rest of the world: the United States is closely related, in point of time, with previous ages; in point of space, with other civilized countries.

  2. *Institutions* are a *growth*, and not a creation: the Constitution of the United States itself is constantly changing with the changes in public opinion.

  3. Our institutions are *Teutonic in origin*; they have come to us through English institutions.

[33] *Ibid.,* 400.

4. The growth of our institutions has been *from local to central:* the general government can, therefore, be understood only in the light of the early history of the country.

5. The *principle of union* is of slow growth in America: the Constitution was framed from necessity, and not from preference.[34]

VI

The greatest achievements of the methods of the pioneer "scientific" historians, and the clearest illustrations of whither their aims and assumptions could lead, are the monumental studies of colonial institutions produced by Herbert L. Osgood, student and colleague of Burgess, and by Charles M. Andrews, trained under H. B. Adams. Here if anywhere is unadulterated devotion to "the fact," especially in Osgood's crammed pages. And here is the cardinal instance of what can be done even if, in accordance with their principle of selection, the "historical fact" be limited to the development of local legal and political institutions. Here is the true American fruit of Bluntschli and Stubbs and Maitland and Maine. Here is the "comparative method" transformed from a speculative evolutionary hypothesis into a factual comparison of the different British colonies. Neither Osgood nor Andrews ever accepted the Teutonic theory. But its core, the basic continuity between English and Colonial institutions, is the controlling assumption of both. Osgood sees English law, administration and imperial policy as the foundation of the colonies, which were a natural outgrowth of the history of England during the middle ages, and preserved their institutional and organic connection; their history is concerned largely with certain medieval survivals. This is the one "correct general idea" Osgood makes central. The whole struggle culminating in the Revolution was but an episode in the development of the English colonial system.[35]

Andrews likewise made central the colonial and British character of the colonies. "The colonial period of our history is not American only but Anglo-American"—"The years from 1607 to 1783 were colonial before they were American or national, and our Revolution is a colonial and not an American problem." This controlling assumption runs through all his volumes; he always insists that colonial history must be approached from the "English end." His magnum opus, not published until the nineteen-thirties, seems particularly conservative because of this thoroughgoing emphasis on the earlier evolutionary idea of continuity, in contrast to the idea of the "mutations wrought by environment" in America which the influence of Turner had made central.

Osgood originally had broad interests in economic history: he had

[34] A. B. Hart, "Methods of Teaching American History," *Methods of Teaching and Studying History,* ed. G. Stanley Hall, 3.

[35] *Bulletin* of the Columbia Department of History (1896), quoted in D. R. Fox, *Herbert Levi Osgood* (New York, 1924), 71-73.

studied under Schmoller and Adolf Wagner. But his position was cautious: "Social and economic forces should be treated as contributing to and conditioning historical development, but the historian must never lose sight of the fact that they operate within a framework of law."[36] In reviewing Osgood's posthumous work, Andrews took him to task for his neglect of economic forces:

> To pay almost exclusive attention to politics, government, and administration and to pass by with only an occasional reference all consideration of economic and social forces, the significance of rising prices, debt, and the cost of living, the growth of regional and radical feeling, and the bearing of commerce and the increase of wealth on legislation is to run at times pretty near the surface and to miss some of the deeper currents of colonial life. . . .
> Professor Osgood's position of viewing all details of his subject from the standpoint of the colonies tends to create in him a disrelish—I would not call it a prejudice—for the British system and all who upheld it, and to make it difficult for him to understand just what was the British outlook before 1763.[37]

On Andrews' charge of anti-British prejudice, it is interesting to read what Osgood himself said of Fiske:

> Two political societies of quite different type were thus brought into conflict, and to the reviewer it seems clear that the historian is bound to do justice to the character and aims of both. . . . The truth is until American historians cease the attempt to defend a dogma, and begin in earnest the effort to understand the aristocratic society which existed in England and the democracy which was maturing here, and the causes of the conflict between the two, we shall not have a satisfactory history either of the colonial period or of the revolution.[38]

Thus does the impartial objectivity of one generation become the biased prejudice of the next.

To complete the story, let us compare this judgment of Andrews on Osgood with the judgment passed in the next decade by a frank employer of methods of economic interpretation on Andrews himself:

> It must be concluded that his history is animated by a conservative spirit. His legalistic approach, his preoccupation with the legal foundation of property rights, and his emphasis upon the role of leaders in colonial history (particularly those of the English upper and upper middle classes) suggests such a conclusion. He assumes that legal and political institutions are the most important elements in the internal history of the colonies, assigning to economic factors a minor role. . . .
> In treating colonial economy he is content merely to describe a few products and activities without probing into the workings of economic forces, without

---

[36] *Ibid.*, 70.
[37] C. M. Andrews, review of Osgood in *American Historical Review*, 31 (1925-26), 536, 537.
[38] Review of Fiske's *American Revolution* (1891), cited in Fox, *op. cit.*, 50*f*.

considering wages, prices, profits, creditor-debtor relationships, and the distribution of income and wealth, and without showing the impact of such factors on law, government, and policy. Without mentioning the productive labor of the servants in New England he describes them as an undesirable, immoral element. . . .

In brief, Professor Andrews has written the history of the legal foundations of colonial government and property rights.[39]

As Professor Nettels points out, "Professor Andrews certainly does not belong to that group of historians who regard themselves as judicial because they refrain from judging." Andrews did not in fact claim to be "objective": "Complete objectivity would be as undesirable as it would be impossible." Yet he also maintained: "Objective history is merely nonpartizan history. To write objectively is merely to write with the detachment of the onlooker rather than with the prejudice of the advocate and to draw conclusions from the evidence itself and not from prepossessions already existing in the writer's mind. History viewed through Whig or Tory spectacles . . . and used to defend a doctrine, a theory, or a philosophy—all such history is a bad guide for the public because it does not tell the truth."[40] Professor Nettels is probably right in suggesting that if ever an historian looked at the past through Tory spectacles, it was Andrews. His whole work is colored by his defense of the British mercantilist policy and by his contempt for the American "radicals" and for the lower classes in general.

In Andrews the "scientific" institutional school had completed the circle. The profession was now so firmly rooted that an historian could afford to give rein to his "strong convictions," and in the process bring out more significant facts than the pure devotees of "the fact." For the moral of the judgments passed by Osgood on Fiske, by Andrews on Osgood, and by Nettels on Andrews, is not only that ways of understanding the past change, and that therefore the historian does not "tell the truth." It is also that in seeking "the truth" in his own way, and in terms of his own assumptions and presuppositions, the historian does manage to add significantly to that store of knowledge we possess about the past.

VII

The first major break with these ideas of the early "scientific" historians came with Frederick Jackson Turner. His paper, "The Significance of the Frontier in American History," read at Chicago in 1893, was, in the words of Beard, "destined to have a more profound influence on thought about American history than any other essay or volume ever written on the

---

[39] Curtis Nettels, review in *New England Quarterly*, 10 (1937), 793-795.

[40] C. M. Andrews, "These Forty Years," *American Historical Review*, 30 (1924-25), 243, 244.

subject."[41] Turner is conventionally identified, much too narrowly, of course, with this frontier hypothesis. Actually, he had an extremely broad conception of history, and of the various approaches and hypotheses by which the past might be illuminated. Although he did not himself follow them all up, there is hardly a way of exploring and interpreting the American past employed by later historians that is not suggested in his writings. And from the first he was clear upon the role of interpretative hypotheses in historical investigation.

Superficially, Turner's great influence came from the fact that he had delivered for American history a Declaration of Independence from the domination of the seaboard historians and their problems of colonial "origins." He broadened its central theme into the building of a continental nation. He encouraged a host of writings on the various phases of American internal expansion, and on the conflicts of the democratic agrarian freehold economy with its rivals in the East and South. Many of his disciples had much narrower perspectives than Turner himself, and went further in identifying a distinctive American "democracy" with the crudities of frontier life—although he cannot be wholly absolved from responsibility for the loose and superficial dilution of the "democratic idea" to cover anything and everything.

More significant in the long run in changing concepts of historical method was the very fact that Turner had dared to advance explicitly not only a new principle of selection, but also a full-fledged hypothesis to guide the investigation and interpretation of historical facts. And he went on to a second, the importance of sectionalism in American life, conceived in intellectual and cultural as well as in economic terms. This hypothesis of the divergent and conflicting interests and ideas of different economic and cultural "sections" or regions has entered deeply into all later investigation of our history. It has colored and cut across even the class-conflict theory of the Marxian 'thirties, and has given a distinctive American stamp to all serious economic interpretations of our national life. Perhaps most important of all, Turner's economic sectionalism for the first time made such economic interpretation respectable.[42]

Finally, in identifying what was distinctively American with the "democracy" of the freeholding frontier, Turner was fully aware that he was making central, for understanding the past as well as for acting in the present, the new problems that had succeeded the earlier ones that still dominated the schools of Adams and Burgess. The issue of national unification had in fact given way to the struggle between the agrarian interests of the Populists and early Progressives against Eastern capitalism. The epic of the slow building of a federal structure out of local institutions

---

[41] Beard, "The Frontier in American History," *loc. cit.*, 359.
[42] *Cf.* Beard's, *An Economic Interpretation of the Constitution of the United States*, 5.

now in Turner likewise gave way to the epic conflict between Jeffersonian and Hamiltonian principles. For those who understood the significance of Turner, "detachment" and sheer worship of "the fact" were over. One might not be committed, like Turner, to the agrarian cause. One might not even distinguish the protagonists in the struggle quite as simply as he did. But one could not fail to perceive the illumination that came from reading it in the light of present problems. It would still take several decades to overcome the institutionalized inertia of the profession. But for those who grasped Turner, the battle was over. Principles of interpretation were fruitful, and they were most fruitful when related to continuing problems.

In actual fact, of course, Turner was not for the first time introducing assumptions into "scientific" history. He was making explicit the assumptions already there. And he was doing it, not by opposing those presuppositions radically, but rather by modifying them in detail. Thus, he did not challenge the accepted principle that the central concern of the historian should be the development of American political institutions. Rather, he viewed those institutions in a new light, as the democracy of the frontier; he turned to the interplay of forces that constituted the history of that development.

Turner had had many discussions at Johns Hopkins with Woodrow Wilson as to what constitutes the distinctive basis of American nationalism.

Thus the advance of the frontier has meant a steady movement away from the influence of Europe, a steady growth of independence on American lines. And to study this advance, the men who grew up under these conditions, and the political, economic, and social results of it, is to study the really American part of our history.[43]

Here too, in transforming the national epic into the history of the shifting West, Turner was actually doing just about what the Easterners had long been doing for their own sections. He was as much if not more of a nationalist than they. He often went as far in identifying Middle-Western with American institutions and attitudes as his teacher William F. Allen, who had a fine enthusiasm for the North-West as the key to the "imperial destiny of the United States," and to its national policy.[44]

This side of Turner has recently come in for a good deal of criticism by Easterners, who speak of the "intra-United States tendency" of Turnerian study, and even of his "isolationism."[45] But two years before his Chicago address, in 1891, Turner himself had written:

[43] *Early Writings of Frederick Jackson Turner* (Madison, 1938), 189.
[44] William Francis Allen, "Place of the North-West in General History" (1888), William Francis Allen, *Monographs and Essays* (Boston, 1890), 110-111.
[45] *Cf.* G. W. Pierson, *Pennsylvania Magazine of History and Biography*, 64 (1940), 449*ff.*, and *New England Quarterly*, 15 (1942), 224*ff.* Pierson gives credit to Richard H. Shryock and Dixon Ryan Fox.

Not only is it true that no country can be understood without taking account of all the past; it is also true that we cannot select a stretch of land and say we will limit our study to this land; for local history can only be understood in the light of the history of the world. There is unity as well as continuity.[46]

Thus from the beginning Turner viewed the development of distinctively American institutions as an extension and modification of the history of Western civilization, though the concern with the American phase gradually came to overshadow for him the larger whole within which it originally had its setting.

Moreover, Turner was as much of a social evolutionist as the other historians of the 'eighties, and even more anxious to make use of biological concepts. But, uninfluenced by the idealistic evolutionary thought of the Germans, he was closer to Darwinian ideas of variation under different conditions. Where those who had studied in Germany, following the European lead, had emphasized the side of continuity with remote "origins," he brought to the fore the modifying influence of the new American environment, its function in selecting and adapting new forms, new institutions, new patterns of thought.

The outcome is not the old Europe, not simply the development of Germanic germs, any more than the first phenomenon was a case of reversion to the Germanic mark. The fact is, that here is a new product that is American. . . . The existence of an area of free land, its continuous recession, and the advance of American settlement westward, explain American development. . . . American democracy is fundamentally the outcome of the experience of the American people in dealing with the West.[47]

Turner seems to have derived his evolutionary ideas more from Darwin than from Spencer: his references to biological theory are direct. But he expanded his evolutionary environmentalism in the direction of the sociologists who were emphasizing geographical influences. He owed something to Buckle, and more to Ratzel and Albion Small;[48] he was early struck by Josiah Royce's study of California as a distinctive "province." There is much in his conception of a "section" that resembles the "region" of the sociologist and the "culture area" of the anthropologist. The firm hold the sectional theory came to obtain was undoubtedly strengthened by its congeniality with that type of thought. Turner himself apparently worked out the idea in relative independence. But his historical hypothesis was part

---

[46] "The Significance of History," *Early Writings,* 57.

[47] Frederick Jackson Turner, *The Frontier in American History* (New York, 1920), 4, 1, 266. *Cf.* Merle Curti, "The Section and the Frontier in American History: the Methodological Concepts of F. J. Turner," *Methods in Social Science,* ed. S. A. Rice (Chicago, 1931).

[48] Fulmer Mood, "Turner's Formative Period," *Early Writings,* 3*ff.*

of a broad movement toward environmentalism in all the evolutionary social sciences, which developed in criticism of the overemphasis on continuity and origins in the generation of Spencer and Tylor.

Turner was no narrow geographical determinist. He specifically denied that any single factor is determinative, or absolutely dictates to man, and he advocated a "multiple hypothesis" scheme of historical interpretation, providing room for "stock," inherited ideals, and spiritual factors.[49] Indeed, his contention was that the conditions of the frontier, on the "hither edge of free land," did not force any particular institutions on men. They rather freed men from the compulsions of habit and law, and made it possible for them to work out new experiments in institutional forms. The frontier was not coercive but emancipating, not a limit to be accepted but a challenge to be faced actively. Turner's social evolutionism saw no automatic process, coming either from a growing "germ" in continuous development or from the pressure of an external environment. He had freed himself both from the evolving *Geist* of the Germans, and from the mechanical progress of the Spencerian sociologists. He was working his way toward that humanistic, experimental, and pragmatic conception of social evolution as the human use of natural conditions and materials, which came to the fore in American social thought around 1910, to find its philosophic formulation in John Dewey, and its exemplification among historians in Carl Becker and Charles Beard.

From the beginning Turner was conscious of the relation between his hypotheses for interpreting the past and the new problems he faced as a Wisconsin Progressive. He made his functional conception of history clear in his early essay of 1891 on "The Significance of History."

The historical study of the first half of the nineteenth century reflected the thought of that age. It was an age of political agitation and inquiry, as our own age still so largely is. It was an age of science. That inductive study of phenomena which has worked a revolution in our knowledge of the external world was applied to history. In a word, the study of history became scientific and political.

Today the questions that are uppermost, and that will become increasingly important, are not so much political as economic questions. The age of machinery, of the factory system, is also the age of socialistic inquiry. . . .

Each age tries to form its own conception of the past. *Each age writes the history of the past anew with reference to the conditions uppermost in its own time.* . . . 'The whole mode and manner of looking at things alters with every age,' but this does not mean that the real events of a given age change; it means that our comprehension of these facts changes.[50]

[49] But *cf.* Shryock, "American Historiography," 37, 38.
[50] *Early Writings*, 51, 52.

In his presidential address to the American Historical Association in 1910, in the midst of the struggle between the Progressives and the Old Guard, he emphasized the close relation between his way of understanding the past and the political struggles among conflicting economic interests central in his own day: "There is disclosed by present events a new significance to these contests of radical democracy and conservative interests."[51] The whole long history of American development was thus brought to a focus in the issues of 1910, and illuminated by them.

This functional conception of the historian's principles of interpretation, so clearly entertained by Turner and applied in his own distinctive hypotheses, led far beyond the particular struggles of the Progressive era in terms of which he himself read the American past. As the crucial issues themselves deepened with growing industrialization, it demanded the further elaboration of those hypotheses. In effecting such an extension, subsequent historians were remaining true to Turner's spirit, however far they might depart from his letter. In 1910 it was natural, and still possible to identify the spearhead of "radical democracy" with the Middle-Western heirs of the old frontier. Another decade, of Wilson and of war, broadened the contest to include as a central protagonist the working class of the great industrial cities. Turner's agrarian perspective began to seem too narrow. Historians like Beard, who had started with an economic regionalism close to Turner's, were led to emphasize the past role of other factors and other economic interests which Turner had neglected but whose historical importance now stood revealed. As the basis and the very texture of American democratic programs shifted more and more to the demands of the urban industrial classes, there stood out in sharper relief the significance, in past conflicts also, of the democratic impulses of Eastern idealism, and of the long story of labor organization.

Thus Turner's own principles pointed to that very extension and supplementation of his particular limited hypotheses which has formed the main task of more recent historical interpretation. With the shifting and broadened incidence of the major economic conflict, Turner's championship of the Middle West and of frontier agrarian democracy came to be balanced by a juster recognition of the importance, in the complex interplay of forces in American history, of other sections and of other economic groups.

During the 'twenties this more adequate and less simplified version of economic sectionalism was still carried on within the framework set by Turner's assumption of the distinctively American character of American history. American problems continued to dominate the historian, and he plunged into an eager investigation of the background of the struggle of competing ideas and economic interests on the contemporary scene. For

---

[51] "Social Forces in American History," *Frontier in American History*, 328.

the great majority this concentration on rather narrowly national issues was even intensified by the depression of the 'thirties. Most historians then reflected the widespread desire to find somewhere in the American past a distinctively American answer to all our economic difficulties. Those who did look beyond the seas turned back in alarm, convinced that our country must be different, and must be kept unique. Turnerian nationalism, conceived primarily in economic terms, but now with a new ideological emphasis on "the American way," seemed everywhere in the ascendant.

To be sure, the 'thirties also saw the rise of new schools of interpretation to challenge this basic nationalism. But it would not be too much to say that even this further break with Turner's underlying assumption was still exemplifying his own functional principle. Face to face with new issues that seemed to them to transcend the too narrow limits of a purely American economic conflict, these minority schools were compelled to understand even the American past in more universal ways and in a broader setting. Thus the Marxians saw America not as unique, but as a cardinal instance of the common pattern of capitalistic development. Their histories consequently abandoned Turner's nationalistic perspective, and tried instead to bring out in the American past all those traits it shared with the general history of Western industrialism. For they were setting out from the problems of a world-wide depression and a world-wide conflict of interests and ideas; they were trying to understand why America too had been swept into the world current. They read American problems in the light of world issues.

In the post-Marxian present, there are many signs that America's radically changed status among the nations, bringing with it a host of new international problems, is provoking a fundamental reaction against the whole nationalistic emphasis that has dominated American historians for a generation. These new and unfamiliar issues will doubtless express themselves in a further reorientation of the way in which historians will understand our past. Indeed, there is already emerging a major conflict between two perspectives for interpreting American history. On the one hand stand those, still in the great majority, who hold to Turner's assumption of a distinctive American development, in economic organization and problems as well as in democratic ideals and ways of life. On the other hand stand those who see the growth of America as an integral part of the history of the western world in which she now holds so commanding and responsible a position. If the second group are likely to increase in number and influence, this is to say, with Turner, that "the conditions uppermost in our own time" have profoundly altered, and that, confronting significantly new problems, we must of necessity find other aspects of our past more basic than those we have recently emphasized. Those who would supplement Turner's own nationalism with such a broader perspective are really vindicating his fundamental conception of historical understanding.

VIII

In Turner are to be found, at least implicitly, nearly all the ideas more recent American historians have pushed further. Above all, he revealed the assumptions of the "scientific" and "objective" school for what they were. In proposing alternatives, he raised the whole question of the basis for choosing principles of selection to be employed. He strikingly illustrated the utility of hypotheses of interpretation. He suggested the expansion of the "field" of history to include social, cultural, and intellectual developments. And he was among the first to conceive the whole enterprise of history in the functional terms of the new humanistic and pragmatic philosophy that was emerging from the American social sciences.

During the decade of the nineteen-hundreds all these suggestions were rapidly exploited in their several directions. Most obvious was the sheer broadening of the possible subject-matter of the historian to embrace any or all aspects of civilization and culture. Lamprecht's visit in connection with the St. Louis Exposition proved a great stimulus to what was loosely called "the new history." These unsettling ferments created alarm in the more institutionalized members of the profession, whose precious traditions went back as far as the eighteen-eighties. Then around 1910 the heretics began to take the offensive, proclaiming their own programs and vigorously attacking in unmeasured tones the presuppositions of the founding fathers of the profession.

At the same meeting of the American Historical Association in 1910 at which Turner read his presidential address on "Social Forces in American History," James Harvey Robinson presented a paper on "The Relation of History to the Newer Sciences of Man." He started a controversial discussion, in which George L. Burr defended the conservatives and George H. Mead supported Robinson. The same year Carl Becker, in his article on "Detachment and the Writing of History," in the *Atlantic Monthly*, had launched the first of his major attacks on "the fact" to which "objectivists" were proclaiming their undying devotion. In the *Popular Science Monthly*, writing on "The Scientific Presentation of History," Lynn Thorndike made similar sharp criticisms of the methodology of the scientific school. In 1910 and 1911 appeared two economic interpretations: A. M. Simons' *Social Forces in American History*, definitely socialist, and Gustavus Myers' *History of Great American Fortunes*. In 1912 Robinson issued a collected volume of his essays on *The New History*. The same year Becker delivered his address on "Some Aspects of the Influence of Social Problems and Ideas upon the Study and Writing of History," perhaps the clearest early statement of the functional and pragmatic view. In 1913 was issued Beard's *An Economic Interpretation of the Constitution*.

A bare list like this suggests how thick and fast the rebels were hurling their shafts against the older "scientific" history. And they won the day. After a few years of vigorous controversy, serious opposition subsided. Enterprising historians were henceforth free, if not exactly encouraged, to select what aspect of the past they might choose, and to employ what principles of interpretation they might find illuminating. Gradually their results ceased to be impugned on the ground that as "historians" they had no right to start with such assumptions. Assumptions came slowly to be judged by the competence and brilliance with which they were used to explore the past, and to be criticized in their own terms in the light of their interpretative value. The older political historians were not indeed driven from the "field." They continued to form the majority, and, like Andrews, to produce very substantial work. But their ideas were now on the defensive. It was generally recognized that they too had principles of selection and methods of interpretation, and those principles and methods now had to justify themselves, like any others, by their fruits.

With this practical recognition of the functional nature of historical knowledge, American historiography had come of age. To be sure, there was to be continuing controversy over the efforts of reflective historians like Carl Becker and Charles Beard to formulate in theoretical terms their conceptions of the historian's enterprise. The profession, even in its outstanding leaders, can hardly be said even as yet to have achieved complete clarity as to its methodological principles. And large numbers, who greatly admire in others the fruits of the practice of a functional history, and perhaps ably carry it on themselves, nevertheless in their own theory of history retain many elements from the assumptions of earlier days. But in this lag the historical profession is scarcely unique. It is notorious that most natural scientists are apt to be none too clear when they try to analyze all that is implied in the very methods they themselves may be so brilliantly exemplifying. In stating their methods, they are very likely to fall back on what they early learned their methods should be, oblivious of how they themselves have improved on what they were taught. In this, historians by and large can well claim that they are thoroughly scientific. Theoretical clarity as to method seems to be possible only after that method has been painfully elaborated in practice.

The major achievements in American history after 1920 are frankly functional; the fact needs no belaboring. They employ principles of selection and of interpretation of which their authors are clearly conscious. That selection and that interpretation have been brought to a focus upon the critical problems that have successively confronted the American people. There are still those who, recognizing this present practice of our historians, regard it with regret as a lapse from the high standards of those who raised American historiography to a position of prestige. This essay, as indeed this whole volume, maintains rather that it is rooted in the nature of the historical enterprise itself. We have endeavored to show that this was in fact the practice of those "scientific" and "objective" founders of the profession in America who in theory denied it. In becoming aware of their controlling assumptions, and in consciously striving to work out hypotheses and principles of interpretation that would contribute most fruitfully to the understanding of basic American problems as they have seen them, our more recent historians have actually been following the lead and carrying on the work of the great pioneers of the last generation. They have been able to do it more critically and more intelligently, because they have realized more clearly just what it is they are doing.

CHAPTER III

WHAT HISTORIANS HAVE SAID
ABOUT THE CAUSES OF THE
CIVIL WAR

By Howard K. Beale

A NALYSIS OF historians' efforts to explain the coming of the American Civil War reveals a surprising variety of attitudes toward that conflict and toward causation in general. In their methods of dealing with causes, historians fall into three groups. Some explicitly raise and answer questions of "why" and "how." Others, without actually dealing with causes, order their material in sequences in which causation is implicit. Still others eschew all effort at interpretation, perhaps because interpretation is to them wrong, impossible, or perilous; they present the Civil War and its antecedents as "merely chaos floating into chaos," as Charles Beard once described the result of refusal to attempt interpretation of historical facts—in itself an interpretation. One can read, for example, eighteen hundred pages of John B. McMaster's cataloguing of information about the three ante-bellum decades without discovering therein any hint or implication of causality.

Even as they begin their work historians differ widely in their predispositions. Some exhibit a cocksureness that brooks no questioning of their possession of all the answers; others display tentativeness and modesty sprung from experience with the difficulty of diagnosing human motives and values. Some authors have attained an impartiality and detachment that make their frames of reference difficult to determine; others, while professing "objectivity," write with patent though unavowed bias; still others frankly confess their own philosophy and then, within its limits, exhibit fairmindedness that approaches the objectivity of the more exact sciences.

Historians, whatever their predispositions, assign to the Civil War causes ranging from one simple force or phenomenon to patterns so complex and manifold that they include, intricately interwoven, all the important movements, thoughts, and actions of the decades before 1861. One writer finds in events of the immediately preceding years an adequate explanation of the War; another feels he must begin his story with 1831 or even 1820; still another goes back to the importation of the first slaves, to descriptions of geographic differences before white men appeared, or to differentiation in Europe between those who settled North and South. For instance, John W. Draper treated at length such subjects as geography, the Negro in Africa, colonization of America, the white man in Europe, the Saxon and Norman invasions of England, and the shift from Roman to Gothic architecture; out of 634 pages of his *American Civil War* devoted to the coming of war, 350 pages dealt with these comparatively remote influences. Moral, ideological, political, economic, social, psychological explanations of the War have been offered. Responsibility has been ascribed both to actions of men and to forces beyond human control. Conspiracy, constitutional interpretation, human wickedness, economic interest, divine will, political ambition, climate, "irrepressible conflict," emotion, rival cultures, high moral principles, and chance have severally been accredited with bringing on the War. There is a Marxian interpretation; also a racist theory.

Certain questions confront every historian of the Civil War who does not merely accept and repeat conventional explanations. First, which facts shall he include? Granted that the Civil War was in a broad sense the consequence of forces and events and experiences that include most of American life and thought prior to 1861 and much of antecedent European and human development, still, if one is to interpret at all, he must choose out of all historical data certain facts that he thinks explain or help to explain the coming of the Civil War. This selection, like all interpretation, necessitates making difficult and sometimes arbitrary decisions. It requires drawing chronological lines back of which the influence is too remote to merit inclusion. It means, too, separating out from the immediate past whatever is necessary to understanding the reasons for the War and distinguishing this material from the nonessential, too meagerly pertinent remainder. One must somewhere break the chain in which A is caused by B which is caused by C which is caused by D into infinity and the equally endless sequence whereby A is interrelated with B which affects C which influences D which modifies E among contemporaneous forces or men.

This process of selection and emphasis involves evaluation and thought, which are more difficult than fact-collecting. It requires a realization that synthesis often proves merely tentative and hence frequently demands modification as times and techniques and horizons change. Any one author's selection may be questioned by scholars of differing backgrounds. Interpretation is challenging to undertake but full of hazard for the historian's reputation; inherent difficulties make some men avoid it. Unfortunately the men best equipped to interpret adequately are sometimes so appalled by human incapacity to interpret satisfactorily that they deliberately seek to avoid interpreting, and the men who do it with assurance sometimes so little comprehend the perils that they are unsuited to do it at all.

Through their selection of facts, even recent historians, on some subjects, have maintained interpretations as opposite as those of their Northern and Southern ancestors of eighty years ago. For example, in 1939 two books on the slavery controversy appeared simultaneously, one by Dwight L. Dumond, born in Ohio, educated in the North, and professor in Ohio and Michigan, and the other by Arthur Y. Lloyd, born in Kentucky, educated in the South, and professor in a Kentucky teachers' college. Dumond wrote with a sympathy for the anti-slavery cause that might have pleased an abolitionist, and Lloyd with an animosity toward it that would have done credit to a pro-slavery Southerner of 1861. Similarly in their 1930 debate over Lincoln's election, Arthur C. Cole, born in Michigan, educated entirely in the North, and professor in Northern universities, and J. G. de Roulhac Hamilton, born in North Carolina, educated in the South except for his Ph.D. training at Columbia, and long-time professor at the University of North Carolina, looked at the same facts and reached the same diverse conclusions as their fellow-sectionalists in 1861. Cole maintained that Lincoln was moderate and the South had nothing to fear from his election so far as slavery in the states was concerned, whereas Hamilton insisted that Lincoln was radical on the slavery issue and there was "every indication" that overt "aggression against slavery" was forestalled only by secession. Implicit in Cole's discussion was a belief that slavery was wrong, and he explicitly stated that the "doom of slavery . . . was sealed . . . by the social and economic forces" of nineteenth century America. Implicit in Hamilton's reply was condemnation of Northerners who opposed slavery. Cole made obvious his disapproval of ante-bellum Southern institutions and Hamilton his dislike of ante-bellum Northern critics of the South.

Secondly arises the problem of relating the underlying forces to specific events. Are the series of dramatic episodes, sometimes labeled "immediate causes," that preceded the Civil War "causes," or are they merely surface manifestations of underlying forces? Did they in themselves affect history or are they merely incidents in the unfolding of more significant phenomena that did?

Thirdly, what is the relationship of the sectional conflict to the War? Can the two be separated? If war need not have arisen from sectional conflict, then which forces were the causes of the conflict and which of the War, and what bearing does one set of causes have on the other?

Fourthly, what influence did the actors who dominated the ante-bellum scene exert upon these historic forces and events?

The answers to these questions in histories of the Civil War, whether implicit or expressed, depend upon the background and training of the writers, upon the time and place in which they lived and wrote, and upon their philosophies of history and of life or their lack of any conscious philosophies.

I

Conspiracy of selfish or wicked men—under what one might call the "devil theory" of history—was once widely accredited, particularly in the period from 1861 to 1900, as a cause of the Civil War. Indeed, some writers have called it *"the* cause." But there are Southern "devils" and Northern "devils," and this conspiracy hypothesis has two faces.

Southern writers describe an aggressive North determined to destroy the South and its institutions. Chief among the offenders, of course, were the abolitionists bent on stirring up servile insurrection and encouraging slaves to escape. The peace of the Union was disturbed by the fanaticism of the abolition attack; forces in the South that might require apology are explained as part of the South's reaction to the unreasoning outburst against it, and may therefore be blamed upon the abolitionists. Important factors that brought on the War were: the *Liberator;* anti-slavery societies; irritating activities of the anti-slavery forces in Congress led by John Quincy Adams and Joshua Giddings in the 'thirties and 'forties; the organized flood of abolition petitions; formation of the Free-Soil Party; efforts to deprive the South of its just gains in the settling of Texas and winning the Mexican War; the persistent reappearance of the Wilmot Proviso; machinations of the New England Emigrant Aid Society; John Brown's activities in Kansas including the "Pottawatomie massacre"; Northern refusal to admit Kansas under the Lecompton Constitution; free-state men's refusal to obey the Fugitive Slave Act; successful work of the Underground Railway; personal liberty laws and slave rescues; attacks on the slave trade and slavery in the District of Columbia; anti-Southern activities of anti-slavery clergy, speakers, and press; charges that Southern institutions and Southerners themselves were evil; organization of the Republicans as a sectional party bent on ruining and then ruling the South; Republicans' espousal of the anti-slavery cause; their circulation of *Uncle Tom's Cabin* and Helper's *Impending Crisis;* attacks of Chase, Seward, and Sumner in Congress; Northern refusal to accept the Dred Scott Decision; reputed Republican intention to destroy slavery in the states; the North's greed for power and determination to aggrandize itself; Lincoln's "radical" anti-slavery, anti-Southern attitudes; Lincoln's election with all it implied in Southern minds; Republican defeat of compromise efforts; attempts to provision Sumter; and Republican determination to "coerce" Southern states. According to this theory, Northerners were persistently aggressive against a South that loved the Union and merely wished to be let alone with proper respect, under the Constitution, for its local institutions. Repeatedly the North violated the Constitution, broke its promises, and repudiated compromise agreements. Northerners were guilty of hypocrisy and sophistry. The phrases "Black Republicans" and "abolitionists," loosely applied, symbolize the attitude of this school of writers.

Unprovoked Northern attack, they maintain, forced the South first to secede, and later to fight, purely in self-defense.

A Northern counterpart of this explanation portrays a conspiracy of slaveholders determined to rule the Union or break it. The plot had been laid long before the War and the conspirators included men in high national offices who used those offices to further their schemes of overthrowing the Constitution they were sworn to serve. The conspirators' aim was, of course, to force the nation to accept slavery and to protect slavery by national power, not only in Southern states but in all territories, and ultimately in Northern states as well. According to the "slaveholders' conspiracy" theory the factors that brought war were much like those named above but with a reverse emphasis. They included: constant attacks on anti-slavery men; the gag resolution by which Congress for a time refused to receive petitions; the effort to censure venerable John Quincy Adams because of his "courageous stand" for "democratic principles"; pro-slavery agitation in Congress; exclusion of free discussion of slavery in the South, violence or threats of violence against anti-slavery advocates in the South, and acts like driving Judge Hoar, official representative of Massachusetts, from South Carolina; plotting to add to slave area by annexation of Texas and by war with Mexico, coupled with failure to insist upon American claims in Oregon, which would be free territory; later efforts to extend slavery by acquisition of tropical possessions; use of the nation's foreign service for pro-slavery ends; attempts to win the national territories for slavery, exemplified in Calhoun's stand on the constitutional position of slavery in the territories; the plotting of Douglas and pro-slavery senators to pass the Kansas-Nebraska Act and repeal the Missouri Compromise, activities of Missourians in Kansas, Buford's organized effort to capture Kansas for slavery, and acts of violence like the "sack of Lawrence"; Buchanan's pro-Southern policy in Kansas and elsewhere including his effort to foist the Lecompton Constitution upon free Kansas; the Dred Scott Decision, described as a conspiracy of slaveholders, Supreme Court, and President; imposition of the obnoxious Fugitive Slave Act upon an unwilling North; kidnaping of free Negroes; smuggling slaves into America and efforts to legalize the foreign slave trade; propagation of pro-slavery arguments and attacks on "free" institutions by Southern clergy, speakers, and press; substitution of a pro-slavery bloc for the old national parties; determination to entrench slavery and federal protection for it in the Constitution; the position of Davis, Atchison, and other pro-slavery men in Congress; the Nashville Convention of 1850 and repeated efforts of Rhett, Ruffin, Yancey, and others to break up the Union; the slavery-bred habituation of Southerners to the use of violence, their brandishing of weapons and threats of duels in Congress,.and the attack upon Sumner with subsequent lionizing of Brooks for it; Southerners' scheming to split the Democratic

Party at Charleston in 1860 in order to insure Lincoln's election so as to force secession on unwilling Southern Unionists; long-continued control of the federal government by Southerners with the aid of their Northern allies and use of that power to settle issues in their own favor to the injury of the North; the slavocracy's determination to hold on to this power or to destroy the Union when they could no longer control it—in short, to rule or ruin; desire of Southern leaders to secede rather than compromise in 1860-1861 and extremists' clever demands intended to defeat compromise while pretending to support it; attack on the Union through secession; seizing of federal properties; and, finally, the firing on Sumter. The attitude of upholders of this view is indicated by their frequent use of "fire-eaters," "slavocracy," "rebels," and, for Northern accomplices, "doughfaces." They charge Southerners with cant and hypocrisy. The North went to war, they say, to defend the Union and the Constitution against unprovoked attack, after repeated violations of the Constitution, breaking of promises, and repudiation of compromise agreements.

Both North and South were flooded with this type of history for years after the War. James G. Blaine, Horace Greeley, John A. Logan, and Henry Wilson were good examples of Northern writers of this type. In 1886 Theodore Roosevelt wrote of the "reckless ambition" of Southern leaders and classed Jefferson Davis with Benedict Arnold. As late as 1904 he still condemned Davis as a traitor. One of the earliest and perhaps the most effective of Southern exponents of the conspiracy view was Edward A. Pollard who put out the first version of his history in 1862. Subsequently, he softened his asperity, but he continued to deny that slavery caused the War and he repeated the charges of Northern aggression in each re-writing. Among numerous Southerners appeared in 1866 one vigorous Northern expounder of the "Northern conspiracy" view. He was Rushmore G. Horton, campaign biographer of Buchanan in 1856, ardent Democrat, and wartime Copperhead. His history, which sold 75,000 copies, was published by Van Evrie, Horton and Company of New York, who also sponsored "anti-abolition tracts."

A second generation finally dropped the sectional bitterness and partisanship sufficiently to produce from about 1890 to 1920 a number of histories in which the authors attempted to see the points of view of both regions. This period saw the appearance of the works of James Schouler, James Ford Rhodes, John B. McMaster, and Southerners of the Dunning school. These writers were still influenced by their parents' feelings sufficiently to understand their own section better than the rival one. They still exhibited unconscious biases, but they were trying hard to ferret out and overcome them. They did abandon the terms "rebel" and "Black Republican" and ceased to talk about abolitionists' and slaveholders' conspiracies. Northerners stopped speaking of the "War of the Rebellion" and some Southerners began dropping "War between the States." Northerners commenced to pay tribute to the character of Lee, Stephens, and Davis. The Southern picture of Lincoln was redrawn.

Contrary to the general trend, occasional recent examples of reversion to the early "devil theory" have appeared. In 1925 two Texans republished Rushmore G. Horton's work of 1866 with its vigorous expounding of Northern aggression and added a dedication to "Copperheads of the North . . . who refused to bow the knee to the *Baal* of commercial and imperialized aggression." And as late as 1941 Frank L. Owsley described as the cause of the War "the egocentric, the destructive, the evil, the malignant type of sectionalism" of the North and "the abuse and villification" with which "the moral and intellectual leaders of the North" attacked "slavery and the entire structure of southern society." "Indeed," Owsley averred, ". . . neither Dr. Goebbels nor Virginio Gayda nor Stalin's propaganda agents have as yet been able to plumb the depths of vulgarity and obscenity reached . . . by . . . abolitionists of note."

Yet many of the new generation of historians of the nineteen-twenties and nineteen-thirties in both North and South have produced histories nearly free from even unconscious sectional patriotism. It required a world war, the passage of sixty years, and the rise of a third generation that for the most part had not known veterans of either army to escape the war-bred conviction that war came through opponents' conspiracy and wickedness. Occasional telltale phrases or inherited attitudes that unmistakably reveal a Northern or a Southern upbringing do crop out. The greater part of this new generation, however, in both sections, have ceased to concern themselves with "blame" for the War and justification of their ancestors and have turned instead to other approaches.

II

As the years passed an increasing number of historians saw the War not as a conspiracy of one group but as a struggle between two groups with irreconcilable interests. It was not until the eighteen-nineties that Frederick Jackson Turner popularized the word "sectional." Yet much earlier than that the War was interpreted as a quarrel between two rival regions. The terms, however, in which the clash of sections is described have changed time after time.

In the first generation, Southerners interpreted the controversy in terms of constitutional theory and Northerners in terms of conflicting moral standards. Between 1861 and 1900, Southerners, particularly leaders in the losing cause, wrote histories and memoirs seeking to justify their own course by maintaining that they fought to protect constitutional principles. The War as described by these men was a contest over types of government. Republicans sought to establish a highly centralized national regime exercising vast powers. Southerners stood firmly on a retention of power in the states where they insisted the framers had meant it to be and where it was the more safely and wisely exercised. A parallel was drawn between the eleven Southern states in 1861 and the thirteen colonies in 1776, both acting on the motive of protecting themselves against oppression. This view denied slavery as a major cause of war and stressed instead the menace of concentration of power in the central government. In his *Constitutional View of the Late War between the States* in 1868 Alexander H. Stephens, while admitting that "slavery, so called," was the "occasion" or "main exciting proximate cause" of the War, insisted it was "not the real cause." In two huge works, he sought to prove that Northern violation of Southern constitutional rights brought on the War and to establish the soundness of the Southern view on state rights and the compact theory of the Constitution. In his *Rise and Fall of the Confederate Government* in 1881 and his *Short History of the Confederate States of America* in 1890, Jefferson Davis, too, argued that slavery was "in no wise the cause of the conflict, but only an incident." It was Northern destruction of the Union as established by the fathers, he contended, and Northern violation of constitutional guarantees that forced Southerners reluctantly to withdraw from a compact, already broken, in which there was no longer safety for them. Both Stephens and Davis defended the right of secession.

Then, as a profession of trained historians arose in the 'eighties and 'nineties, a generation of scholars interested in political and constitutional problems assumed leadership and further emphasized constitutional issues. For example, Hermann E. von Holst, though primarily concerned with the slavery issue, called his work a "constitutional" history and devoted considerable space to discussion of the constitutional aspect of the conflict. Of this group, however, John W. Burgess was the dean. His *Middle Period* in 1897 and his *Civil War and the Constitution* in 1901 constituted a masterly attack on the position so painstakingly presented by Stephens and Davis. Burgess maintained that the Southern doctrines of state sovereignty and secession were supported neither by sound constitutional theory nor by "sound political science" and he blamed Southern leaders for the War. Burgess's Tennessee birth and background might have led one to expect him to agree with Stephens and Davis, but he had happened to come from the strongly Unionist portion of Tennessee and he had served in the Union Army. Subsequent training in a German university then had intensified and given scholarly backing for his youthful devotion to nationalism.

In Northern histories during this period from 1861 to 1900, slavery as a moral issue played the role that loyalty to the compact theory and state rights did among Southerners as an explanation of the sectional clash. For a generation or two after the War most Northern writers talked of the "irrepressible conflict" between freedom and slavery. Slavery had been planted in the Constitution, so this version ran, but Northerners came to realize that it was contrary to the principles of American democracy and had to be extirpated. First the abolitionists and then more moderate men became aroused over the evil nature of the institution and the wickedness of men who would profit by slavery. *Uncle Tom's Cabin*, contact with fugitive slaves, political agitation of the subject, and clerical denunciation of human bondage finally aroused the Northern conscience to a determination to prevent its extension and as speedily as possible to destroy slavery itself. Only thus could the national conscience be cleared. Southern defense of slavery as a positive good with supporting Biblical authority for it merely intensified the North's conviction of its own righteousness. Just as early Southern historians condemned abolitionists as fanatics, so these Northern writers praised them as moral crusaders. The great exponents of the moral conflict view were men like Blaine, Greeley, Giddings, and Wilson, who had participated in the conflict, and late nineteenth century historians like Draper, von Holst, Alexander Johnston, Rhodes, and Schouler; Albert Bushnell Hart, Henry W. Elson, and numerous other later men long accepted their interpretation and continued to expound it. These men pointed to the stressing of slavery in resolutions of secession conventions as Southern proof of their contention that slavery caused the War.

About the turn of the century, the emphasis began to change. Nearly everyone in every period had stressed the importance of the abolition campaign if only as an irritant to Southerners and conservative Northerners, but following World War I a generation of historians impressed with the importance of economic motivation came to deny that slavery as a moral issue was an important cause of the War. Charles and Mary Beard led the way. Others accepted this rejection of moral motivation until, in the nineteen-thirties, Gilbert H. Barnes and Dwight L. Dumond restudied the anti-slavery movement and came to the conclusion that the moral issue of slavery and the abolitionist propaganda were after all important. Barnes abandoned the narrow focus of William Lloyd Garrison, but he showed how objection to slavery on moral grounds, as part of a larger religious movement, reached thousands of Northerners and exerted greater influence than his immediate predecessors had admitted. He described the steps by which the religious impulse of the day was translated into the anti-slavery movement and then was broadened into a general crusade against the South. Though Owsley has quarreled with Dumond's restatement of the old thesis, Charles W. Ramsdell, Avery O. Craven, and other recent writers have acknowledged the anti-slavery impulse, in this broader religious enthusiasm that Barnes described, as one facet of a complexity of causes of the War.

Slavery described in terms other than morality has continued important in historical interpretation. Thus the slavery controversy has been variously pictured as a rivalry of political systems and of men aspiring to public office, as a struggle of political philosophies for supremacy in the nation, as a conflict of competing social systems each endangering the other, and as a clash of economic interests. Some have stressed the mutual jealousy of two labor systems and have said the quarrel arose because both the slaveowner on the one hand and the nonslaveholding farmer and wage-earner on the other feared the effect of the rival labor system upon his own. In 1939 Roger W. Shugg insisted that Louisianians did fight to defend slavery as a necessary police system that "assured social and political dominance to all white people" and as a provider of "cheap labor for planters" that "exempted them from manual work, and afforded a comfortable way of living."

However they have interpreted slavery, most historians have agreed that westward expansion precipitated a crisis in the sectional conflict. Over the status of slavery on the trans-Missouri frontier and in foreign territory that Americans annexed or coveted came the clash. There compromise proved impossible. So most histories have described as important in the coming of war the acquisition of Louisiana, Texas, California, and New Mexico and subsequent efforts to acquire tropical lands, and also the Missouri Compromise, the Compromise of 1850, Douglas's popular sovereignty campaign, the struggle over Kansas, the Dred Scott Decision, Douglas's Freeport Doctrine, and the inability of compromisers who could settle everything else to agree upon what to do about slavery in the territories. Some have felt the compromises were futile. Others have believed that the Kansas-Nebraska Act's abandonment of the old compromise solutions made war inevitable. Some have denounced Calhoun for precipitating the issue in irreconcilable form. Others have blamed later Southern extremists, or anti-slavery Republicans like Chase, Seward, and Sumner, or Douglas's ambition, or Buchanan's ineptitude, or Taney, or Lincoln, or Davis for setting in motion forces that made the territorial problem insoluble. Still others have said the conflict in the territories had been irreconcilable from the first acquisition of land in Louisiana. Many Northern writers have agreed with Lincoln that the struggle would have gone on until the land was all free or all slave and that the trend until 1860 was toward the country's becoming all slave, and have felt that this tendency made war necessary. Southern writers who have denounced Lincoln because his "house divided" speech indicated a determination to destroy slavery everywhere have still justified Southern secession, either on the ground that slavery to exist required federal protection as a right in all the territories, or else because slavery had to expand to survive. Indeed, Calhoun in the debates of 1836 and 1837 had said about what Lincoln did in his "house divided" speech.

Frederick Jackson Turner and followers of his, such as Walter P. Webb, might really be set apart from Northern and Southern historians alike in their stressing of frontier influences upon the slavery issue. Turner thought it was the Western "area for expansion which gave the slavery issue its significance in American history." By 1840, Western settlers had occupied most of the best land east of the ninety-eight degree meridian. West of that line inadequate rainfall rendered agriculture difficult as practiced by either slaveholders or nonslaveholding farmers. Scarcity of adequately watered, unoccupied land, consequently forced both free-soil and slave states into a competitive struggle over room for expansion elsewhere. Thus, Western conditions, historians of the West have urged, intensified the sectional controversy back East.

All agree it was over the quarrel about territories and new possessions that efforts at peaceful solution within the Union broke down in 1860-1861.

III

Since World War I, historians have tended to shift emphasis from conspiracy, state rights arguments, and slavery, all three, and to talk in terms of broader political, economic, or social conflict. This does not mean that earlier writers failed to see economic and social issues or that recent writers have discarded slavery, as causes of war. Simply the emphasis has changed.

In a period when courses in civilization and histories of civilization and studies of cultures have become popular, some writers talk of the Civil War as a collision of civilizations or cultures. Historians as different as Frank L. Owsley in 1930 and Thomas C. Cochran in 1942 have portrayed the clash in cultural patterns. But culture and civilization are large terms. There are more specific explanations.

One is a stressing of the spirit of nationalism. This historic force, powerful all over the western world, took possession of North and South in different degrees. Western development and Northern economic interest and growth created practical conditions that gave many Northerners a sense of American nationality lacking in the South. Hence Webster's appeal, itself influenced by these forces, struck response in the North but left the South cold. The South, for its part, was divided among men like the mountain Unionists loyal to an American nationality, other men like Davis himself strongly influenced by nationalism but in whom it assumed an aggressively Southern form, and still others untouched by and opposed to this nineteenth century phenomenon in either its American or its Southern form. On the whole, in spite of particularists who dissented in both North and South, the War became a contest of nationalisms, a Southern and an American variety. Pollard emphasized this in 1867. Channing tried to express it in his title, "The War for Southern Independence." Harry J. Carman, Jesse T. Carpenter, Robert S. Cotterill, Benjamin B. Kendrick and Alex M. Arnett, Samuel E. Morison and Henry S. Commager, Henry T. Shanks, and Nathaniel W. Stephenson have pointed to this fact of separate Southern nationality.

Some writers have found seeds of war in the wide differences between the social systems of North and South. To them slavery was essentially a manner of organizing society. Southerners felt that a social order based on a slave class at the bottom provided the greatest stability and happiness for workers and upper classes alike. It created leisure that permitted development of leadership and culture. Southerners blessed with this "superior" social system were contemptuous of democratic Northerners and Northerners in turn were jealous of the "superiority" of Southerners they encountered in the national capital. Consequently clashes occurred. Northern historians have emphasized rather the merits of social democracy and the evils that an aristocratic system entailed for the vast majority who were not great planters. In any case, here was a struggle between aristocracy and democracy, with ante-bellum Southerners convinced of the social idealism of the slave system and a youthful social democracy in the North belligerently proclaiming a new day for the common man. Even had Southerners become convinced that slavery was undesirable as a social system—or economically unprofitable—still, under any system but slavery, the social problem of handling Negroes who were not only slaves but members of another race and densely ignorant would have been stupendous. Harvey Wish has analyzed George Fitzhugh's conviction that "the universal paternalism of an ordered society" provided by slavery was "the only practical alternative to world-wide communism." The world had to choose, Fitzhugh believed, between "the security of the feudal ideal and the chaos of liberalism." Herbert Aptheker, after a detailed study of slave revolts, concluded that fear of slave insurrection influenced most phases of ante-bellum Southern history and that rebelliousness among Negro slaves was "exceedingly common" and did play a part in bringing on emancipation. Many historians have felt it was the social dread of free Negroes and the inability to see how blacks could be controlled socially or made to do labor effectively, if free, that created the insurmountable obstacle to all consideration of emancipation. Economics had little to do with defense of slavery, Morison and Commager have told us in a passage that did not appear in 1927 in the original *Oxford History* by Morison alone; "slavery was simply a social necessity for keeping the negro population in its proper place." Ulrich B. Phillips, indeed, called determination that the South should remain "a white man's country" the "central theme" of Southern history.

Then there was the political phase of the conflict. Politics was important per se. Initially the national parties, strong in both sections, had helped bind the Union together. Each party had sought issues that would elect candidates dependent upon votes in both sections and had avoided issues that would weaken either its Northern or Southern wing. The breakup of these old national parties and the emergence of a purely sectional Republican Party were ominous. Republican gains in 1856 and 1858 and the split in the Democratic Party paved the way for war. Some writers, as has been pointed out, have believed the final cleavage of the Democratic Party was engineered by Southern extremists who hoped in this way to insure Douglas's defeat and thereby to acquire, in Lincoln's election, a weapon with which they could coerce reluctant fellow-Southerners into secession. In any case, the Lincoln election is accredited by most historians as the immediate cause of secession, sometimes because of what it really implied for the South, sometimes because of what Southerners believed it implied.

Maintenance of the balance of power in the United States Senate, now hopelessly destroyed, had long been deemed essential by Southern leaders. Northerners, on the other hand, had always resented the extra power and "rotten boroughs" created for Southern white men by the three-fifths rule.

Political ambition of individuals has been described as a cause of dissension. For instance, an aggregation of disappointed office-seekers united to form the Republican Party; repudiated Southerners used extremist doctrines to stage comebacks. Rivalry of Buchanan and Douglas, neither of them anti-slavery men, contributed to the disruption of the Democratic Party. Some have seen in secession a brave plunge to attain freedom from political oppression that awaited Southerners within the Union; but others have adjudged it bad sportsmanship in defeat, revealing determination to retain the power and emoluments outside the Union that Southerners had now lost within it. Unhappiness over seeing patronage within Southern states taken away from those long accustomed to dispense favors played its part—and some writers feel that Douglas's election was as much feared on this score as Lincoln's.

The slavery issue itself, other historians have maintained, was mainly a focus for attack on political enemies. Northern politicians employed it to overthrow and Southerners to sustain Southern political power. Cotterill believed Southern secessionists used "the anti-slavery menace as a bogie man" to frighten Southerners into accepting an already arranged program. Some historians have contended that the issue of slavery in the territories was not really of practical importance to either North or South: climate barred slavery anyway; Kansas never had any slaves to speak of; and, when they had the power just before the War to frame territorial acts as they pleased, Northerners imposed no Wilmot Proviso on Colorado, Nevada, or Dakota. Indeed, Ramsdell in 1929 contended that by 1860 slavery had reached its natural frontiers. "There was . . . no further place for it to go." Hence "there was no longer any basis for excited sectional controversy over slavery extension." If these views are correct, mere prestige and "sectional honor," on the one hand, and desire of politicians to make political capital, on the other, stirred up the dispute over territories. According to one view, settlement of the conflict in Kansas and unsuitability of the remaining territories to slavery embarrassed the Republicans by depriving them of their only issue and forced them to seek issues in more radical stands. Then again the Republican refusal to accept compromise in 1860, which many writers have felt plunged the nation into war, was necessitated by purely political considerations. Yielding on the territorial issue, however wise it might have been, would, this thesis runs, have destroyed the Republican Party by violating its chief campaign pledge and destroying its raison d'être.

Several historians have pointed out that the election of 1860 failed to register the wishes of the people, who in both sections were overwhelmingly opposed to extreme measures. Shugg has described how in Louisiana the minority of slaveholders that did favor secession were able to overrule a majority that were opposed or indifferent, not through conspiracy, but by exercise of powers they had always possessed in a planter and commercial oligarchy. The Beards called attention, too, to the balance of power that a small group of extreme anti-slavery men held at given times and places in crucial Northern elections. In Louisiana Shugg found politics confused in 1860 by the tendency of influential men to follow national leaders on the basis of old loyalties that had little to do with current issues. Recently, Craven has maintained that the election was fought within each section on local issues irrelevant to the major national problem.

Rival political theories, too, have been suggested as a cause. The North represented political democracy and the South an aristocracy in which a small group of large slaveholders held the power. Stephenson emphasized this rivalry of democracy and aristocracy. Dodd pictured a struggle for "the rights of men" represented by Lincoln "as against the rights of property" represented by Davis. War came, Dodd felt, out of an irritating disparity between "healthy moral, even radical, forces" of Northern democracy and a South that "no longer believed in democracy." Here was the old fight between popular rights and political privilege for the "rich and well born." Burgess in 1897 wrote of a conflict between the Northern ideals of progress and the perfectibility of man and a pessimistic Southern view that only a few men are intelligent or good and hence all others must be subjected to rule by the few. Historians friendly to the South have argued that the South stood for the principle of protection of a minority against tyranny of the majority, for which Calhoun tried to provide a philosophy and a formula. When this protection became impossible inside the Union, the discontented minority, exercising its basic political right of self-determination, separated from the majority.

Several recent writers have spoken of the Civil War as revolution. To some this term means an unsuccessful effort of Southerners to change our political system into one where the minority rules. The Beards and likeminded writers since the 'twenties have seen, rather, a successful revolution in which a Northern industrial group seized power from an agrarian group that had long held it. The Beards have pointed out that this is none the less political revolution because the opposed economic interest groups were separated by geographic instead of class lines.

IV

Certainly one of the most fundamental revisions of Civil War history was made in the 'twenties by historians who followed the Beards' lead in interpreting the Civil War as an economic conflict. The period subsequent to the appearance of Charles Beard's revolutionary *Economic Interpretation of the Constitution* in 1913 saw a whole school of economic interpretation arise, dominate the scene for a decade or two, and then recede from its ascendancy to a place along side other schools of interpretation, not, however, without leaving an indelible mark on Civil War historiography and on most other areas of historical research. To be sure, this emphasis on economic motivation was not new. Madison in the *Federalist* gave classic expression to it years before Marx was born, and Marx with a different slant and greater stress upon dogma long antedated Beard. Indeed, Jefferson Davis in Senate debate had very nearly stated the Beardian thesis. Others had pointed out the economic conflict without employing the Beards' concept of a revolution: James Spence in 1862, Edward A. Pollard in 1862 and 1867, Jefferson Davis in 1881, Alexander Johnston in 1885, John A. Logan in 1886, John M. Harrell in 1899, Henry W. Elson in 1904, W. Birkbeck Wood and J. E. Edmonds in 1905, George S. Merriam in 1906, John H. Latané in 1910, and Emerson D. Fite in 1911.

In his significant but often overlooked *Social Forces in American History* in 1911, Algie M. Simons had presented a well developed economic interpretation of history two years before Beard's more famous book appeared. As early as 1903, moreover, in an almost unknown essay, *Class Struggles in America*, Simons had published a brief and oversimplified interpretation of the Civil War that suggested the conflict of economic groups later described by the Beards and the economic interpretationists of the 'twenties. Simons said the War resulted from class antagonisms between North and South. The Emancipation Proclamation was "simply a war measure." Abolitionism was important chiefly because it made Western farmers and

Eastern wage-earners believe they had an interest in the struggle between capitalists and slaveholders. "In any society the exploiting class must control the government if its exploitation is to continue." Hence the Southerner was right in assuming that, if he lost control of the government, there "was no hope for him except in secession and the formation of a government which he could control." "The Civil War," Simons concluded, "was simply a struggle by the capitalist class of the North to maintain the ruling position not only over the North but over the South as well."

Nevertheless, it was under the influence of Charles and Mary Beard that economic interpretation burst into full flower. According to this school, the Civil War arose from a new phase of the old conflict between business and agriculture. With the coming of the industrial revolution to America a new industrialism arose beside the older commercial interest and finally superseded it as the rival of agrarianism. The new industrialism sought from the federal government aid that planter interests and Western farm interests opposed. So long as West and South stood together the new industrialism was powerless, though growing in strength. But, partly through the new economic ties created by railroad building of the 'fifties between Northeast and Northwest and partly by a political bargain Republican managers engineered between the elections of 1856 and 1860, a majority of Northwestern farmers were won to an alliance with Northeastern industrialists against their former allies in the agricultural South. In return for Western backing of a protective tariff, the Northeast agreed to support Western land policies that it had previously joined the Southeast in opposing. Both tariff and free homestead planks appeared in the Republican platform of 1860. The West had sought free homesteads on the frontier and internal improvements. Also, for years Northern business men had favored and Southern Democrats had opposed a national bank, "sound" money, federal support of business enterprise and New England fishing interests, ship subsidies, federal grants to railroads and other internal improvement projects, and tariff protection for American manufacturers. A Democratic Party dominated by able Southerners had for many years controlled the federal government and had thereby prevented enactment of these measures. The Census returns of 1850 showed the South foredoomed to ultimate defeat, convinced Southern leaders that they could not long continue their control within the Union, and made Northern leaders in turn exultant and uncompromising. Northern business was anxious to gain control of the government as soon as possible to enact laws supporting its ventures. Slavery was used as a point of attack with popular appeal, but the real basis for opposition to the slave power was economic. Secession and war came and, when the strife was over, Southern and Democratic power had been broken and Northern industrialism was in the saddle. The United States had entered upon a long period of control of government by business with the industrialists' wishes enacted into law in place of the old planter views that had dominated ante-bellum legislation. This was revolution.

It is interesting to find Southerners before the Civil War, on the one hand, and Blaine in 1884, on the other, pointing out economic motivation represented in the North's tariff aims long before men of the nineteen-twenties were to stress it. Blaine, indeed, wrote in his *Twenty Years in Congress* that "large consideration must be given to the influence of the movement for Protection" in "reviewing the agencies" that "precipitated the political revolution of 1860." Interestingly, too, in 1944 in their *Basic History of the United States,* the Beards omitted all mention of their "Second American Revolution" hypothesis of 1927 that had given them such far-reaching influence on Civil War historiography. In describing the 'fifties they gave other than economic factors somewhat more relative importance than they had in 1927. Charles Beard wrote in 1933 a critical review of a book that avoided interpretation and attacked the author for believing that "impressionistic eclecticism is the only resort of contemporary scholarship." Yet writing in 1944 he and Mrs. Beard avoided all explicit interpretation of the coming of the Civil War. In spite of this reticence, the selection and arrangement of their facts make it obvious what they thought were the causes.

Economic forces were given added strength in the North, some historians have contended, by the Panic of 1857, which Northerners could attribute to the recently enacted lower tariff rates. Carman in 1934 and Hicks in 1937 pointed out that the Panic strengthened Southern extremists and left the North more hurt than the South. Channing writing in 1925 believed that the effects of the Panic injured the Democratic Party in the North. Hacker in 1940 and Hicks found that its effects made government aid to industry seem imperative. Craven has shown how Northerners blamed the South for Northern economic ills.

On the other hand, historians like the Beards, Channing, Cole, Cotterill, Craven, Phillips, Russel, Shanks, Sitterson, and Van Deusen have described the Southern side of the economic picture. Apparently and in comparison with its own past, the South was well off in the 'fifties, and yet Southerners were troubled. The North was growing alarmingly and, in population, wealth, and economic power, was far outstripping the South. Through the one-crop system and failure to do their own carrying and manufacturing, Southerners were paying Yankees for these services a disproportionate share of the returns on Southern agriculture. Forgetting that the actual tariff had been enacted by Southern votes and was lower than duties had been in three decades, the South's political spokesmen complained that the tariff drained Southern profits into Northern pockets. In reality, the

South was worried less by existing conditions than by fear of what Republican control might do to the tariff in the future. Southern dependence on Northern capital led to a continuance of the old creditor-debtor controversy. The distribution of the nation's wealth between North and South was inequitable. In popular parlance, the South was tired of living in vassalage to the North; it was determined to cease being a colony of the Northern business empire. From the Civil War to the present this factor has been discussed, and as late as 1937 and 1942 has been particularly stressed by Walter P. Webb and Benjamin B. Kendrick respectively. Besides, much of the older South was suffering from soil exhaustion and competition with the virgin soil of Western plantations. Many Southerners felt that expansion of slavery into new regions was essential, and some favored reopening of the slave trade as a further remedy. Commercial conventions frequently met to study remedies but did little to follow up plentiful proposals made by convention speakers. The South tended to attribute its economic ills to Northerners, and extremists urged economic independence, obtainable, they said, only after secession.

There was also a conflict in labor systems. Northern wage-earners were afraid of the competition of slave labor. Many Northerners felt that the South was blocking national, meaning Northern, progress; that it was impeding the operation of Manifest Destiny, that is, the spread of Northern democracy and nonslaveholding farmers. Southern slaveholders, on the other hand, were afraid of the effect upon their slaves of contact with free workers and free-state farmers.

Besides the Beard school of economic interpretationists, there are the Marxists, James S. Allen, Herbert Aptheker, and Richard Enmale, and a onetime editor of the *Marxist Quarterly,* Louis M. Hacker. In the little they have written on causes of the Civil War, none of them has distorted historical reality to shape it to a preconceived Marxian mold as Du Bois did with the facts of Reconstruction. Allen and Hacker, both writing in 1937, presented about the same picture that the Beardians painted except that Allen and Hacker used somewhat different terms. For instance, they, like Simons a generation earlier, spoke of a conflict between the slavocracy and *capitalists*. Aptheker insisted that "the anti-slavery struggle broadened into a battle for democratic rights of white people" and that slaves frequently "received aid from white people, generally in the lower economic groups." Enmale in 1937 attempted to show the rudiments of a class struggle involving labor by pointing out that American labor played a part in the struggle against the slavocracy. He pictured the slavocracy as conducting a "counter-revolution" and talked of a coalition of farmers and wage-earners organized to crush it. He also pointed out that the First International and British labor supported the North. Charles Wesley, on the other hand, has shown that American labor was hostile toward free Negroes in the North as well as in the South. Morison in 1927 and Stephenson in 1918 also called attention to participation of the American working class in overthrowing slavery but without seeing in this a "class struggle." Shugg contended that in Louisiana, in spite of many confusing factors, slaveholders tended to urge, and small farmers and city workers to oppose, secession. Enmale suggested an alliance between merchants and financiers in the North and slaveholders in the South. He was troubled because anti-war feeling had been strong among workers who should have supported the class struggle of the Civil War. He felt, however, that labor pacifism had not been spontaneous. It had been manufactured by pro-slavery mercantile interests who played on fears of workers that war would bring unemployment. Allen declared the War was "a revolution of a bourgeois democratic character, in which the bourgeoisie was fighting for power against the landed aristocracy." Long before these recent Marxists, Benjamin E. Green, a Southerner writing in 1872, had maintained that slavery elevated the common people of the South, had accused Northerners of monarchism, and had listed as a cause of the Civil War "the irrepressible desire of capital to cheapen labor."

In spite of the vogue of the economic interpretationists, Andrew C. McLaughlin of an older generation still believed in 1935 that slavery was the *chief* cause of the War. Morison alone in 1927 and together with Commager in 1942 maintained that it was the cause of secession. While not neglecting the economic conflict, Henry H. Simms felt in 1942 that "political and psychological rather than economic factors played the paramount role." And James G. Randall in 1937 and 1940 seriously questioned the validity of the whole economic interpretation.

V

The Negro's views on the Civil War would be interesting, but in their preoccupation with the history of their race, Negroes have written little on the larger aspects of American history. Frederick Douglas's autobiography published in 1882 puts him in the group that sees the War as a conspiracy of slaveholders. It is rabidly pro-Northern. George W. Williams in his *History of the Negro Race in America*, appearing the same year, wrote from a pro-abolition point of view and treated the War as a struggle over the moral issue of slavery. He tried to explain why there were not more slave insurrections and included an interesting chapter on the role of the Northern free Negro in the anti-slavery movement. Charles Wesley in *Negro Labor in the United States* found slavery the major issue of the War, but pointed out that neither Northern labor nor Northern soldiers nor Southern slaves realized what "the real issue" was. In a detailed study of the failure of the Senate Committee to agree upon a compromise that might have prevented war in 1860-1861, Clinton E.

Knox decided in 1932 that responsibility for failure had to be shared jointly by Lincoln and the Republican Party. He came also to the conclusion that the real grievance of the South was not such concrete matters as loss of fugitive slaves or failure to obtain protection for slavery in the territories but "the hostile sentiment of the North toward slavery." He offered the comment that compromise was impossible because such a grievance could not be settled by "any human concessions" and since "popular sentiment" would eventually have risen again to overthrow any compromise made.

Unless one includes incidental material in Charles Wesley's *Collapse of the Confederacy,* the present author has found, even among works touching only briefly on the period, only one study by a Negro that is not focused entirely on the Negro. In an interpretive article of 1933, George W. Brown showed that some of the South's ablest leaders were secessionists, that a "rising sense of [Southern] nationalism" stimulated the South to dislike of Republican attacks on it, that the South was far from united and extremists had to work hard to "precipitate a revolution," and, finally, that only in the Gulf states was the opposition of a slave-based economic system to commercialization strong enough to persuade states to secession as a remedy. Both Wesley and Brown, when they do turn to general topics, so detach themselves from race bias that no one unacquainted with them would guess they are Negroes.

VI

Writers who feel that free choices of men were important have analyzed the part various leaders played in bringing on armed conflict, and old judgments of these leaders have been modified as war feeling has died out and scholarly researches have provided new understanding. Even Rhodes, in spite of his anti-slavery background and preponderant use of Northern sources, dealt more sympathetically with men whose cause he thought wrong than had earlier Northerners.

Decreasing sectional feeling and greater perspective have gradually won for John Quincy Adams, doggedly fighting for the cause of liberty in Congress, a rather more enviable reputation than either friends or foes gave him earlier. Calhoun, always great to Southern writers, has grown in stature with the years. Northern writers have ceased denouncing him as the leader of a conspiracy. Historians of whatever point of view have come to recognize the greatness of his mind, his prophetic vision, the importance of his political philosophy. He is now usually pictured as a man devoted to the Union but also to the interests of his state and region, trying desperately to reconcile these conflicting loyalties by safeguarding slavery within the Union and by solving the problem of protection of minorities against majority tyranny. In short, he was trying not to destroy but to save the Union by removing the conflict that would otherwise destroy it. Recent writers like Craven still make him share responsibility for bringing on war. But his motives and abilities are no longer questioned. Webster, too, has been exonerated, at least from the bitter charges of the *Ichabod* view of him, by restudy of his relation to the Compromise of 1850.

Fire-eaters and abolition leaders have lately been more critically treated than they were in earlier years by admiring fellow-enthusiasts, but yet more understandingly than early writers of the opposition found possible. Of all leaders of the period, however, the most unsympathetic handling by current writers has been reserved for these two groups and for certain anti-slavery political leaders like Chandler, Chase, Sumner, and Wade. Few historians have liked Sumner, but some have respected him for his ability and sincerity. In recent years Northerners have ceased praising Sumner's "courageous" verbal attack on the South, and denouncing Brooks's "cowardly" assault on him, and Southerners have stopped damning Sumner and lauding Brooks. Most historians, like some contemporaries in both North and South, have come pretty generally to regret the action of both men and to feel that both should bear heavy responsibility for making peaceful agreement more difficult. Yet, even today, most Southerners find it easier to understand Brooks and Northerners Sumner, so strong are cultural influences. The debate as to whether Sumner was really seriously injured or was shamming to get sympathy will have to await Laura A. White's biography for a possibly definitive answer.

Republican leaders were once all lumped together, but recent re-examination of their motives has tended to separate them into various categories of conservatism and radicalism. Attention to economic factors has revealed that, of Republican extremists, some were essentially conservative except for radical views on slavery based on a desire to serve their own economic aims, whereas others like Stevens and Julian were thoroughgoing social and economic radicals.

Davis long suffered at the hands of Northern historians and of Southern protagonists of his rivals and enemies. Gradually, however, scholarly research has made of him a not always wise and rarely lovable but still responsible statesman. He is pictured, not as a promoter of secession, but rather as a representative, in the late 'fifties at least, of a conservative group in the South. Strongly pro-Southern, he none the less hoped, until almost the last, to avert secession by winning concessions within the Union.

Buchanan's indecision and ineptitude have generally been blamed for failure to stem in time the rising tide of secessionism, and some writers have felt that if Lincoln or Douglas could have entered the White House in November, 1860, the Union might have been saved without war. Yet George T. Curtis as early as 1883, Horatio King in 1895, and John

Bassett Moore in 1908 defended Buchanan. More recently Philip G. Auchampaugh in 1926, James G. Randall in 1937 and 1940, Frank W. Klingberg in 1943, and Roy F. Nichols, as a result of yet unpublished researches, have carried his rehabilitation further. They have suggested that he was following a consistent and definite policy that might have succeeded and that, in any case, he more nearly represented the will of the people North and South than did Southern extremists or radical Republicans who criticized him. In 1942 David M. Potter restudied Seward and credited him, during Lincoln's "perilous silence" of November to March, with able leadership in efforts to save the Union by conciliation.

Some students of the period have blamed Douglas for breaking the peace and loosing in the Kansas-Nebraska Act the forces that led to war. Rhodes in 1892 judged him severely. Historians have debated at length whether ambition for the presidency, concern for a Pacific railway to promote his own and his constituents' economic interests, use of him by Southerners cleverer than he, an honest desire to produce a formula for a permanent peace in the slavery feud, or just moral and political obtuseness explain his opening of Pandora's box. As men have attained greater freedom from wartime prejudices that led Confederates and Republicans alike to hate middle-of-the-road statesmanship, and as the evidence has been thoroughly examined and sifted, Douglas has been given new character credentials and a more significant place in history. Fiske and McMaster in 1902 and Burgess in 1897 partially defended him. So did Channing in 1925. The major task of rehabilitation, however, was performed by Frank H. Hodder from 1899 to 1936, by George Fort Milton in his *Eve of Conflict* in 1934, and by Avery O. Craven in several works published in the last six years.

Lincoln is still an enigma, subject to strong disagreement. The hatred expressed by early Southern writers is gone. So, too, among most serious historians, is the peculiar brand of hero-worship sponsored for political reasons by generations of Republican political writers. His claims to greatness after the War began seem little questioned today but do not concern us here. About his part in the coming of war, there is still controversy. Some see in Lincoln a statesman who perceived and gave popular voice to the fundamental issues of his day, a leader whose abilities brought the nation through crisis to preservation of the Union and elimination of slavery. Others, however, picture him in the ante-bellum years as a skilful politician whose cleverness turned every situation to his own and his party's advantage. Milton, Craven, Mary Scrugham in 1921, and William E. Baringer in 1937 have stressed his shrewdness as a politician. Did his "house divided" speech call to the nation's attention a fundamental truth and set in motion a series of events that ultimately resolved the conflict in favor of union and freedom instead of disunion and extension of slavery over the whole nation? Or did the speech merely call Abraham Lincoln to public attention in such a way as to put him finally in the White House and make war inevitable? Did his debates with Douglas clarify a great public issue that Douglas was beclouding and thereby lead to saving the Union? Or did Lincoln in these debates merely win for himself the presidency at the expense of precipitating a bloody war that Douglas as president might have avoided without loss to the nation? Did Lincoln's refusal to sanction compromise in December, 1860, save the country from further conflict over slavery in new territories to be acquired and preserve the Union from ultimate disruption or subjection to the rule of slaveholders made powerful through expansion? Or did it merely precipitate a war that could otherwise have been avoided without destruction of the Union? And what of Lincoln's attitude on Sumter? Answers to most of these questions have differed according to each author's point of view and his judgment of basic human values.

VII

Yet a few other reasons given for the coming of war need mentioning. One is conflict between a romanticism that characterized the South and a practicality or materialism of the North. Differences in manners, even failure to understand each other's conception of a "gentleman," led to misunderstanding. In 1862 William Taylor, a Californian living in London, ascribed the War to Divine intervention. In his *Cause and Probable Results of the Civil War in America,* Taylor declared that the War was brought by God as "a severe chastisement of the American nation for national sins," as discipline "in the school of adversity" so that the nation might attain "humble permanent greatness," and as a means to the "providential end" of overthrowing slavery.

A number of writers have pointed to the suppression of civil liberties in the South as a cause of the War. The threat to civil liberties aroused many Northerners who themselves disliked anti-slavery men but were alarmed at the attack on fundamental American rights. Important, too, these authors have felt, was the effect upon the South of shutting off the possibility of criticizing slavery, since only through criticism and discussion of the merits and evils of slavery could the South itself have solved from within the slavery problem, thus removing the possibility of war from that source.

Historians seeking causes of the War and recognizing the differences between North and South, have sought reasons why North and South became so different. Contrasts in climate, soil, and other geographic factors are one explanation popular with historians whom Ellen Churchill Semple and Frederick Jackson Turner have made conscious of the influence of geography upon history. Peculiar adaptability of staple crops to Southern soil and climate and of Negro labor to the growing of staples, coupled with the rich return from staple production and the ready supply of African Negroes, led in colonial days to a development of Southern people and life distinct from those of the North. Even before the nation was founded, many differences grew up between the colonists in the two regions. The industrial revolution is another factor that has appealed to writers interested in economic motivation. It brought the South the cotton gin, enlarged markets for its staple crops, and surpluses of capital in industrial areas for loans to promote Southern expansion. On the other hand, it brought industrialism to the North. Hence it increased the dissimilarity of the sections.

Racism has had its exponents. Hinton Rowan Helper, writing soon after the War, expressed it in an extreme form. It appears, too, in George Fitzhugh's late writings. "It is a gross mistake," said Fitzhugh in 1861, "to suppose that abolition alone is the cause of dissension. . . . The Cavaliers, Jacobites, and Huguenots who settled the South, naturally hate, contemn, and despise the Puritans who settled the North. The former are master races, the latter, a slave race, the descendants of the Saxon serfs. The former are Mediterranean races, descendants of the Romans. . . . The Saxons and Angles, the ancestors of the Yankees, came from the cold and marshy regions of the North; where man is little more than a cold-blooded, amphibious biped." Indeed, Wish, Fitzhugh's recent biographer, believes that Fitzhugh's ideal "system" "belongs within the ideological orbit of contemporary Fascism." "From Fitzhugh to Mussolini," says Wish, "the step is startlingly brief."

In 1923 a Virginian with a Johns Hopkins Ph.D. presented a racist doctrine of the origin of sectional differences—interesting indeed in the year when an unsuccessful Putsch first brought Hitler and *his* creed of racial superiority to the world's attention. According to Hamilton J. Eckenrode, the Nordic race, distinguished by "predominance in war and political capacity, together with love of adventure," had become "tropicized" in the Lower South where "the natural relationship is that of master and servant." The Southern Nordic had lost "northern respectability and idealism, . . . sourness, hardness, avarice." He had gained "towering race pride and an inclination to ride over racial groups considered inferior." He was "recovering his primeval character, . . . reverting to the type of masterful man which had imposed its will so long on the world." "The Southerner was a type as yet new in history: he was the one real creation of America." He felt "revulsion for the mechanistic, egalitarian North." "This change in the Nordic race . . . in the hot lands of America, unhampered by European restraints," was the "main cause of the Civil War." The War was "a struggle between that part of the Nordic race which was prepared to renounce its tradition of mastery for equality, modernism and material comfort and that part of the race which was resolved, despite modernity, to remain true to its ruling instincts."

Most authors have not written so explicitly as Eckenrode, but racism is implicit in the writings of numerous historians dealing with this period. In some it takes a form that the sociologist calls Anglo-Saxonism, somewhat less extravagant than the Nordicism of Eckenrode; in others it appears in a more general form as belief in racial superiority of whites. It is implicit, for example, in the writings of historians as various as Horton and Pollard in early days and Phillips more recently and affects their interpretation of history.

Various writers have called attention to differences in sectional characteristics that made it hard for Northerners and Southerners to get along with each other. For instance, in 1866 Horton spoke of the North's dangerous views and "traitorous desire to overthrow the free Government of the United States." These attitudes he ascribed to British influence and to a carry-over of Tory principles of 1776, that had come down through John Adams to the Lincoln Republicans, who were merely carrying out in America "the British free negro policy." William W. Handlin, in a book of 1864 published in Louisiana, pointed out the danger of votes in the hands of peoples who have not property and responsibility. In 1896 Edward Ingle spoke of the ante-bellum fear of "the populating of the South by a no-property class from the North." Ann E. Snyder in 1890 found part of the trouble in an ante-bellum North's jealousy of the "broad, liberal, free . . . noble civilization" of the South, which, "narrow and lacking in breadth of judgment" as they were, Northerners "could not appreciate." Numerous writers have suggested that the North's humanitarian reform impulse made Northerners difficult fellow-countrymen. Some have indicated that "gentlemen" found it hard to cope with Northerners' bad manners and their failure to respond to the requirements of a gentleman's code of honor. Others have felt that the large foreign immigration to the North considerably increased Northern anti-slavery sentiment and Eckenrode said it increased sectional differences by weakening the Nordic strain in Northerners.

On the other hand, historians have pointed out qualities that made Southerners difficult. One was extreme sensitiveness to criticism. Von Holst spoke of the South's "consciousness of weakness"; Cole and James Truslow Adams saw a Southern "inferiority complex"; Morison and Commager noted "a strong, emotional sense of insecurity." Cotterill in 1936 maintained that, while many Northerners came to America to escape from persecution or oppression, most Southerners fled from nothing and consequently had no inferiority complex and therefore were aggressive. Eckenrode is proud of the aggressiveness they showed. Occasional writers through the years have called attention to Southerners' economic jealousy of the North. Dodd said the politicians and "to an extent, too, the South generally" were jealous of everything Northern. Intellectual backwardness, lack of education, illiteracy, and absence of the habit of reading or thinking have been severally credited to ante-bellum Southerners. Some writers have felt that Southerners' ideas about "chivalry" and their tendency to settle arguments by force were sources of trouble in relations with Northerners. More than one writer has spoken of the "madness" of Southern extremists. Gay and the poet Bryant in 1881 in their *Popular History of the United States* revealed perhaps more of their own sectional bias than of the character of Southerners when they described the North's dread of "the supremacy of an ill-born, ill-bred, uneducated, and brutal handful of slaveholders over a [Northern] people of a higher strain of blood, with centuries of gentle breeding, and a high degree of moral and intellectual cultivation behind them."

VIII

Historians have been baffled trying to decide why Southerners wanted to withdraw or thought they could succeed in leaving the Union. Southerners believed in the right of secession. They felt aggrieved. But why did they choose to exercise the right and why did they feel that secession would remove the grievance? Some writers point out a series of illusions that made chances of success seem more likely than they were. Thus Southerners believed that Northerners were unwilling to fight and would prove weak in warfare; they thought the Northwest needed the South as a market for its products and was dependent on whoever held the mouth of the Mississippi; they counted on Northwesterners of Southern origin to swing that contested section to the South's side or keep it neutral; and they were certain that Cotton was King and could command aid from European countries subject to its rule. Some historians have felt that the South was bluffing to gain concessions; others that she expected to remake a more happy union with abolitionists eliminated; still others that she thought she would have greater bargaining power outside than in the Union. Besides, there were the fears she entertained as to what would happen if she did not secede: that Southern Unionists would be controlled against former leaders of the South by Lincoln's or Douglas's patronage; that support of nonslaveholders would gradually be lost; that the Border States would abandon slavery; that her own sons would become free-soilers if they migrated into territories where there were no slaves. Too, she feared slave insurrection, injury from Republican rule, and uncertainty of her future if she stayed in the Union. Some have maintained she seceded to safeguard her property, or to protect her social system, or to defend her liberties threatened by oppression. Others have insisted she left because only in that way could she retain actual prosperity—or avert serious decline in it. Southern extremists dreamed of riches of a great slave empire when, freed from the North, the South could absorb territories to the southward. Obviously, motives varied. Lincoln's election signalled secession for some states. Other states left and many individuals took a stand for the Confederacy only after the firing on Sumter and Lincoln's call to arms forced them to side with South or North in an already existent war. Large numbers of Confederates went along only because, after war came, there was nothing else to do. Thus a majority of people, who loved the Union, were led by a minority to leave it.

IX

Secession would not have led to war except for the North. Northerners denied the right of secession. But why did they wish to prevent secession? Even when these questions are answered some historians feel they must still ask how and why war came. Under Buchanan, states had already announced their secession, had seized federal property, and had joined in creating a new Confederacy. Yet there was no war. And most people of both sections wanted peace and believed there would be no war. How then did attempted secession and Northern denial of its validity lead under Lincoln to war that had not come under Buchanan?

The outbreak of fighting over Sumter, it has been generally agreed, consolidated behind their respective governments a Northern and a Southern people hitherto badly divided. Northern writers have tended even into recent times to say that the South precipitated this final break by ordering the firing on Sumter and have proceeded to debate whether this was the deliberate choice of responsible leaders or a rash decision of extremist subordinates who misinterpreted or deliberately exceeded their powers. Southerners have generally accredited Lincoln's attempt to provision Sumter with responsibility, and some have concluded that this action resulted rather from undue influence upon him by radicals in his party than from his independent initiative. Recently, however, two other hypotheses have been championed.

The older one lays armed conflict at Sumter to Lincoln's own deliberate decision. Edward A. Pollard even as early as 1862, Samuel W. Crawford in 1887, Percy Greg in 1892, Clement A. Evans and James Schouler in 1899, and Mary Scrugham in 1921 suggested that Lincoln had calculatingly manoeuvered the South into striking the first blow. Channing worked out the hypothesis more elaborately but, with his usual caution, omitted this, like so many of his interesting spoken intuitions, from his printed volume. Edgar Lee Masters in 1931, Craven in 1936 and 1942, Carl Russell Fish in 1937, Milton in 1941, and Simms in 1942 have also stated this view in one form or another. But it was Charles W. Ramsdell, entirely independently of Channing, who worked out a detailed statement and, with the added support of Browning's diary, which was unavailable to Channing, dared publish it. Though Randall, one of Lincoln's current biographers, has rejected it, many have accepted the Ramsdell interpretation. Ramsdell's thesis was briefly this: Lincoln felt bound by solemn oath to preserve the Union. He was convinced that this could be done only by armed victory over the South. If he did nothing the nation would disintegrate. If he took the initiative in using force, Northerners would not support him. He must somehow manoeuver the South into armed attack that could be dramatized. So, against the judgment of most of his official advisers, he planned the provisioning of Sumter, conscious that whatever the outcome, he would gain his point. He kept the secret of his intent so well that only after seventy-five years did sufficient evidence come to light to justify a careful historian in charging Lincoln with deliberate provocation of war. The provisioning "failed," but Lincoln rejoiced to intimates that, as he foresaw, it had "succeeded"—in its larger object of outmanoeuvering the Confederates into striking the first blow and thereby consolidating for him Northern opinion behind a war most Northerners did not want.

Potter, after thorough searching of contemporaneous materials, offered a new explanation. Lincoln, Seward, and other responsible Republicans were eager, he maintained, to avoid war. Lincoln's failure to assume leadership between election and inauguration he considered unfortunate. As president, however, Lincoln pursued a definite policy. His "rejection of compromise did not mean the rejection of peace." If the Upper South could be kept in the Union, if both coercion and admission of the right of secession could be avoided, and if meantime the Republicans could demonstrate in practice that their administration did not endanger Southern institutions, then powerful Unionist forces in all the slave states would bring a voluntary reconstruction of the Union without compromising the question of slavery in the territories and without war. Some one symbol of federal authority must be maintained for the sake of national and Republican prestige. Pickens, however, would do as well as Sumter with less risk of precipitating war. Lincoln was ready therefore to yield Sumter if he could by evacuation keep Virginia in the Union, or he was ready to evacuate Sumter just to ease tension if he could keep Pickens. The unexpected exhaustion of Anderson's supplies and unanticipated failure to establish federal authority at Pickens before a decision had to be made at Sumter forced Lincoln's decision to provision Sumter. Even then, his notification of South Carolina and his promise not to re-enforce were meant to prevent, not to provoke, hostilities. According to Potter, aside from certain faults of loose administration, the "policy was executed with great skill." Lincoln failed to preserve the Union short of war without compromise chiefly because he and other Republicans overestimated Southern Unionism and failed from the first to take Southern secessionism seriously.

X

In the last two decades a series of questionings of the inevitability of war have led to a new revision. Indeed, as early as 1887 Percy Greg, an Englishman, doubted whether war need have come out of the sectional conflict, and in 1897 and 1901, while voicing his reprobation of the Kansas-Nebraska Act and John Brown's activities, Burgess expressed the same doubt. Except for these two, however, every writer the present author has found questioning the inevitability of the Civil War has written between the two twentieth century world wars. This timing may be accidental, but it seems to indicate that the feeling of disillusionment and futility after World War I may have affected attitudes toward wars in general. When Channing in 1925 raised the issue of needlessness of war, he restated the old view that slavery would have disappeared and that the South would have met economic ruin even without war. Ramsdell pointed out in 1929 that slavery, "a cumbersome and expensive system," must shortly have begun to decline and would, from its own unprofitableness, have disappeared in a generation without the "frightful cost" of war. In 1932 Dodd pointed to the suppression of all "authoritative objection to the dangerous trend of the plantation system" by denying to "teachers and scholars the function of free criticism," and asserted that, except for this silencing of discussion, "one of the most cruel and most needless of wars" might have been avoided. Dumond, Max Farrand, Hicks, Milton, Russel, and Henry T. Schnittkind have also questioned whether war need have come.

It is, however, Avery O. Craven and James G. Randall who have developed a new revision out of this questioning. They began by asking: Was war inevitable? Was the conflict irrepressible? If war was needless, why did it come? If inevitable, at what point and for what reasons did it become so? Craven in an article of 1936, then Randall in a book of 1937, then Craven in books of 1939 and 1942 and Randall in three articles of 1940 answered elaborately that war was unnecessary. In support of this view they presented what might be called a psychological interpretation that ranks in importance with the earlier economic interpretation.

Neither Craven nor Randall ignores or neglects the various conflicts, cultural, social, economic, political, constitutional, philosophical, moral, that divided North and South in the eighteen-fifties. Both are familiar with the influences that made the sections so different. Neither offers a blanket cause for the War. Indeed, both men, profiting by the work of the many historians who have gone before, give able syntheses of all of these forces. To be sure, earlier writers, too, have recognized and described the excitements, passions, and fears of the period. Craven and Randall depart from previous explanations in ceasing to assume that because the two sections employed different labor systems and had developed different cultures, social systems, economic interests, political aims, constitutional theories, philosophies of life, and codes of morality along geographical lines they had necessarily to settle the resulting conflicts through war. They wonder why other serious and similar disputes between nations and between sections of the American nation were resolved short of war while the one of 1861 required four years of fighting to settle.

These new revisionists hold that, among the complex and manifold factors dividing North and South, it was psychological forces and not the nature of the issues themselves that brought on war. Emotional considerations such as hatred and other passions, reformers' zeal, fanaticism, intolerance of things distasteful or different, pride, sectional "honor," crimination and recrimination, religious enthusiasm, and a sense of mission controlled both sections. Lack of proper means of intercommunication intensified ignorance. Southerners failed to distinguish mild anti-slavery men from abolitionists. Northerners took isolated episodes and conditions and generalized them into exaggerated pictures of the slave system. Each section misunderstood the other. Increasing excitement prevented rational processes from functioning. A majority of sane men in both sections were swept aside and silenced. Agitators in both regions, clergymen, editors, speakers, politicians seeking personal advantage, all joined to whip up emotions. Overbold leaders went further than they originally intended. In Congress, fire-eaters' threats and vituperation of Sumner and his anti-slavery fellows, boasts, insults, fisticuffs, calls to duels, brandished pistols, a caning and language so insulting as to provoke a caning, were not conducive to calm solutions of social and economic differences. Sectional honor and pride often required actions that carried no concrete advantage to either rival, sometimes injury to both. For instance, there was no real issue in the "irreconcilable conflict" in the territories, for, with all the victories over anti-slavery men the South could imagine, slavery would not have been profitable in the territories that remained to be settled, and the North needed no Wilmot provisos to exclude it.

Slavery was used as a point of attack or defense by every demagogue. Under its cloak, tariff, internal improvements, ship subsidies, banking policies could be fought over. The words "slavery" and "anti-slavery" became symbols. "Slave power," "Bully Brooks," "Uncle Tom," "Black Republicans," "Bleeding Kansas" became slogans of high emotional power. Craven shows how these phrases were used as abstractions that gave moral value to local material needs of both sections, and how slavery was used as an arouser of passions that made all issues hard to settle. "All contests became part of the eternal struggle between right and wrong." Citizens with social or economic grievances of a local nature sublimated those grievances into hatred, not of the local forces responsible, but of the rival section of the country, which was blamed for all these ills. So a "blundering generation" stumbled over its emotions into needless war about a "repressible conflict."

XI

In conclusion, a few generalizations are pertinent:

1. This study has illustrated the difficulty and danger of all generalizing about historians or about history. In spite of an already great caution about generalization, the present author, before he began his study, would have made, from his knowledge of a few outstanding historians, several simple generalizations with a feeling that those, at least, were justified. After thorough reading of most that has been said about the causes of the Civil War, he hesitates to generalize at all, for he has discovered that history writing falls into no *simple* chronological or ideological pattern, if indeed into any pattern. Hence, these few generalizations are offered with tentativeness and humility.

2. No "new" interpretation is really new or unique. (a) Every idea the author had thought a contribution of recent historical scholarship, he found in one or several nineteenth century historians. Indeed, every explanation of the War presented by historians with the benefit of hindsight, even the Beardian thesis and the recent Craven-Randall explanation, was comprehended and stated before the War occurred. (b) Few of the points of view historians present can be attributed to a single person's influence. There were always several people who voiced them who had almost certainly not got them from each other or from one common originator.

3. Historians have generally failed to make several distinctions that would be helpful. (a) Most of them, even recent writers, have mixed fundamental forces and trivial incidents rather indiscriminately without proper evaluation. (b) Rarely have they differentiated underlying from immediate causes. (c) Only a few have distinguished causes of the sectional conflict from causes of secession, or either from causes of the War. (d) Even fewer have explicitly faced the question whether the men whose activities they all discuss really influenced history at all. Most historians have given no hint whether choices of men or impersonal determinisms, economic or otherwise, brought on the Civil War, or, if both were important, how they were related.

4. Standards of writing history were affected by the War. (a) For several decades after 1865 in histories on both sides, the extreme views of

ante-bellum days were given by war the sanction of orthodoxy, whereas the saner, more moderate views held by the majority in both sections before the resort to arms were discredited by war and hence by historians. (b) On various historical questions military victory made the victor's views correct and invalidated the contentions of the vanquished. Not only the Supreme Court but many historians accepted this verdict of armed force, instead of applying the criteria of history in reaching historical decisions. (c) Because war left the South seriously weakened, the victorious North produced for a generation most of the history that was not sheer apology of defeated leaders, and hence, temporarily and outside the South at least, established historically its views of the conflict. (d) War-stimulated patriotic fervor and the prestige of victory led Northerners to feel in the post-bellum era that history fair to the defeated South was unsound. Similarly, the need for bolstering hurt pride and an inability to admit even partial responsibility for the tragedy war had brought upon the defeated South led Southerners to regard special pleading as sound history. Then, at length, in reaction against earlier biases, some younger historians of both sections, contrary to general trends, began in the nineteen-twenties and nineteen-thirties to lean over backward in criticism of their own section's ante-bellum past. Certain reviewers have come to praise a Southerner who condemns Southern, and a Northerner who condemns Northern leaders or attitudes and to charge with bias one who defends his own section's past, without applying criteria of fair-mindedness or "objectivity" that would prevail in other fields of history. A war of eighty years ago still affects historical standards.

5. Perhaps no historian fully escapes his background. In the case of the Civil War, peculiarly persistent sectional feelings and traditions about that conflict have given the historian's early environment a particularly telling influence. (a) Even in recent times, most historians have been affected consciously or unconsciously by a Northern or Southern background or a reaction against one or the other, by an internal conflict of both influences, by a leaning over backward to avoid unfairness that in turn becomes partiality in reverse, or by the enthusiasm of a convert to an adopted sectional allegiance. Occasionally, special factors such as Burgess's origin in a Unionist fragment of the South or Horton's Copperheadism have complicated the effects of sectionalism. Many historians have degenerated into mere sectional apologists. Very few have attained or fallen heir to complete detachment from geographic or traditional influences. (b) Two authors of equal honesty, sincerity, and scholarly training, each believing he has been completely "objective," may use the same historical material to arrive at diametrically opposed statements of what each believes is historic "fact." This is possible in dealing with such matters as judgments about individual men, analyses of popular opinion or human

motives, evaluations of the pro-Northern, middle-of-the-road, or pro-Southern point of view, or assessments of the importance of the North's and the South's grievances against each other. It is possible, too, in weighing anti- and pro-slavery contentions about territories, deciding how much of a threat to the South Lincoln's election was, or determining the reasonableness or wisdom of secession or prevention of it. It happens where a choice in emphasis must be made between human rights of the Negro or well-being of the small farmer or free wage-earner, on the one hand, and, on the other, protection of property in slaves or solution of the social problem inherent in the free Negro in Southern society. Even the historian who tries to avoid interpretation must exercise subjective judgment in choosing and emphasizing his facts. Hence even in "objective" history, the historian's own attitude toward the place of the Negro in human society, toward the relative importance of property and human rights, or toward the desirability of an agrarian or an urban way of life becomes significant, as does his belief in or distrust of democracy or aristocracy. So, too, do accidents in his education, the mores under which he grew up, his contact with or isolation from ways of doing and thinking different from those of his own locality, his own devotion to or rebellion against what he has known, his preference for maintaining the status quo or seeking an improved society, his own social and economic status, his personal happiness or unhappiness, his grandfather's defeat or victory in civil war eighty years ago. All these factors subtly but profoundly influence history writing, since historians are all human beings as well as scholars. (c) Textbook writers and their publishers with an eye on sales, have frequently yielded to public opinion in one or both sections by including some items and omitting others, not because of historical soundness or importance but because they would please or offend sectional patriots. Sometimes publishers have sought favor in both sections by suggesting that an author from one section associate with himself a co-author from the other. At other times separate texts have been published for the two sections. (d) The Northern and Southern biases, pronounced in the first generation, grew milder in a second generation farther from the War, and weaker still in third and fourth generations, but have usually persisted, except where conflicting loyalties cancel each other out or confuse the picture. (e) The same historian has sometimes changed his interpretation or emphasis over a period of years as did the Beards between their histories of 1927 and 1944, Hacker between the time when he was an editor of the *Marxist Quarterly* and the present, and Randall between his book of 1937 and his articles of 1940.

6. Several groups that might have been expected to present particular points of view have displayed no peculiar bias in treating the causes of the Civil War. (a) Southern agrarians have written much as other

Southerners have. (b) Marxists have not here molded history into dogmatic patterns as they have in dealing with Reconstruction. (c) Few Negroes have dealt with the subject, but the writing of those who have is often indistinguishable from that of their white fellows. (d) No great foreign historian, if Von Holst is classed as an American, has made a first-hand study of the causes of the Civil War. Foreigners who have discussed the subject have been free from some of the unconscious biases of American writers, but have usually accepted the interpretations, and often the philosophy, too, of Northern or Southern writers of their time. For example, Percy Greg, writing for Englishmen in 1887, pretty closely followed the "Northern aggression" view of contemporary Southerners. (e) The present author was unable to discover any marked correlation between Ph.D. degrees or university professorships and fairmindedness. "Trained historians" have produced a good deal of unbiased history, but they have also provided striking examples of prejudice.

7. Historians have found the causes of the Civil War bafflingly complex. No simple explanation is possible. Early writers found simple answers more satisfying than have later ones. The tendency has been from simple explanations to many-sided ones until recently the picture has become complicated indeed.

8. Still, in spite of this complexity and of numerous exceptions to the prevailing trend, successive periods have seen successive hypotheses receive special emphasis. (a) The "conspiracy" explanations of a rival North and South appear most commonly in the decades just after the War when wartime emotions were still strong. They have become rarer in the twentieth century. (b) In this same first generation, 1861-1890, the constitutional conflict was stressed, for the most part by Southerners who remembered and tried to justify Southern contentions in ante-bellum political debates, though also by Von Holst, an immigrant. Between about 1890 and World War I, constitutional and political factors seemed important to scholars of *both* sections. Perhaps this emphasis resulted from the domination of public life by sectional jealousies and party politics in that period before men had become aware of the importance of contemporary economic developments. Since World War I, few have felt that the constitutional issue was of prime importance, though one of the latest writers, Simms in 1942, does stress the political conflict. (c) Slavery as a moral issue was usually emphasized by late nineteenth century Northerners still under the influence of ante-bellum humanitarians. It ceased to seem important to writers in the early decades of the twentieth century, but was revived by Barnes and Dumond in the nineteen-thirties. Among twentieth century writers, under the spell of material prosperity and economic determinism, reformers and moral issues have gone decidedly out of favor. Recently, historians have been inclined to look critically

upon "agitators" of causes, whom nineteenth century writers often admired. (d) Economic interpretation developed under Beard's leadership from 1913 until the early 'thirties. This was the period when men had become conscious of the power of "big business" and when progressivism of the two Roosevelts, La Follette, and Wilson had arisen to protect men against that power. So far as the history of the Civil War was concerned in the late 'thirties the economic interpretation waned in influence and fell back to take its place beside several other emphases. (e) Later, at a time when men were feeling the futility of one world war and facing the possibility of another, a psychological interpretation was sponsored by men persuaded that the sectional conflict could have been solved by other means than war, if emotional forces had not made the use of reason difficult. Writers of this view emphasize more than do others the causes of war as distinct from the causes of conflict. In showing that sectional conflict was turned into war because emotion overcame reason, they still have not shown why emotions rather than reason prevailed, and hence still have not presented a final answer. (f) Textbook writers usually have lagged behind other historical writers in accepting new points of view. (g) Individual historians have provided occasional surprises. For instance, Blaine stressed economic forces long before the economic interpretation school arose. So, too, Henry Adams and Edward Pollard in 1861 and 1862, almost contemporaneously with the events they described, wrote with some heat and much bias, but considerable insight. And Edward Channing, provincial Bostonian and conservative as he was, emphasized in his ivory tower many of the economic motives and psychological factors generally not stressed until after he published his volume, and even then chiefly by historians with whom no one would have suspected Channing of agreeing.

9. Historians of this war have failed to deal adequately with the relation of individual men to the coming of war and the problem of human blundering as a cause of war. Randall spoke of "the blundering generation" but his and Craven's emphasis was upon group emotions rather than individual men's decisions. Numerous studies of leaders have been written. Ramsdell and Potter have raised and sought to answer questions about Lincoln's role prior to the firing on Sumter. For the most part, however, historians of this period who have studied individual men have been preoccupied with justifying, rehabilitating, or unmaking individual reputations rather than with the basic problem of the influence of leadership and the blundering of leaders that David Lloyd George, Sidney B. Fay, and George P. Gooch, for instance, stressed in the causation of World War I. Perhaps the relative decline of economic determinism in recent historical interpretation and the importance popularly ascribed to leadership, good and bad, on both sides in World War II may lead to a new probing of the Civil War period for light on the role of leadership in

bringing on that conflict. In any case, the two-fold problem still awaits study and an answer: (a) How important were individual actors as opposed to impersonal forces and (b) to what extent were avoidable human blunders a cause of this war? Were individual men responsible or did inexorable forces bring war and were the men merely puppets of these forces? Could different actions or decisions of men have prevented it? If men made the War, then what men and through what decisions and what actions? Which men could have prevented the War and when and how? In short, was this war the end result of interacting determinisms or did the free will of free men and their blunders in exercising that free will influence its coming and the time of its coming?

10. Study of what historians have said were the causes of this particular war makes one skeptical of all simple explanations of all wars. The fact that early historians were so sure that this war was fought over the moral issue of slavery, for high constitutional principles, or as a matter of self-defense against an aggressive opponent, and that later historians have largely discarded these simple and high-principled "causes" raises questions about other wars in other times and places. Indeed, the fact that nearly all happenings of the 'fifties and all differences between North and South have been discussed as causes of the War, warrants wondering whether one could not accumulate equally impressive causes of wars that never occurred; it arouses speculation whether an equally impressive list of likenesses between North and South and reasons why war could *not* occur between them might not be compiled out of the same 'fifties. In short, one comes away from such a study inquiring with Channing, Craven, Dodd, Ramsdell, and Randall whether war need have come at all, except for human blundering, and whether, since it did come, the great social forces or "fundamental causes," or in their turn the more recently stressed psychological forces, really explain its coming.

11. Conclusions about this particular historical problem have been constantly changing ever since the events occurred, as available data and men's environment, techniques, and philosophies have changed. Particular theses have been discarded or modified. Emphases have shifted. Almost certainly men's conclusions will continue to change in the years ahead with resulting revisions of anything written now.

12. This study has encouraged the present writer, however, to believe that the repeated efforts to discover the "truth" about causes of the Civil War have been fruitful and that both the methods and the quality of history have improved in the period analyzed. (a) Limitations inherent in a study of human activities prevent the historian's becoming an exact scientist in the sense in which the physicist or biologist is a scientist. The historian is limited by the accident of survival of materials. He is handicapped by the faults of observation of the man who preserved the record.

He cannot check his conclusions by experiment; human motives and attitudes cannot be measured as can heat or heart beats. Still, this study indicates that the acquisition of "scientific tools," the more systematic sifting and evaluating of evidence, and the constant striving toward never-fully-obtainable objectivity or fairmindedness have brought us closer than we were to a clear and true picture of the causes of the Civil War. Growing recognition of the complexity of the causes of human action and of the problems of history would seem to suggest, if an analogy with the biological sciences is pertinent, a decided step forward. The recording of history is thousands of years old, but, with a few rare exceptions, American historians have employed the "scientific tools" only in the last sixty to seventy years. The fault, indeed, is not so much in the meagerness of accomplishment as in the grandeur of expectation. Actually, constant seeking for explanations of the War, digging out new materials, and presenting even soon-to-be-modified conclusions have been decidedly worth the time and trouble, for these efforts, in combination, *have* gradually created the more complex, yet clearer and more nearly accurate picture of today. (b) Increasing recognition of the degree to which an historian's personal point of view affects his history has led to greater efforts to analyze and control, or at least avow, the subjectivity of the writer. In much of the writing on the Civil War there has been little correlation between claims to objectivity and freedom from prejudice. Heralded "objectivity" has too often turned out to be mere unawareness of individual prejudice or else an unwitting reflection of the prevailing prejudice of the period or region. Freedom from a point of view is not often possible; consciousness of one is. Happily, consciousness of points of view is more common than formerly. This study has furnished some evidence that writers with a determined philosophy of life of which they are fully conscious and which they make clear to the reader stand a better chance of approaching "objectivity" than did the older writers who, if they used "scientific tools," thought themselves completely "objective."

13. In view of the manifold difficulties in attaining objectivity, the impossibility of finding answers of scientific exactitude to questions about the history of human activities and motivations, the disparities among conclusions of the most diligent and honest workers, and the constantly shifting kaleidoscope of hypotheses about the causes of the Civil War, it is pertinent to ask whether so much study of a detail of history is defensible. The present writer, after making this analysis, believes with renewed conviction that it is. Though caution and full awareness of the dangers even in unconscious distorting of history to support current views are essential, still, if one approaches it humbly, with a desire to learn rather than to bolster already held theses, knowledge of history can teach this or any generation a great deal about itself and its problems. Ap-

proached with speculative capacity and some cognizance of potential analogies, a concentrated study of a small fragment of the past such as the causes of an American civil war may add to the student's wisdom, not only about the causes of that war but about the causes of all wars; indeed, about human motives and human actions in any time or place. Study of the past, therefore, may increase the individual's capacity to meet current problems intelligently. Multiplied manifold this individual capacity could help society as a whole to avoid repeating mistakes of past generations and to plan for a better future. This purpose probably is better served by historians and students who, with due caution and humility, do attempt to interpret and explain the past than by those who merely catalogue what happened.

PERTINENT WRITINGS OF AUTHORS MENTIONED

(This list does not purport to be a complete bibliography of the causes of the Civil War. It includes only a portion even of the works used for this study. Only authors specifically mentioned in the essay are included. For each of these the books and articles that proved useful are named. Where more than one edition was used, the date is that of the earliest obtainable.)

ADAMS, HENRY: "The Great Secession Winter of 1860-1861," Massachusetts Historical Society, *Proceedings*, XLIII (1909-1910), 660-687.

ADAMS, JAMES TRUSLOW: *America's Tragedy*, 1934; *The Epic of America*, 1931; *History of the United States*, 1933; *The March of Democracy*, 2 vols., 1932-1933; *The Record of America*, with Charles G. Vannest, 1935.

ALLEN, JAMES S.: *Reconstruction. The Battle for Democracy (1865-1876)*, 1937.

APTHEKER, HERBERT: *American Negro Slave Revolts*, 1943; *The Negro in the Abolitionist Movement*, 1941; *The Negro in the Civil War*, 1938; *Negro Slave Revolts in the United States, 1526-1860*, 1939.

ARNETT, ALEX M.: *The South Looks at Its Past*, with Benjamin B. Kendrick, 1935; *The Story of North Carolina*, 1933.

AUCHAMPAUGH, PHILIP G.: *James Buchanan and His Cabinet on the Eve of Secession*, 1926; *Robert Tyler, Southern Rights Champion, 1847-1866. A Documentary Study Chiefly of Ante-Bellum Politics*, 1934; a biography of James Buchanan (in preparation).

BARINGER, WILLIAM E.: "Campaign Technique in Illinois—1860," Illinois State Historical Society, *Transactions for the Year 1932* (*Illinois State Historical Library Publication*, no. 39), 202-281; *A House Dividing; Lincoln as President Elect*, 1945; *Lincoln's Rise to Power*, 1937.

BARNES, GILBERT H.: *The Antislavery Impulse, 1830-1844*, 1933; "Introduction" to *Letters of Theodore Dwight Weld, Angelina Grimké Weld, and Sarah Grimké, 1822-1844,* I, v-xxvii, with Dwight L. Dumond, 1934.

BEARD, CHARLES A.: *The American Party Battle,* 1928; *America Yesterday,* with Roy F. Nichols and William C. Bagley, 1938; *An Economic Interpretation of the Constitution of the United States,* 1913; *A First Book of American History,* with William C. Bagley, 1920; *A History of the American People,* with William C. Bagley, 1918; "Review" of Arthur M. Schlesinger's *The Rise of the City, 1878-1898,* in the *American Historical Review,* XXXVIII (July, 1933), 779-780.

BEARD, CHARLES A. and Mary R.: *A Basic History of the United States,* 1944; *History of the United States,* 1921; *History of the United States. A Study in American Civilization,* 1929; *The Making of American Civilization,* 1937; *The Rise of American Civilization,* 2 vols., 1927.

BLAINE, JAMES G.: *Twenty Years of Congress. From Lincoln to Garfield,* 2 vols., 1884-1886.

BROWN, GEORGE W.: "Trends toward the Formation of a Southern Confederacy," *Journal of Negro History,* XVIII (July, 1933), 256-281.

BROWNING, ORVILLE H.: *Diary* (Illinois State Historical Library, *Collections,* XX and XXII), Theodore C. Pease and James G. Randall, editors, 2 vols., 1925-1933.

BRYANT, WILLIAM CULLEN: *A Popular History of the United States, from the First Discovery of the Western Hemisphere by the Northmen, to the End of the First Century of the Union of the States,* with Sydney H. Gay, 4 vols., 1876-1881.

BURGESS, JOHN W.: *The Civil War and the Constitution, 1859-1865,* 2 vols., 1901; *The Middle Period, 1817-1858,* 1897.

CARMAN, HARRY J.: *Historic Currents in Changing America,* with William G. Kimmel and Mabel G. Walker, 1938; *A History of the United States,* with Samuel McKee, Jr., 1931; *Social and Economic History of the United States,* 2 vols., 1930-1934.

CARPENTER, JESSE T.: *The South as a Conscious Minority,* 1930.

CHANNING, EDWARD: *First Lessons in United States History,* 1903; *A History of the United States,* 6 vols., 1905-1925; *A Short History of the United States,* 1900; *A Students' History of the United States,* 1898; *The United States of America, 1765-1865,* 1896.

COCHRAN, THOMAS C.: *The Age of Enterprise. A Social History of Industrial America,* with William Miller, 1942.

COLE, ARTHUR C.: *The Era of the Civil War, 1848-1870* (Centennial History of Illinois, III), 1919; *The Irrepressible Conflict, 1850-1865* (A History of American Life, Dixon R. Fox and Arthur M. Schlesinger, editors, VII), 1934; "Lincoln's Election an Immediate Menace to Slavery in the States?" *American Historical Review,* XXXVI (July, 1931), 740-767; *Lincoln's "House Divided" Speech. Did It Reflect a Doctrine of Class Struggle? An Address Delivered before the Chicago Historical Society on March 15, 1923,* 1923; "The South and the Right of Secession in the Early Fifties," *Mississippi Valley Historical Review,* I (December, 1914), 376-399; *The Whig Party in the South,* 1913.

COMMAGER, HENRY S.: *America—the Story of a Free People,* with Allan Nevins, 1942 (reprinted as *The Pocket History of the United States*); *Growth of the*

American Republic, with Samuel E. Morison, 2 vols., first edition, 1930; latest edition, 1942.

COTTERILL, ROBERT S.: *The Old South. The Geographic, Economic, Social, Political, and Cultural Expansion, Institutions, and Nationalism of the Ante-Bellum South*, 1937.

CRAVEN, AVERY O.: *The Coming of the Civil War*, 1942; "Coming of the War between the States," *Journal of Southern History*, II (August, 1936), 303-322; *Democracy in American Life. A Historical View*, 1941; *Edmund Ruffin, Southerner. A Study in Secession*, 1932; *The Repressible Conflict*, 1939; "Southern Attitude toward Abraham Lincoln," Illinois State Historical Society, *Papers in Illinois History and Transactions for the Year 1942*, 1944; "The South in American History," *Historical Outlook*, XXI (March, 1930), 105-109.

CRAWFORD, SAMUEL W.: *The Genesis of the Civil War. The Story of Sumter, 1860-1861*, 1887; republished as *The History of the Fall of Fort Sumpter*, 1896.

CURTIS, GEORGE T.: *Constitutional History of the United States from Their Declaration of Independence to the Close of the Civil War*, 2 vols., 1889-1896; *Life of Daniel Webster*, 1870; *Life of James Buchanan, Fifteenth President of the United States*, 1883.

DAVIS, JEFFERSON: *The Rise and Fall of the Confederate Government*, 2 vols., 1881; *A Short History of the Confederates States of America*, 1890.

DODD, WILLIAM E.: *The Cotton Kingdom. A Chronicle of the Old South* (*Chronicles of America Series*, Allen Johnson, editor, XXVII), 1919; *Expansion and Conflict*, 1915; "The Fight for the Northwest, 1860," *American Historical Review*, XVI (July, 1911), 774-788; *Jefferson Davis*, 1907; "Letter to the Editor," *Chicago Tribune*, July 15, 1932; *Lincoln or Lee. Comparison and Contrast of the Two Greatest Leaders in the War between the States*, 1928; *Statesmen of the Old South. Or, from Radicalism to Conservative Revolt*, 1911.

DOUGLASS, FREDERICK: *The Life and Times of Frederick Douglass, Written by Himself. His Early Life as a Slave, His Escape from Bondage, and His Complete History to the Present Time, Including His Connection with the Anti-Slavery Movement*, 1881.

DRAPER, JOHN W.: *History of the American Civil War*, 3 vols., 1867-1870.

DU BOIS, W. E. BURGHARDT: *Black Reconstruction. An Essay toward a History of the Part Which Black Folk Played in the Attempt to Reconstruct Democracy in America, 1860-1880*, 1935.

DUMOND, DWIGHT L.: *Anti-Slavery Origins of the Civil War in the United States*, 1939; "Introduction" to *Letters of James Gillespie Birney*, I, v-xxiii, 1938; "Introduction" to *Letters of Theodore Dwight Weld, Angelina Grimké Weld, and Sarah Grimké, 1822-1844*, I, v-xxvii, with Gilbert H. Barnes, 1934; *The Secession Movement, 1860-1861*, 1931; *Southern Editorials on Secession*, 1931.

ECKENRODE, HAMILTON J.: *Jefferson Davis, President of the South*, 1923.

EDMONDS, MAJOR J. E.: *A History of the Civil War in the United States*, with W. Birkbeck Wood, 1905.

ELSON, HENRY W.: *A Child's Guide to American History*, 1909; *A Guide to United States History for Young Readers*, 1910; *History of the United States of America*, 1904; *History of the United States of America*, 5 vols., 1905;

School History of the United States, 1906; *Sidelights on American History*, 2 vols., 1899-1900; *The Story of Our Country*, 2 vols., 1910-1911; *United States, Its Past and Present*, 1926.

EVANS, CLEMENT A.: "The Civil History of the Confederate States," *Confederate Military History*, C. A. Evans, editor, 1899, I, 247-570.

FARRAND, MAX: *The Development of the United States from Colonies to a World Power*, 1918.

FISH, CARL RUSSELL: *The American Civil War. An Interpretation*, 1937; "The Decision of the Ohio Valley," American Historical Association, *Annual Reports* (1910), 153-164; *The Development of American Nationality*, 1913; *History of America*, 1925; *History of the United States*, 1934; *The Rise of the Common Man, 1830-1850* (*A History of American Life*, Dixon R. Fox and Arthur M. Schlesinger, editors, VI), 1927.

FISKE, JOHN: *A History of the United States for Schools*, 1894; *Modern Development of the New World*, with John B. McMaster (*A History of all Nations*, XXIII), 1902.

FITE, EMERSON D.: *History of the United States*, 1916; *The Presidential Campaign of 1860*, 1911; *The United States*, 1923.

FITZHUGH, GEORGE: "The Black and White Races of Men," *De Bow's Review*, XXX (April, 1861), 446-456; "Chotank, Alexandria—A Dive into Herculaneum," *ibid.*, XXX (January, 1861), 77-93; "The Huguenots of the South," *ibid.*, XXX (May and June, 1861), 513-521; "The Message, the Constitution, and the Times," *ibid.*, XXX (February, 1861), 156-167; "The Pioneers, Preachers, and People, of the Mississippi Valley," *ibid.*, XXX (March, 1861), 257-275; "Wealth and Poverty—Luxury and Economy," *ibid.*, XXX (April, 1861), 399-407; scattered articles in *De Bow's Review*, 1861-1862, 1866-1870, 1879-1880.

GAY, SYDNEY H.: *A Popular History of the United States, from the First Discovery of the Western Hemisphere by the Northmen, to the End of the First Century of the Union of the States*, with William Cullen Bryant, 4 vols., 1876-1881.

GIDDINGS, JOSHUA R.: *History of the Rebellion*, 1864.

GREELEY, HORACE: *The American Conflict: A History of the Great Rebellion in the United States of America, 1860-'64: Its Causes, Incidents, and Results: Intended to Exhibit Especially Its Moral and Political Phases, with the Drift and Progress of American Opinion Respecting Human Slavery from 1776 to the Close of the War for the Union*, 2 vols., 1864-1866; *Recollections of a Busy Life: Including Reminiscences of American Politics and Politicians, from the Opening of the Missouri Contest to the Downfall of Slavery, to Which Are Added Miscellanies...*, 1868.

GREEN, BENJAMIN E.: *The Irrepressible Conflict between Labor and Capital: A Brief Summary of Some of the Chief Causes and Results of the Late Civil War in the United States, As Presented in the Translator's Preface to Adolphe de Cassagnac's History of the Working and Burgher Classes, in Which the Origin, Nature and Objects of the Much Calumniated French Commune Are Historically Explained*, 1872.

GREG, PERCY: *History of the United States from the Foundation of Virginia* to the *Reconstruction of the Union*, 2 vols., London, 1887; also an American edition, Richmond, Virginia, 1892.

HACKER, LOUIS M.: "The American Civil War: Economic Aspects," *Marxist Quarterly*, I (April-June, 1937), 191-213; *The Triumph of American Capitalism. The Development of Forces in American History to the End of the Nineteenth Century*, 1940; *The United States. A Graphic History*, with George R. Taylor, 1937.

HAMILTON, J. G. DE ROULHAC: *Benjamin Sherwood Hedrick (James Sprunt Historical Publications*, X), 1911; "Lincoln's Election an Immediate Menace to *Slavery* in the States?" *American Historical Review* XXXVII (July, 1932), 700-711; *Party Politics in North Carolina, 1835-1860 (James Sprunt Historical Publications*, XV), 1916; *Reconstruction in North Carolina*, 1906 and 1914 editions, 1-36; "The South in Political Parties, 1789-1860," *The South in the Building of the Nation*, IV (Franklin L. Riley, editor, 1909), 219-338.

HANDLIN, WILLIAM W.: *American Politics, a Moral and Political Work, Treating of the Causes of the Civil War, the Nature of Government, and the Necessity for Reform*, 1864.

HARRELL, JOHN M.: "Arkansas," *Confederate Military History*, Clement A. Evans, editor, 1899, X, part 2.

HART, ALBERT BUSHNELL: "American Social Characteristics" and "Plantation Life," *Social and Economic Forces in American History*, A. B. Hart, editor (1915), 313-345; *Essentials in American History (from the Discovery to the Present Day)*, 1905; *National Ideals Historically Traced (The American Nation. A History*, A. B. Hart, editor, XXVI), 1906; *New American History*, 1917; *Salmon Portland Chase (American Statesmen*, John T. Morse, Jr., editor), 1899; *School History of the United States*, 1918; *Slavery and Abolition, 1831-1841 (The American Nation. A History*, A. B. Hart, editor, XVI), 1906.

HELPER, HINTON ROWAN: *Nojogue. A Question for a Continent*, 1867; *Noonday Exigencies in America*, 1871.

HICKS, JOHN D.: *The Federal Union. A History of the United States to 1865*, 1937; *A Short History of American Democracy*, 1943.

HODDER, FRANK H.: "The Authorship of the Compromise of 1850," *Mississippi Valley Historical Review*, XXII (March, 1936), 525-536; "Genesis of the Kansas-Nebraska Act," State Historical Society of Wisconsin, *Proceedings* (1912), 69-86; "Propaganda as a Source of American History," *Mississippi Valley Historical Review*, IX (June, 1922), 3-18; "The Railroad Background of the Kansas-Nebraska Act," *ibid.*, XII (June, 1925), 3-22; "Side Lights on the Missouri Compromises," American Historical Association, *Annual Reports* (1909), 151-161; "Some Aspects of the English Bill for the Admission of Kansas," *ibid.* (1906), I, 199-210; "Some Phases of the Dred Scott Case," *Mississippi Valley Historical Review*, XVI (June, 1933), 3-22; "Stephen A. Douglas," *Chautauquan*, XXIX [new series XX] (August, 1899), 432-437.

HOLST, HERMANN E. von: *The Constitutional and Political History of the United States*, 8 vols., 1876-1892; *John Brown*, 1888; *John C. Calhoun (American Statesmen*, John T. Morse, Jr., editor), 1882.

HORTON, RUSHMORE G.: *The Life and Public Services of James Buchanan, Late*

Minister to England and Formerly Minister to Russia, Senator and Representative in Congress, and Secretary of State, 1856; A Youth's History of the Great Civil War in the United States, from 1861 to 1865, New York City, 1866; A Youth's History of the Great Civil War in the United States (War between the States) from 1861 to 1865, Dallas, Texas, 1925.

INGLE, EDWARD: *Southern Sidelights. A Picture of Social and Economic Life in the South a Generation before the War,* 1896.

JOHNSTON, ALEXANDER: *History of American Politics,* 1879; *A History of the United States for Schools,* 1885; *A Shorter History of the United States for Schools,* 1890; *The United States. Its History and Constitution,* 1889.

KENDRICK, BENJAMIN B.: "The Colonial Status of the South," *Journal of Southern History,* VIII (February, 1942), 3-22; *The South Looks at Its Past,* with Alex M. Arnett, 1935.

KING, HORATIO: *Turning on the Light. A Dispassionate Survey of President Buchanan's Administration, from 1860 to Its Close. Including a Biographical Sketch of the Author, Eight Letters from Mr. Buchanan Never before Published, and Numerous Miscellaneous Articles,* 1895.

KLINGBERG, FRANK W.: "James Buchanan and the Crisis of the Union," *Journal of Southern History,* IX (November, 1943), 455-474.

KNOX, CLINTON E.: "The Possibilities of Compromise in the Senate Committee of Thirteen and the Responsibility for Failure," *Journal of Negro History,* XVII (October, 1932), 437-465.

LATANÉ, JOHN H.: "The Diplomacy of the United States in Regard to Cuba," American Historical Association, *Annual Reports* (1877), 217-277; *The Diplomatic Relations of the United States and Spanish America,* 1900; "The Economic Causes of the Civil War," in *The South in the Building of the Nation,* V (James C. Ballagh, editor, 1910), 656-668; *A History of the American People,* 1930; *A History of the United States,* 1918; *The United States and Latin America,* 1920.

LLOYD, ARTHUR Y.: *The Slavery Controversy, 1831-1860,* 1939.

LOGAN, JOHN A.: *The Great Conspiracy: Its Origin and History,* 1886.

MASTERS, EDGAR LEE: *Lincoln, the Man,* 1931.

MCLAUGHLIN, ANDREW C.: *A Constitutional History of the United States,* 1935; *A History of the American Nation,* 1899; *A History of the United States for Schools,* with Claude H. Van Tyne, 1911; *Lewis Cass (American Statesmen,* John T. Morse, Jr., editor), 1891.

MCMASTER, JOHN B.: *A Brief History of the United States,* 1907; *A History of the People of the United States during Lincoln's Administration,* 1927; *A History of the People of the United States from the Revolution to the Civil War,* 8 vols., 1883-1913; *Modern Development of the New World,* with John Fiske (*A History of All Nations,* XXIII), 1902; *A Primary History of the United States,* 1901; *A School History of the United States,* 1897 (republished as a *New Grammar School History of the United States,* 1903).

MERRIAM, GEORGE S.: *The Life and Times of Samuel Bowles,* 2 vols., 1885; *The Negro and the Nation. A History of American Slavery and Enfranchisement,* 1906.

MILTON, GEORGE FORT: *Conflict. The American Civil War,* 1941; *The Eve of*

CAUSES OF THE CIVIL WAR

Conflict. Stephen A. Douglas and the Needless War, 1934; *The Use of Presidential Power, 1789-1943,* 1944.

MOORE, JOHN BASSETT: "Editorial Note" in *The Works of James Buchanan, Comprising His Speeches, State Papers, and Private Correspondence,* J. B. Moore, editor, 12 vols., 1908-1911, I, v-vii.

MORISON, SAMUEL E.: *The Growth of the American Republic,* with Henry S. Commager, 2 vols., first edition, 1930; latest edition, 1942; *The Oxford History of the United States, 1783-1917,* 2 vols., 1927.

NICHOLS, ROY F.: *America Yesterday,* with William C. Bagley and Charles A. Beard, 1932; *The Disruption of the American Democracy* (in preparation); *Franklin Pierce, Young Hickory of the Granite Hills,* 1931; *The Growth of American Democracy: Social: Economic: Political,* with Jeannette P. Nichols, 1939.

OWSLEY, FRANK L.: "The Fundamental Cause of the Civil War: Egocentric Sectionalism," *Journal of Southern History,* VII (February, 1941), 3-18; "The Irrepressible Conflict," *I'll Take My Stand. The South and the Agrarian Tradition,* by twelve Southerners (1930), 61-91; "Origins of the American Civil War," *Southern Review,* V (1939-1940), 609-626.

PHILLIPS, ULRICH B.: "The Central Theme of Southern History," *American Historical Review,* XXXIV (October, 1928), 30-43; *The Course of the South to Secession. An Interpretation by Ulrich Bonnell Phillips,* E. Merton Coulter, editor, 1939; "The Economic Cost of Slave-holding in the Cotton Belt," *Political Science Quarterly,* XX (June, 1905), 257-275; "Georgia and State Rights. A Study of the Political History of Georgia from the Revolution to the Civil War, with Particular Regard to Federal Relations," *American Historical Association, Annual Reports* (1901), II, 3-224; *The Life of Robert Toombs,* 1913; "The Literary Movement for Secession," in *Studies in History and Politics Inscribed to William A. Dunning* (1914), 31-60; "Racial Problems, Adjustments and Disturbances," *The South in the Building of the Nation,* IV (Franklin L. Riley, editor, 1909), 194-241; "The Slavery Issue in Federal Politics," *ibid.,* IV, 382-422; "The Southern Whigs, 1834-1854," in *Essays in American History Dedicated to Frederick Jackson Turner,* Guy Stanton Ford, editor (1910), 203-229.

POLLARD, EDWARD A.: *The First Year of the War,* 1862; new edition, 1863; *Lee and His Lieutenants, Comprising the Early Life, Public Services, and Campaigns of General Robert E. Lee and His Companions in Arms with a Record of Their Campaigns and Heroic Deeds,* 1867; *Life of Jefferson Davis with a Secret History of the Southern Confederacy, Gathered "Behind the Scenes in Richmond." Containing Curious and Extraordinary Information of the Principal Southern Characters in the Late War, in Connection with President Davis, and in Relation to the Various Intrigues of His Administration,* 1869; *The Lost Cause. A New Southern History of the War of the Confederates. Comprising a Full and Authentic Account of the Rise and Progress of the Late Southern Confederacy—The Campaigns, Battles, Incidents, and Adventures of the Most Gigantic Struggle of the World's History. Drawn from Official Sources, and Approved by the Most Distinguished Confederate Leaders,* 1866; new editions in 1867 and 1890; *The Lost Cause Regained,* 1868; *Southern History of the Great Civil War in the United States,*

1863; new edition in 2 vols., 1866; *Southern History of the War. The First Year of the War,* 1863.

POTTER, DAVID M.: *Lincoln and His Party in the Secession Crisis (Yale Historical Publications,* XIII), 1942.

RAMSDELL, CHARLES W.: "The Changing Interpretation of the Civil War," *Journal of Southern History,* III (February, 1937), 3-27; "The Frontier and Secession," in *Studies in History and Politics Inscribed to William A. Dunning* (1914), 61-79; "Lincoln and Fort Sumter," *Journal of Southern History,* III (August, 1937), 259-288; "The Natural Limits of Slavery Expansion," *Mississippi Valley Historical Review,* XVI (September, 1929), 151-171; "The Secession Movement," *Reconstruction in Texas (Columbia University Studies in History, Economics and Public Law,* no. 95), 1910, 11-20.

RANDALL, JAMES G.: "The Blundering Generation," *Mississippi Valley Historical Review,* XXVII (June, 1940), 3-28; *The Civil War and Reconstruction,* 1937; "The Civil War Restudied," *Journal of Southern History,* VI (November, 1940), 439-457; *Lincoln the President: Springfield to Gettysburg,* 2 vols., 1945; "When War Came in 1861," *Abraham Lincoln Quarterly,* I (March, 1940), 3-42.

RHODES, JAMES FORD: *History of the Civil War, 1861-1865,* 1917; *History of the United States from the Compromise of 1850,* 7 vols., 1893-1904; *Lectures on the American Civil War, Delivered before the University of Oxford in Easter and Trinity Terms 1912,* 1913.

ROOSEVELT, THEODORE: *Thomas Hart Benton (American Statesmen,* John T. Morse, Jr., editor), 1886; Theodore Roosevelt, Oyster Bay, New York, to Colonel George Harvey, Harper's Weekly, New York City, Sept. 19, 1904, Roosevelt MSS.

RUSSEL, ROBERT R.: *Economic Aspects of Southern Sectionalism, 1840-1861 (University of Illinois Studies in the Social Sciences,* XI, nos. 1 and 2), 1924; "The General Effects of Slavery upon Southern Economic Progress," *Journal of Southern History,* IV (February, 1938), 34-54; "The Pacific Railway Issue in Politics Prior to the Civil War," *Mississippi Valley Historical Review,* XII (September, 1925), 187-201; "A Revaluation of the Period before the Civil War: Railroads," *Mississippi Valley Historical Review,* XV (December, 1928), 341-354.

SCHNITTKIND, HENRY T.: *The Story of the United States. A Biographical History of America,* 1938.

SCHOULER, JAMES: *Eighty Years of Union, Being a Short History of the United States, 1783-1865,* 1903; *History of the United States of America, under the Constitution,* 7 vols., 1880-1913.

SCRUGHAM, MARY: *The Peaceable Americans of 1860-1861. A Study in Public Opinion (Columbia University Studies in History, Economics and Public Law,* no. 219), 1921.

SEMPLE, ELLEN CHURCHILL: *American History and Its Geographic Conditions,* 1903; *Influences of Geographic Environment, on the Basis of Ratzel's System of Anthropo-Geography,* 1911.

SHANKS, HENRY T:. *The Secession Movement in Virginia, 1847-1861,* 1934.

SHUGG, ROGER W.: *Origins of Class Struggle in Louisiana. Social History of White Farmers and Laborers during Slavery and After, 1840-1875,* 1939.

SIMMS, HENRY H.: "A Critical Analysis of Abolition Literature, 1830-1840," *Journal of Southern History*, VI (August, 1940), 368-382; *A Decade of Sectional Controversy, 1851-1861,* 1942; *Life of Robert M. T. Hunter. A Study in Sectionalism and Secession,* 1935.

SIMONS, ALGIE M.: *Class Struggles in America,* 1903; third edition "revised and enlarged" and changed, 1906; *Social Forces in American History,* 1911.

SITTERSON, J. CARLYLE: *The Secession Movement in North Carolina* (James Sprunt Studies in History and Political Science, XXIII, no. 2), 1939.

SNYDER, MRS. ANN E.: *The Civil War from a Southern Stand-point,* 1890.

SPENCE, JAMES: *The American Union. Its Effect on National Character and Policy, with an Enquiry into Secession, as a Constitutional Right and the Causes of Disruption,* 1861; second edition, 1862.

STEPHENS, ALEXANDER H.: *A Compendium of the History of the United States from the Earliest Settlements to 1872,* 1872; revised editions in 1883 and 1885; *A Comprehensive and Popular History of the United States Embracing a Full Account of the Discovery and Settlement of the Country . . . ,* 1882; *A Constitutional View of the Late War between the States. Its Causes, Character, Conduct and Results. Presented in a Series of Colloquies at Liberty Hall,* 2 vols., 1868-1870; *The Reviewers Reviewed. A Supplement to the "War between the States,"* etc., *with an Appendix in Review of "Reconstruction," So Called,* 1872.

STEPHENSON, NATHANIEL W.: *Abraham Lincoln and the Union. A Chronicle of the Embattled North* (Chronicles of America Series, Allen Johnson, editor, XXIX), 1918; *An American History,* 1913; *The Day of the Confederacy. A Chronicle of the Embattled South* (Chronicles of America Series, Allen Johnson, editor, XXX), 1919; *A History of the American People,* 2 vols., 1934; *Lincoln. An Account of His Personal Life, Especially of Its Springs of Action as Revealed and Deepened by the Ordeal of War,* 1922; *A School History of the United States,* 1921; "Southern Nationalism in South Carolina in 1851," *American Historical Review,* XXXVI (January, 1931), 314-335; *Texas and the Mexican War. A Chronicle of the Winning of the Southwest* (Chronicles of America Series, Allen Johnson, editor, XXIV), 1921.

TAYLOR, WILLIAM: *Cause and Probable Results of the Civil War in America. Facts for the People of Great Britain,* 1862.

TURNER, FREDERICK JACKSON: *The Early Writings of Frederick Jackson Turner,* Edward E. Edwards, compiler, 1938; *The Frontier in American History,* 1920; "Report of the Conference on the Relation of Geography and History," American Historical Association, *Annual Reports* (1907), I, 43-48; *The Significance of Sections in American History,* 1932; *The United States, 1830-1850. The Nation and Its Sections,* 1935.

VAN DEUSEN, JOHN G.: *The Ante-Bellum Southern Commercial Conventions* (Trinity College Historical Society, Papers, XVI), 1926; *Economic Bases of Disunion in South Carolina* (Columbia University Studies in History, Economics and Public Law, no. 305), 1928.

WEBB, WALTER P.: *Divided We Stand. The Crisis of a Frontierless Democracy,* 1937; *The Great Plains,* 1931.

WESLEY, CHARLES H.: *The Collapse of the Confederacy,* 1922; revised edition, 1937; *Negro Labor in the United States, 1850-1925,* 1927.

WHITE, LAURA A.: "Charles Sumner and the Crisis of 1860," in *Essays in Honor of William E. Dodd*, Avery O. Craven, editor, 1935; *Life of Charles Sumner* (in preparation); "The National Democrats in South Carolina, 1852 to 1860," *South Atlantic Quarterly*, XXVIII (October, 1929), 370-389; *Robert Barnwell Rhett: Father of Secession*, 1931; "The United States in the 1850's As Seen by British Consuls," *Mississippi Valley Historical Review*, XIX (March, 1933), 509-536.

WILLIAMS, GEORGE W.: *History of the Negro Race in America from 1619 to 1880. Negroes as Slaves, as Soldiers, and as Citizens. Together with a Preliminary Consideration of the Unity of the Human Family, an Historical Sketch of Africa, and an Account of the Negro Governments of Sierra Leone and Liberia*, 1882.

WILSON, HENRY: *History of the Rise and Fall of the Slave Power in America*, 3 vols., 1872-1877.

WISH, HARVEY: *George Fitzhugh. Propagandist of the Old South*, 1943; "The Revival of the African Slave Trade in the United States, 1856-1860," *Mississippi Valley Historical Review*, XXVII (March, 1941), 569-588.

WOOD, W. BIRKBECK: *A History of the Civil War in the United States*, with Major J. E. Edmonds, 1905.

CHAPTER IV

PROBLEMS OF TERMINOLOGY IN HISTORICAL WRITING

The Need for Greater Precision in the Use of Historical Terms Illustrations

By CHARLES A. BEARD
and
SYDNEY HOOK

SINCE HISTORIOGRAPHY has a certain domain peculiar to its interest and a certain degree of independence and integrity those who work at it confront inevitably problems of terminology: the meanings of the terms used and the necessity of attaining as much precision as possible in the use of terms. Emphasis upon and a study of historical terminology therefore become a matter of prime concern in writing history, in communications among historians, in training students, and in attaining the highest degree of exactness in descriptions, statements, and narrations offered to historians and the general public. The fact that recent discussions of "meanings" in many quarters have bordered on hair-splitting, if not worse, in no way absolves historians from the obligation of having a care for the choice and use of terms appropriate to their thinking and writing.

As compared with mathematics, the physical sciences, and indeed some of the other social sciences, historiography suffers from many disadvantages. Of course, even like the physical sciences, meanings and thought in historiography have their origins in the remote history of the human race, and still rest in part upon popular usages and "common sense" assumptions. But a number of circumstances have militated against the development of a special terminology in historical studies.

First of all it is widely assumed that any literate person can "write history" if he or she can set about the collection and ordering of historical "facts." It would not be regarded as absurd if a junior high school student or a college freshman or even a brilliant journalist attempted an "outline of the first World War" or drew "conclusions" or "lessons" from that highly complicated aggregation of human actions and experiences. But it would be generally recognized as both absurd and presumptuous if even a very learned scholar utterly ignorant of mathematics and the terminology of physics should undertake to expound or to prove or disprove the equivalence of heat and mechanical work.

The development of mathematics and physics has been accompanied by the development of terms the meanings of which are for practical purposes universal in all languages. A right angle, whatever the words for it in given languages, is a right angle for all people of all times who have an elementary competence in such matters. Even in some of the humanistic studies, such as philosophy and economics, terms have been created for dealing with particular themes. For example, when philosophers are discussing concepts and the term "pure idealism" is used, they know fairly well just what they are talking about. Again if an economist refers to "marginal utility," his colleagues have a reasonably precise knowledge of what he is talking about. Indeed for several of the humanistic studies, philosophy and sociology for instance, excellent dictionaries have been prepared by competent hands; and all who have occasion to work in one or another of these domains may readily avail themselves of the advantages offered by such handbooks.

In the development of historiography, to be sure, many special terms have been evolved, such as, "paleography," "diplomatics," "original sources," "secondary authorities," and "calendar." But these pertain to the methodology rather than to the thought of historiography. The broad question of correct terms for the actual writing of history has received relatively little consideration at the hands of historians and this lack of agreement on terms is responsible for no little confusion in the composition of historical works.

Historians are also beset by the special disadvantage that arises out of the fact that history comprehensively conceived covers not only events, personalities, ideas, and interests in the conduct of ordinary affairs but also the development of the natural sciences, philosophy, history, economics, politics, and so forth. Thus the historian is called upon to use the words of the marketplace, forum, and battlefield—and the words of philosophy, natural science, and political economy. Besides, he confronts the difficulties involved in the translation of other languages into his own. With regard to technical terms—for example "right angle," "pure idealism," "government"—he has little difficulty; but in the case of words of wide and common usage he encounters obstacles that are almost, if not sometimes entirely, insurmountable.

Even in writing about his own country, in which the difficulties of translation from other tongues may not occur, the historian, if as cautious as he should be, becomes entangled in the matter of choosing the most exact words appropriate to the subject matters of each sentence, paragraph, chapter, and work. To paraphrase a warning uttered by Wilhelm von Humboldt more than a hundred years ago, when one attempts to tell the story of the simplest and most insignificant affair and is firmly resolved to describe it as it actually happened, one soon discovers that, without exercising the highest care in choosing and measuring words, little determinations or decisions will become involved in the operation and introduce falsities or uncertainties. Moreover language is so constituted that expressions free from equivocal meanings and varying associated sentiments can scarcely be found, if at all, for giving a literally true account of a simple series of events, to say nothing of events, ideas, and interests highly complicated in nature. To historians conscious of what they are trying to do and conscientious in their regard for their office, language difficulties are often so perplexing as to induce utter despair. Only those who "write without fear" can avoid the issues of terminology.

In its efforts to introduce more consistency into the operations of historiography by securing agreements on a number of propositions relevant to the subject, the committee faced the problem involved in trying to develop a more exact terminology for use in writing history. A proposition to compile a dictionary of historical terms was discussed in committee meetings, but lack of funds and time soon led to an abandonment of the idea. Still convinced that something should be done at least to emphasize the problem and bring it before historians for their consideration, the committee decided to attempt a limited and modest experiment. It was not unaware of the difficulties, or even the humor, likely to arise in making definitions. It recognized that any definition is likely to be more or less arbitrary, but it was firmly of the opinion that unless "we know what we are talking about we cannot talk to any point or have any understanding of one another's views."

By a process of discussion, choice, and elimination, the committee decided upon an experiment with fifty words or terms frequently used in the writing of history or in works on historiography. It engaged Mrs. Wallace K. Ferguson to collect from historical works numerous illustrations of the ways in which each of these fifty words have been used. As an aside it may be said that the results were fearful and wonderful. At the same time, the committee engaged Professor Sidney Hook, a specialist in philosophy who has written on certain phases of history and the social sciences, to study the fifty words in question, correlate Mrs. Ferguson's findings, and formulate definitions as exact as possible for historical purposes.

After attempting to carry out these suggestions, Professor Hook, at a long conference with the committee, made it evident to the members that no self-consistent definitions of the fifty historical terms could be based on an analysis and synthesis of the meanings given to them by numerous historians. Thereupon, the committee requested Professor Hook to formulate his own definitions taking such account as he could of the illustrations afforded by Mrs. Ferguson's collection from the writings of historians. This assignment also proved to be impossible, for the varied and conflicting usages of the terms by historians could not be reconciled with one another or with those prevailing in general or in philosophy in particular.

Unwilling to drop the problem of terminology, indeed more convinced than ever that it deserved serious attention in connection with any effort to give more exactness to historical work, the committee finally made two decisions: to make this brief statement on the subject for the purpose of giving emphasis to its importance; and to print Professor Hook's definitions as he formulated them, without attempting to reformulate them in the "light" of the usages which are practiced by or should be practiced by historians.

ILLUSTRATIONS

By SIDNEY HOOK

Accident. See *Chance.*

Analogy

An analogy is a comparison which, on the basis of certain points of resemblance between two cases, suggests the existence of some further resemblance selected because of its relevance to the purposes of the comparison. As a figure of speech it functions as a metaphor to enliven and enrich historical style, e.g., when a revolution is described as a "storm that shook the land" or as a "fever" through which society has passed. As an argument it is formally worthless and never logically compelling. An argument from analogy can be countered usually with another argument from analogy which leads to a diametrically opposed conclusion. E.g., when an analogy has been drawn between colonies and children to suggest the duty of accepting the rule of the mother country, it can be countered with an analogy between colonies and matured offspring whose subsequent growth depends upon independence of their parents.

At best an analogy can only suggest a plausible conclusion whose validity must then be established on other grounds. The uncritical use of analogies is the bane of much historical writing, particularly when the resemblances lack clear definition or when they are blurred and presented as *identities.* The two most pervasive analogies in historiography are those drawn from biology and physics. For example, "cultures are organisms and world-history is their collective biography" (Spengler). "This country will yet be viewed and reviewed as an organism of historic growth, developing from minute germs from the very protoplasm of state-life" (H. B. Adams). The belief that society is an organism is an old but fanciful notion. It can only be seriously entertained by closing the eye to all the respects in which a group of separate individuals differs from a system of connected cells, and by violently redefining terms like "birth," "reproduction," and "death." The organismic analogy has often been used to suggest that class distinctions in society are natural and should be perpetuated in the interest of social health; but it can also be used to show that social differentiations develop out of capacities common to all cells. The same observations hold for analogies drawn from physical science. When history is spoken of as a "system of elements in unstable equilibrium," or when the relations between social institutions are described as "parallelograms of forces," or when it is said, "Even as the chemist and physicist, we [the historians] talk of practice in the laboratory" (J. F. Rhodes), strictly taken, there is nothing in the subject-matter of social and historical behavior which corresponds to these terms. When they are not strictly taken, certain meanings associated with their use in the fields where they are legitimately employed are smuggled into the historical account, and give a misleading impression—more often to the writer than to the reader—of scientific exactness. A man who talks about "social vectors" does not necessarily know more than one who talks about people who grow cotton for market, and he may conceivably know less. Biological analogies of "adaptation," "struggle for existence" and "survival" lead to additional confusion because ethical or value judgments are often read into them. For example: "There may be reason to conclude that an inscrutable law of nature, at last involving us, has long been and now is evolving results. It is one more phase of natural evolution, working itself out, as in the case of Rome, 25 centuries ago, through the survival and supremacy of the fittest" (C. F. Adams).

The program, announced but never carried out, of trying to *deduce* social or historical relationships from laws of physics, physical chemistry, thermodynamics or biology, so that the first set of relationships would appear as special cases of the second, is *not* reasoning by analogy and is not subject to the above strictures. But it is obvious that social and historical knowledge can be won without waiting for the happy day when such deduction is successful, and that the reliability and validity of historical knowledge does not depend upon the possibility of finding overarching laws in the natural sciences from which we can deduce this historical knowledge.

Sometimes historians speak of "analogies of historical experience" when they are drawing parallels or making comparisons between two historical events; e.g. The French and Russian Revolutions. This use of the term "analogy" must be carefully distinguished from the preceding senses. Not only is it legitimate, it is indispensable for purposes of historical generalization to draw comparisons and parallels between historical events. (See *Cause.*) Analogies between two historical events can be properly evaluated only when we make explicit the defining properties of the class of events of which both are declared to be members. E.g., if a revolution is defined in terms of changes in class-power or transformation of property relations, historical analogies drawn between the Russian and French Revolutions will have greater validity in determining the truth about an hypothesis concerning the nature of revolutions than an historical analogy between the

American and the Russian Revolution. However, if a revolution is defined in political terms, the analogy between the American and Russian Revolution may be relevant.

Cause

An ambiguous and difficult term of varied and complex meaning. Should be used by historians with circumspection in contexts that show clearly what they intend by the use of the term. There is no common agreement on the philosophical analysis of its meaning. The chief schools divide over the question whether the causal relation manifests a relation of *necessity*, logical or ontological, or of uniform sequence or invariant association. When members of the second school do use the word "necessary" in connection with causal attributions, they insist that the meaning of necessity can be adequately defined in terms of uniform succession in contradistinction to members of the first school who hold that we require a notion that is sui generis.

Nonetheless, the word "cause," or some synonym for it like "the consequential order" of events in a process, is employed in every day affairs, in all branches of science, and in the writings of all historians. All intelligent behavior which seeks to control the present or predict the future exhibits an implicit belief in some causal connections.

Cause and effect, and cause and consequence (where the latter refers to a related or relevant temporal succession) are strictly correlative terms. That an event has causes or effects is a postulate of scientific inquiry.

For practical purposes that grow out of the need to master a situation or solve a problem, the cause of an event is regarded as that aspect or factor of the phenomenon under investigation which must be changed to produce a desired or adequate result. E.g., "The cause of this man's pain is a stone in the bladder" or "The cause of the civilian population's flight to underground shelters is the approach of enemy planes." The presence of other relevant conditions is always presupposed. Without the nervous system there would be no pain, and unless it was assumed that enemy planes act differently from friendly planes, there would be no flight. But none of these other relevant conditions, taken individually or collectively, is sufficient to account for the pain or the flight. The presence of the stone in the bladder is a *necessary* condition for the occurrence of this particular kind of pain; the presence of enemy planes a *necessary* condition of this kind of flight. The stone together with a number of other factors in the first case, enemy planes together with a number of other factors in the second case, constitutes a *set of factors which is sufficient* for the occurrence respectively of the pain and the flight.

Since every historical occurrence involves the interaction of several elements, we cannot intelligibly speak of *the* cause of the occurrence if by that term we mean the sole or exclusive element. But usually "the cause" of an event, as used by historians, means not the only cause but "the most important cause" (see below, p. 114) among a complex of causal conditions, or the condition which was most decisive to what occurred, or which made the difference between what occurred and what would probably have occurred in its absence.

The quest for causes can best be conducted when the investigator has a clear idea of the problem to which he is seeking an answer. Sometimes the appearance of divergence among historians in assigning causes to an event, say "The growth of American civilization," is due to the fact that different things are understood by the phrase, so that what we have is a series of different answers to different questions. Sometimes the question itself is ambiguous. E.g. "Why is the American college curriculum four years in length?" may mean an inquiry into its origins, or into its continuing functions which account for its survival. Sometimes different answers to the same question may all be true because the question may be asked from the points of view of different fields of interest. E.g. to the question "Why did the Supreme Court make this decision?" the jurist, social psychologist, and historian will give different but mutually compatible answers. "Cause" will mean for the first a set of legal principles, for the second a set of motives, for the third the set of relevant historical antecedents justified by his hypothesis.

Within the field of history, an inexpugnable element of selection enters into the choice of the historical problem to be investigated. But once the problem is selected and clearly defined, the attribution of causes is either true or false and *in principle* ascertainable although in practice we may not at any moment know enough to provide the answer. This is sometimes obscured by the assumption that it is the business of the historian to account for *every* aspect of the event under examination. Since the number of aspects of anything is indefinitely large, this is impossible. A scientific explanation of a phenomenon is never a total explanation in the sense that it is an exhaustive answer to all possible questions that may be put from all possible centers of selection or interest. Knowledge is nonetheless reliable for being piecemeal or partial. What is sometimes called "the totality of historical actuality" is no more the subject-matter of the scientific historian than the "totality of the actuality" of a falling body is the subject-matter of the physicist.

The historical causes of an event are usually sought among its temporal antecedents rather than among its simultaneous conditions and consequences. When the evidence points to a particular antecedent as the cause of an event, it is sometimes claimed that the causal antecedents of the first antecedent must necessarily be included among the causes of the event. But since antecedents can always be discovered for every antecedent, this is tantamount to saying that the series of countless antecedents which constitutes the history of the universe is a relevant cause of the event. Inasmuch as the history of the universe is a necessary antecedent of all events that may be investigated, it would be impossible to provide a differential explanation of any specific event. The striving to achieve the utmost truth about any aspect of the event is something quite different from a quest for the utmost truth about the *whole* event. Nor does such striving commit us to the pursuit of truth about the totality of all events. Investigators will agree that a given event will have a certain effect. The fact that this effect has further effects does not destroy the first admission. The effects of effects may be investigated just as the antecedents of antecedents may be investigated. But if one admits that a process has a *relative terminating point*, then since cause and effect are strictly correlative terms, one is logically bound to admit that a process has a *relative initial point*, beyond which one need not go for the purposes of the problem in hand.

No historical account that goes beyond the form of a chronicle can be written without the assumption of causal connection. And no historical chronicle exists in which assumptions of this character are not implicit. It may therefore serve some purpose to state briefly the basic features of the general pattern of inquiry that is followed in all fields in which we can distinguish between truth and fiction. It is the presence of this pattern of inquiry which makes a historical account scientific, and *not* the use of the specific methods of physics, biology, or psychology.

Every statement of causal connection is an hypothesis. Only in the light of this hypothesis and its implications, do we know what data to look for in order to verify or refute it. Let F be the event we seek to explain; d, e, l, p . . . those antecedents among which we are seeking the cause: H the hypothesis that e is the cause of F. Whenever it can be shown through a series of experimental controls, that in the absence of d, l, p . . . , F still occurs; that in the presence of e, F always occurs; that in the absence of e, F never occurs; and that F varies concomitantly with e; then we are warranted in concluding that e is *probably* the cause of F. Note, however, the following: (1) In the course of investigation, F, the particular situation whose problematic character is the starting point of inquiry denotes an instance of a class of events. (2) d, e, l, p . . . are selected from an unlimited number of antecedents because of some prior knowledge, or assumption of knowledge, of what is or may be relevant to F or to a *similar* class of phenomena. (3) The hypothesis that e is the cause of F has been established by *eliminating* alternative hypotheses that the other factors are necessary conditions for the occurrence of the event. (4) The conclusion is only probably true because theoretically there may be some other factor x, which for all tested cases fulfils all the conditions satisfied by e but which in some future instance of F may be discovered to be present when e is absent. (5) The probability of the conclusion is increased in various ways: by increasing the range of the antecedents of F and eliminating them successively; by predicting new knowledge that could not be reached at the time by rival hypotheses; or by using the hypothesis as an instrument of action to solve difficulties or remove blockages in the problems and situations similar to those provoked by the original inquiry.

The nature of history makes impossible controlled experiments which vary the component factors of a situation. Nonetheless the above rules for determining the presence or absence of causal connections in historical sequences are applicable, subject to the following considerations: (1) An historical event which is regarded as absolutely unique or novel, that has no points of significant similarity with the other events, is outside the scope of historical understanding or explanation. As soon as the historian formulates an hypothesis about the cause of an event, he converts that event into an instance of a more or less loosely constructed class of similar events from the recorded past or present experience. (2) The historian therefore never approaches a problem with an empty stare or an empty head. On the basis of his knowledge of other historical instances, past and present, of the phenomenon under investigation, he selects a group of relevant or plausible antecedent factors, which appear to be relatively exhaustive, in order to test his hypothesis that one of them, or a combination of them, is more decisive than the others. (3) In place of the controlled experiment, he uses the method of historical comparison and hypothetical construction. Historical comparison involves constructing a class of instances and proceeding, along the lines indicated above, to eliminate alternative hypotheses. This is very difficult because the antecedent factors are rarely, if ever, completely absent from the different instances considered. The validity of the historian's findings will therefore depend upon his ability to discover a method of roughly measuring the relative strength of the various factors present. This method must be logically independent of his own hypothesis since its validity is in question. The method of hypothetical construction which supplements the method of historical comparison consists in envisaging the historical consequences that would have ensued if a given antecedent event had not occurred and in giving an answer, of varying degrees of probability, in terms of approximate regularities observable in other instances. The degree of probability marks the difference between wild speculation and well grounded likelihood. Thus it is overwhelmingly likely that America would have been discovered even if Columbus' ships had foundered, quite likely that the Civil War would have come about at a later date if Fort Sumter had not been fired on, and unlikely that the Russian October Revolution would have been successful without Lenin. Inability to answer hypothetical questions contrary to fact about the past is a mark that we do not have knowledge of historical connections just as inability to answer hypothetical questions about the present or future in any other field is evidence that we do not have knowledge of connections in those fields. Where our answer is well grounded either for the past or present or future, it is based on the assumption of causal relations between events. (4) Conclusions about historical causes are only probable because generically all statements of fact are probable, and specifically, because classes of historical events are vaguely and loosely constructed, their instances are few in number, the number of antecedents in each instance is large, in varying degree all antecedents are present in almost all instances so that they cannot be completely eliminated, and they interact with each other to a greater extent than do antecedent factors in nonhistorical fields. (5) The probability of causal judgment in history is increased by retrospective prediction, i.e., an inference on the basis of the judgment that something about the past, not yet known to be true and not predictable by alternative hypotheses, will be confirmed by certain operations, e.g., excavation, finding of documents, etc.

The term "decisive" or "basic" or "underlying" or "most important" cause of an occurrence, where used by a critical historian, is the sign of a *comparative* judgment concerning the relative antecedent factors of an occurrence. It is an elliptical way of saying that some necessary condition is *more* decisive (or basic, etc.) than some other conditions. It would help matters if this ellipsis were avoided and the other conditions were explicitly stated in relation to which the first condition was called more decisive. A condition is more decisive than others when events of this type take place more frequently than events of other types in relation to the type of occurrence under investigation. Therefore the particular occurrence would be much more improbable if the condition called decisive did not occur than if any of the other conditions to which it is being compared did not occur. Thus, Lenin's activity in the Russian October Revolution was more decisive than, say, Stalin's because it was a necessary condition for the success of the Revolution and represented a factor less easily replaced than the factor Stalin represented; or, in the application of labor-saving devices in industry, the quest for profit was historically more decisive than the particular inventors of these devices because the quest for profit was a necessary condition of the application whereas there is good reason to believe that most of these labor-saving devices would have been invented by other individuals if their actual inventors had not lived. In general, a factor is more decisive than others in any situation if it enables us to predict the development of the situation, and of more aspects of the situation, *more reliably* than predictions based on other factors. In the study of historical situations this prediction is a retrospective prediction or post-diction; it is more fruitful in leading to the discovery of new knowledge than predictions based on factors regarded as less decisive.

An examination of the actual procedure of historians and their knowledge-claims shows that there is little dispute about some kinds of causal attributions in studies of narrowly circumscribed historical sequences but a great deal of dispute about more inclusive ones. Thus, few historians differ on the causes of the fall of Vicksburg and its effects on the fortunes of the Civil War but they are much more at variance over the causes and effects of the Civil War. Similarly, most historians agree on the reasons which led Pope Urban II to convoke the Council of Clermont in 1095, at which he appealed for a crusade against the infidels. But there is no such unanimity among them concerning the causes and effects of the Crusades. It would be helpful to isolate the typical difficulties which arise as we go from one level of complexity in historical statements to another. But this situation in the field of history should not lead us to deny the possibility of scientific history because in the fields of the natural sciences we can observe something very similar. Thus Snell's law of refraction in optics is accepted by all physicists; but they may be in vehement disagreement with each other as to whether this is more adequately explained by the wave theory of light or the corpuscular theory; both the followers of Newton and those of Einstein will accept Galileo's laws of freely falling bodies although they will differ strongly concerning an inclusive theory of gravitation. Perhaps the real difficulty, as Ernest Nagel suggests, is that in *no* domain does there exist an explicit procedure for weighing evidence with respect to *all* types of statements, of whatever degree of generality.

The antecedent of an event which, on the hypothesis of the historian, is relevant not to the occurrence of the event but to its date or occurrence at a *given* time, is usually called *the occasion* in contradistinction to the cause. E.g., if the historian believes that World War I resulted because of the economic and political conflicts of interest among the great powers, he will characterize the assassination of the Archduke at Sarajevo as the occasion of the war. Sometimes the term *proximate* or *immediate* cause is used interchangeably with *occasion* but only if it is contrasted with remote or underlying causes, not with final or nonempirical causes.

Chance, Accident, and Contingency

There are various senses of the term "chance" and "contingency," not all of which are relevant to historiography.

(1) The contingent is that which is given or found in brute actuality, whose existence is not logically necessary and whose nonexistence is not logically impossible. In this sense everything that exists has a contingent aspect.

(2) The chance and the contingent are sometimes made synonymous with "uncertainties" arising from incalculable complexities. E.g. "The superiority of force is often checked by the proverbial contingencies of war" (Sumner).

(3) The contingent is "the uncaused," something which cannot be explained in terms of itself or in terms of its antecedents.

(4) The contingent or chance event is sometimes regarded as a *trivial* occurrence which has given rise to *great or momentous* consequences. E.g. "My alloted time . . . could easily be filled with a mere enumeration of instances where great and general effects are asserted to have followed upon certain accidental or personal causes" (Cheyney).

(5) The contingent is an event whose antecedents are irrelevant or unrelated to the development of a selected theme or sequential series but whose consequences affect this development. Thus from the point of view of the history of American Indian culture, the coming of the white man would be a "chance" or "contingent" event and from the point of view of a history of European migrations, the existence of Indian settlements in America would be a chance event. The narrower or more restricted the theme or sequence under investigation, the greater will be the number of events regarded as chance. E.g. "The temporary triumph of (Robespierre's) philosophy was in part the accident of fate, dependent on such chance things as the weakness of the king and the treason of Dumouriez" (E. N. Curtis).

(6) In its clearest use, chance is the unpredictable intersection of two series of events, only one of which is historical, i.e., concerned with the activities of human beings as members of a social group in pursuit of their aims. That event is a chance event which has historical effects but not historical causes, e.g., the tidal wave at Lisbon, the destruction of Pompeii, the Black Death. No amount of social and historical data would have enabled the historian to predict or foresee these events, although *after* they have occurred social and historical data would enable the historian to explain why these events had certain historical consequences rather than others.

The characterization of an event as a chance event entails a denial that there is one all inclusive system of events in which *all* events can be historically ordered. It therefore involves a conception of history narrower in scope than "the study of everything that happens." It does not necessarily breach the postulate of determinism. Chance events in history are not uncaused events but events, some of whose antecedents or causes are not directly related to determining strand or strands which they twist or snarl in ways that cannot be foretold by a knowledge of the earlier patterns of these strands alone. It follows that the more classes of events the historian considers as integral parts of his province of inquiry, the fewer chance happenings he will recognize provided that he is able to predict the time of the intersection of the different determining strands.

Change, Development, Progress

One of the causes of intellectual confusion in historical writing is the practice of using these terms interchangeably.

(1) *Change* is any difference in position, form, quality. Change is always relative to some thing, measure, or standard which in relation to the changing thing either does not change or is changing at a different rate. If there were only one thing in the world, it would be meaningless to assert or deny change of it. *Historical* change always implies differences in the behavior of human beings as members of a social group or differences in the behavior and organization of things and institutions which condition changes in human behavior.

(2) *Development* is any change which has a continuous *direction* and which culminates in a phase that is qualitatively *new*. The term "development" should be used to characterize any series of events in thought, action or institutional arrangements which exhibits a directional, cumulative change that either terminates in an event marked off by recognized qualitative novelty or exhibits in its course a perceptible pattern of growth. Sometimes the term "evolution" is used as synonymous with "development"; but it would be preferable to speak of "evolutionary change" when the development is gradual, and "revolutionary change" when the development is hurried and sudden when compared to the rates of change of similar series in an earlier time period.

(3) *Progress* is a development favorably evaluated from the standpoint of a human interest, end, or ideal. It is the point at which the historian runs up his ethical flag. E.g. "The road to the true frontier, toward progress and independence was barred by the plantation belt which enclosed many of the poor white areas" (Buck). Whether a development is progressive or not cannot be intelligently determined until the historian makes explicit what his value-judgments are. Where there is prior agreement on value-judgments (e.g., that the elimination of disease is a good), we can speak of objective or verifiable progress, (e.g., "modern medical science has made great progress"). But whether or not the elimination of disease is a good is not objectively verifiable by the same specific methods by which the historian determines that medical progress has taken place. When the historian speaks of progress, it is wise for him to specify the respect in which progress has taken place in order to bring implicit value-judgments to the surface. Very often the context of a historical account will reveal that what the historian means by "progress" is identical with the meanings of either "change" or "development." But even more often the term is used in such a way as to run together conceptions which, in the interest of clarity, should be distinguished. E.g. "Progress may be stemmed for a time but it cannot be permanently stopped by force" (Andrews); "Yet in reality no great progressive movement needs justification at our hands, for great causes justify themselves and time renders the decision" (idem). From this it follows that anything which fails to survive cannot be progressive, that all lost causes are bad causes, i.e., unprogressive. But it is questionable whether the writer intended to assert this.

Civilization and Culture

Two of the most widely used and abused terms in the historian's vocabulary—but abused only insofar as the historian confuses the descriptive or factual and normative or value senses of the terms. In view of the history and varied usage of these words, the notion that they have one proper or legitimate meaning which is violated by anyone who departs from it, is arbitrary and quaint. But these usages must, of course, be distinguished and writers should explicitly, or by context, clearly indicate what usage they are following.

In popular discourse, the term "civilization" is often a crude value term used to contrast one's own society with other societies called "uncivilized." Sometimes it is used to characterize one phase of the same society as distinct from other phases, or some people in present society as opposed to others. In this sense, the term "uncivilized" tells us less about the societies and peoples so characterized, aside from the fact that they are objects of negative value-judgments, than the Greek use of the term "barbarian" or the Christian use of the term "heathen," which also expressed value-judgments but at least had a clear objective connotation. We knew who the "barbarians" or "heathen" were and why they were so designated.

Among contemporary anthropologists, the terms "culture" and "civilization" are usually used interchangeably in order to escape from the necessity of making moral judgment about different societies before studying them. Some anthropologists (Malinowski) prefer to reserve the term "civilization" to designate some special types of culture. Lewis H. Morgan, the pioneer American anthropologist, uses the term "civilization" for a stage of society which is marked by the use of written records. In an effort to keep the term "civilization" neutral, most anthropologists, following Tylor, prefer to speak not of "lower" or "higher" civilizations but of "early" or "primitive" and "modern" civilizations, distinguishing them only by their locus in time and space. They resort to denotative definition, as e.g., "What then is civilization? Our attitudes, beliefs and ideas, our judgments and values; our institutions, political and legal, religious and economic; our ethical code and our code of etiquette; our books and machines, our sciences, philosophies and philosophers—all of those and many other things and beings, both in themselves and in their multiform interrelations, constitute our civilization. In many of these things it differs from the civilizations of antiquity and from those other remote ones of pre-history" (A. Goldenweiser). This also serves as a denotative definition of culture. Others beside anthropologists use "culture" and "civilization" interchangeably. In the following sentence the word "culture" can be substituted for the word "civilization" without altering its intended and logical meanings in the slightest; "The disappearance of the great civilizations of Central and South America and that of Central Africa does indeed appear to present as irrefutable evidence of the perishable character of a civilization as the continuity of Chinese civilization appears to present of its persistence" (C. Brinkmann).

When "civilization" is used as a value-term and "culture" is used as a descriptive term, cultures are said to *become* more or less civilized in virtue of the presence or absence of some idea, institution, or mode of behavior regarded as "progressive" by those who use the term. The specific content of what constitutes progress or decline would constitute a specific people's conception of civilization. "This idea of civilization [in the U.S.], in a composite formulation, embraces a conception of history as a struggle of human beings in the world for individual and social perfection—for the good, the true, the beautiful—against ignorance, disease, the harshness of physical nature, the forces of barbarism in individuals and in society" (C. A. Beard).

Sometimes "culture" and "civilization" are both used as value-terms that are distinguishable from each other. This usage has been made current by Spengler, who distinguishes, not without inconsistency, between "culture" an early phase of growth, marked by creativity, freshness and life in all phases of human activity, and "civilization" a later phase of rigidity, into which the first phase is destined to pass, characterized by petrifaction of institutions and mechanical routines of thought.

Contingency. See *Chance.*

Culture. See *Civilization.*

Destiny, Fate, Predestination

A metaphysical concept which has no place in empirical history. An event is destined or fated if its occurrence is literally inevitable or inexorable or necessary no matter what its antecedent events may be. Thus, in the Greek tragedies Oedipus is predestined to kill his father no matter how hard he struggles to avoid his fate; in Calvinist theory a man is elected or damned independent of works; in certain types of Marxism, socialism is inevitable regardless of the defeats of the proletariat; in Spengler, civilization and extinction is the inescapable fate of all cultures. This conception of an overriding necessity in human affairs is completely alien to the scientific conception of causal connections between events—connections which are not inevitable but evitable. The scientific prediction that an event will occur is always *conditional* upon the occurrence of certain antecedent events in whose absence the event in question does not occur. The occurrence of the event, even if the antecedent events takes place, is *probable* yet never certain, because (a) the relation between antecedent and consequent is empirical, not logical, and no one can guarantee that the kind of connection we have observed in the past must continue to hold for the future, (b) an event from a different system may intervene and prevent the reasonably expected consequence to follow the antecedent event, and (c) as a special case of (b), the foreknowledge of a consequential pattern may permit or invite preventive measures or control.

Some types of determinism, called monistic, organic or absolute, of which Hegel's is the most notable, attempt to differentiate themselves from fatalism by admitting that the occurrence of an event depends upon the occurrence of antecedent events but insist that these antecedent events as well as their antecedents, etc., are *all* logically necessary. Everything that exists, on this view is inevitably what it must be, nothing could have been different in the past, there are no alternatives in the present or future, possibility is unreal, and if *anything* in the world had been different in any respect, *everything* in the world would have been different. This makes the world one big event or closed system in which time plays no part and in which every thing and creature has a logically inevitable role to play out even before it comes into being. This is fatalism en bloc and at one stroke. The assumption that the world is of this character is based on metaphysical or religious faith, not scientific evidence. On the contrary, it is incompatible with the logic of scientific inquiry which presupposes that it is possible to discover truths about events in relatively isolated systems without taking the whole universe into account.

Development. See *Change.*

Dialectic

A philosophical term of great antiquity that has been used by many different philosophers and some historians in varied senses. These senses where they are relevant to history and historiography may be conveniently classified into two divisions. A—Senses of the term which refer to the pattern of actual historical and social change. B—Senses which identify it with a method of understanding historical and social change.

A—Dialectic as pattern of change

(1) Dialectic is a pattern of pendular rhythm or an eternal, repetitive seesaw between polar ideas, interests, movements and institutions. According to this conception, every tendency in action or thought swings through an arc whose highest point is the beginning of a return swing in an opposite direction. E.g., convention leads to revolt and revolt to convention, peace to war and war to peace, despotism to democracy and democracy to despotism, etc. This use of a mechanical analogy is designed to call attention to the *periodicity* of historical and social change in some particular respect since it is never asserted that the oscillations carry a culture back to the *identical* place or state from which it started. It cannot do justice to

continuities, cumulative developments, and transitions from one society to another.

(2) Dialectic in the Hegelian and orthodox Marxist sense is a pattern of dynamic self-development, in the cosmos as well as in history. The pattern is one of continuous development marked by phases of arrest, reaction, and revolutionary transformation which are integral to the historical process. Its geometrical analogue is not the straight line, or circle, or pendulum but the spiral which combines some features of all the others. There are three chief characteristics of the dialectic as an historical process: (a) The negative moment, the phase of reaction, or the evil, in an historical process is the chief motor force of development. It is idle to deplore it, for out of it all subsequent good flows. It is *die List der Vernunft*, the Cunning of Reason, by which what are conceived to be the predestined Ends of History work themselves out. Just as the flower is fertilized by the bee which robs it of its honey, so the underlying Purpose of History is realized through transitory evils. (b) The process of historical development, which consists of a series of successive syntheses of opposing moments (thesis and antithesis) has on the whole a progressive direction conceived to be objective, irreversible, and "higher" in an ethical sense. What is later in time, is better in quality. (c) All historical and cultural phenomena are interrelated with each other (and with everything else in the cosmos) and are, at varying rates of change, all embraced in the sweep of development.

(3) Dialectic designates the perennial fact of opposition and struggle between men, classes, and nations. Although included in the sense of dialectic in A(2)—where it seems inconsistent with the Hegelian belief that historical development stops with the Prussian State and the orthodox Marxist belief that it stops with the classless society—it may be held independently.

(4) Dialectic is the process of *interaction* between objective conditioning features of the human environment and man considered as the active agent in the historical process. Human action, informed by ideals and propelled by interests, introduces changes in the original historical situation whose difficulties provoke action. The dialectical nub of the process is considered to be the element of *creative redetermination* produced in the world and the self by human activity, and the subsequent modification of human nature by the control of things and institutions.

B. Dialectic as a *method* of understanding historical and social change.

(1) Dialectic is an intellectual procedure which regards *all* elements of a culture as necessarily *interrelated* in one cultural pattern. This interrelatedness is not asserted as a heuristic or guiding principle subject to *piecemeal* verification but as a dogma validated by intuition (e.g., Spengler).

(2) Dialectic is the logic of totality. In this sense, the dialectic method maintains that it is theoretically impossible to formulate abstract laws of human and social behavior which can be applied to the study of a given cultural totality without necessarily modifying these laws in the light of the organic interrelationships of that particular culture. Insofar as we can speak of laws every "seamless web of culture" has its own law. This sense of dialectic is already implicit in B(1) but is distinguished because of the importance of its specific denial that we can intelligently speak of invariant laws of social behavior for all societies.

(3) Dialectic is the technique of thinking according to which every historical judgment, of fact or value, implicitly implies its contradictory. These contradictories together, instead of cancelling each other out, logically involve another judgment in which they are reconciled. This is the famous Hegelian *dialectischer Dreitakt* by which our understanding is corrected and advanced in its march towards comprehension of the total historical actuality.

(4) Dialectic is the method by which certain antecedently believed ideas about the Ends of History are established by showing that these Ends or Ideals are involved in every true judgment of historical fact. It is bound up with the belief that history has a goal which will inevitably be realized, that temporary setbacks and defeats are necessary to the ultimate triumph of man's "highest" ideals (which always turn out to be one's own).

Economic

Like all basic terms "economic" is used in a loose way and trails a cloud of vague meanings behind it. It is often defined as a discipline which treats of "social phenomena centering about the provision for the material needs of the individual and organized groups" (E.R.A. Seligman). This would make economic phenomena coextensive with almost the whole of cultural life except those activities that minister to the spirit; and the difference between spirit, mind, body and matter involves troublesome metaphysical distinctions. When the historian talks about the influence of economic factors upon other aspects of social life or on historical development, he may mean one of at least five different things, which, although related, should be distinguished. A great many controversies about the role of economic factors in history are aggravated by a failure to recognize the different senses of the term.

(1) "Economic" sometimes designates a class of personal motives, viz., desire for wealth, more particularly, money. Historians who believe that economic motives are more prevalent or stronger than other motives are committed to a psychological thesis.

(2) "Economic" is sometimes used to designate tools, techniques,

processes and the "know-hows" of production. One may hold to this meaning and remain neutral about the character and distribution of human motives.

(3) "Economic" may refer to the presence or absence of land and raw materials like coal, oil, and gold. Where historical importance is assigned to them, it is assumed that human beings want them: "Gold in the ground is a cipher for a study of society so long as we are doing nothing and not tending to do anything in connection with it. Gold that does not exist is an important factor when we are in turmoil of chasing for it" (Bentley).

(4) "Economic" may refer to social relations of production which are not material things or psychological motives but a set of institutional rules —e.g., feudalism or capitalism—that govern the production and distribution of wealth. In this fourth sense, it is not asserted that human motives are economic in the first sense but that whatever the predominant pattern of human motivation in any period—selfish or unselfish, pacific or aggressive, this-wordly or other-wordly—its predominance is to be explained by the character of the social relations of production.

(5) There is another sense of "economic" which must be distinguished from the four senses enumerated above: "economic" as interchangeable with "efficient," e.g., "the economic organization of government." Economists and others employ the term "economic" in this sense when they are referring to the best allocation of resources to satisfy a set of given diverse wants.

Fact

As generally used in historical study and writing, apart from considerations of ontology, fact, as indicated by *factum*, from which it is derived, means a thing done, an action, deed, event. Abraham Lincoln's taking of the oath of office as president on March 4, 1861, is an historical fact. Fact is also something known to have had a given character; "The Civil War in the United States was long drawn out and was costly in lives, money and property." "Fact" is also a particular truth, often involving many other particulars, known by actual personal observation, by authentic oral testimony, or by authentic recordings: e.g., "There was a decline of the death rate in the City of New York between 1870 and 1940."

When more carefully considered, it will be clear that there are no "facts" in *rerum natura* or in history when considered as a process of events in space and time. Facts have to be *established* in the course of inquiry, but no inquiry is possible except on the assumption that we are already in possession of some facts garnered by earlier inquiry, each one of which *may* be doubted but not all of them together. Facts never speak for themselves but only *to* someone who has an hypothesis which he wishes to test. To collect facts in the hope that they will lead to truths is idle except when such collection is guided by an hypothesis or classificatory scheme. Often the collection of facts is guided by an implicit hypothesis which becomes evident when we ask: Why collect *these* facts and not others? This is concealed by such statements as: "At the very beginning of all conquest of the unknown lies the fact, established and classified to the fullest extent possible at the moment" (G. B. Adams).

Every fact which the historian establishes presupposes some theoretical construction. Even the "date" of an event, as distinct from its givenness, involves the conceptual scheme of the calendar, and the measurement of time as related to a center of reference. Since this scheme is common to all historians, no theoretical difficulties about the dating of events are raised when sufficient evidence is at hand to attach dates to events. There is only a difference of degree of generality and validity between facts and hypotheses and theories. What in relation to some data is an hypothesis, like "The blood circulates through the body," may become after subsequent verification a fact. Facts about things and events and relationships are expressed in propositions, none of which is certain. The propositions which express facts may roughly be distinguished into three fundamental classes: (1) propositions which express a fact about perceptual data or observable properties, like "This is a small, shiny, round golden object"; (2) propositions which interpret the observable properties, like "This is a Roman coin circulated in the age of Augustus"; (3) propositions which assert a determinate connection, either of invariance or of statistical probability, between classes of propositions interpreting observable properties, like "Whenever gold is used as currency, there will be severe penalties for tampering with its weight" or "The presence of gold coins is usually a sign of a centralized government."

In historical analysis propositions of the third type are more *difficult* to establish than those of the second but the fundamental method of establishing them is in principle the same. It is sometimes suggested that particular facts may be established as objectively true by scientific methods but that general facts or hypotheses or theories which relate particular facts cannot be established as objective truths. Yet every assertion of a particular fact, established by scientific method, presupposes the objective truth of facts of greater generality, and intelligent denial of assertions purporting to state objective truths in history must be based on other facts, particular or general, believed to be objectively true. That Caesar crossed the Rubicon is a fact that may be more easily ascertainable than the motive which led him to do so. But the attribution of some motive to Caesar, in the light of the evidence, is better grounded than the attribution of others. What makes one attribution better grounded than another is the coherence of the hypothesis with other facts we know about Caesar, about the state of Rome, about other Romans, about men in situations similar to that of Caesar, and ultimately its instrumental efficacy in enabling us to solve the problem which stimulated inquiry. The procedure does not differ in principle from scientific investigation of the behavior and motives of our contemporaries.

Charles Peirce suggests that evidence warranting the assertion of a fact should be considered not as a single chain of causally related elements, which would be no stronger than its weakest link, but as a cable of relatively independent causal strands whose strength, as evidence, is greater than the sum of the strands taken singly.

Fate. See *Destiny.*

Force

Frequently with a prefix, as "political," "economic," "moral," "religious" or "social." As used in historiography, it is a metaphor which historians, unable to express the idea directly in precise descriptive terms of something exercising a historical effect or influence, employ for convenience in dealing with human activities and situations. It is defined by Henry Adams as "anything that does, or helps to do work." Even so it is elusive and should not be used (see *Analogy*) unless the context gives a certain degree of concreteness to it, indicating the particular economic (or political, social, religious) interests of individuals, classes, and groups, which find outlet or expression in particular actions or types of actions. For example, "The steel, woolen, and tin-plate manufacturing interests, in conjunction with other powerful economic forces, were enlisted in the support of the McKinley tariff bill."

Frame of Reference

Sometimes called "scheme of reference" or "presupposition" or "personal equation." The historian's frame of reference loosely refers to the set of principles which guides him in the selection of his problem, the organization of his materials, and the evaluation of his findings. Some confusion has resulted from a failure to distinguish these elements.

(1) In one sense, a "frame of reference" is an hypothesis as to what constitutes the determining factor or factors in the problem or situation to be explained. It can be used interchangeably with the term "theory." Unless one denies the possibility of objective historical knowledge, a "frame of reference" in this sense is in principle open to objective confirmation or disproof of varying degrees of probability through the employment of scientific method.

(2) In another sense, a "frame of reference" is what determines the historian's selection of his hypothesis, and sometimes the selection of

the *kind* of historical problem he investigates. The "frame of reference" here may be a desire by an historian to glorify a church, nation or party, to improve mankind, to influence the making of history in one direction rather than another, or to further the truth as he understands it, or what not. This may be called the historian's personal bias or prepossession and it *may* lead him not only to select his particular hypothesis but to distort, exaggerate and omit relevant evidence in testing his hypotheses. But the possession of bias or passion on the part of the historian does not preclude the possibility of his achieving objectivity in testing his hypothesis any more than a physician's passion to relieve men from the ravages of a disease or a chemist's desire to achieve money or fame or destroy his country's enemies precludes the possibility of the discovery of a medical or chemical truth. The prepossessions of Pasteur's work on antitoxins was that God in his infinite goodness could not have created a scourge for mankind without at the same time creating a remedy. And this did not prevent Pasteur from rigorously testing his hypothesis. On the other hand, Kammerer's zealous belief that the salvation of mankind depended upon the possibility of transmitting acquired traits of the somaplasm to the germplasm led him, consciously or unconsciously, to "cook" the evidence of his experiments. The more *aware* the historian is of his frame of reference in this second sense, the less likely he is to let it interfere with the validation or invalidation of his frame of reference in the first sense. For an historian to have a driving bias, conscious or unconscious, is merely to be human; for an historian to have a driving bias which leads him to a hitherto neglected aspect of an historical phenomenon that may be fruitfully explored, is to have genius or perhaps luck; for an historian to be able to distinguish between what inclines him to his hypothesis— its causes in his biography—and the evidence for or against it—its logical grounds—is to be scientific.

(3) In a third sense, "a frame of reference" may indicate the scope of the historian's interest, i.e., those things in the furniture of heaven and earth which he intends to include in his account. The "frame of reference" of a social historian will be wider than that of an historian of prices; it will be one thing if he limits himself only to political events and another thing if he includes geographical, demographical, and technological factors. No "frame of reference" can include everything, and the findings of two different frames of reference, *if* true, will be compatible with each other. If the findings are logically incompatible, then either one or both of the historians have violated the canons of scientific method.

(4) A fourth sense of "frame of reference," related to, but distinguishable from, the second sense, is the philosophy of life or value by which the historian expresses his judgment of what is of most worth. No one can prove such a judgment by historical findings alone. When an historian de-

plores, exalts, laments, he tells us what kind of a man he is but this does not guarantee his findings nor is it entailed by them. When James Harvey Robinson writes: "History would seem, in short, to condemn the principle of conservatism as a hopeless and wicked anachronism," it is not history which condemns the principle of conservatism but James Harvey Robinson. It would be possible to show agreements on many historical questions between, on the one hand, Robinson and, on the other, Savigny and proponents of the historical school who invoked history as a support for the principle of conservatism.

Generalization

Sometimes employed in historical writing to designate the action of describing, or a description, under one proposition or formula, of certain characteristics or relationships common to a number of individual personalities, facts, or events. To be distinguished in this sense, from the making of explicit hypotheses and fictions. A generalization is a statement that can be checked for accuracy and authenticity by reference to records of the particulars covered by it. Example: "All the wars here discussed were preceded by a fall in prices on the London Stock Exchange and by a rise in the number of trade union members reported as unemployed." To be distinguished also from what are called "loose generalities."

Predestination. See *Destiny.*

Progress. See *Change.*

Scientific Spirit. See *Cause.*[1]

Understanding

In respect to history, there are two generic schools of thought concerning the nature of understanding.

(1) The first school asserts that historical understanding is a species of scientific understanding in general, and that scientific understanding is theoretically equivalent to "explanation." The criteria of adequate explanation are *formally* the same for all events and processes under investigation. An event or process is explained if it can be shown that it follows from a set of relevant antecedent events regarded as determining conditions (cf. *Cause*). Explanation is of varying degrees of generality but always involves the assumption of some general laws or statistical generalizations relating classes of phenomena, to one of which the event or process belongs. Historical understanding differs from other forms of scientific understanding (physical, biological, etc.) only in respects which reflect differences in the subject-matter to be understood; (a) historical under-

[1] See also below, 134 [ed.'s note].

standing operates with categories derived from human activity in social contexts rather than from the behavior of material particles; (b) both the general laws which are invoked in historical understanding as well as the findings advanced are relatively more vague and less reliable than is the case in physics and biology; (c) the particular methods and techniques of historiography in ascertaining evidence, as distinct from the logic of evidence, need have no relation to the specific methods and techniques of other disciplines.

(2) The second school asserts that historical understanding is not a species of scientific understanding but is of a radically different kind. The object of historical understanding is the unique individual concrete event. It is achieved not by introducing general laws or relevant antecedent events but by an act of "intuition," "imaginative identification," "empathy," or "valuation" which makes the historical occurrence plausible or intelligible. The adequacy of the historical understanding is determined not by external criteria, coherence of verifiable evidence, simplicity of hypotheses, predictability, etc.—at best these lead to preliminary operations on the matter to be understood—but by a self-certifying insight. Usually associated with this position, but not logically entailed by it, is the view that the understanding of history necessarily reflects the scheme of credibility which the historian carries around in his head, that this scheme is essentially dependent upon the times and culture in which the historian lives, that it varies as these vary, and that therefore each age must rewrite the past according to its own scheme of credibility even when no new historical data have been uncovered. When to this is added the belief that these different histories are equally valid this doctrine is known as historical relativity, and implies that "historical truth," as distinct from scientific truth, is truth for one's own age. When the historian's scheme of credibility is made dependent not only on his times and culture but on his class, vocation, nation, personality, historical truth is so relativized that it becomes truth for the particular historian and the question which of two conflicting historical interpretations in any given age is true becomes a question concerning the truth of two conflicting philosophies or schemes of credibility. Such questions are usually declared to be outside the province of scientific decidability, and are assimilated to questions that arise when the "truth" of works of art is discussed.

The fundamental issues between these two schools of historical understanding are obviously issues of philosophical analysis. But from the point of view of the practicing historian certain considerations are in order.

First, both in assembling and evaluating his materials in relation to an historical theme or problem, and in judging other historical accounts, the historian must differentiate between historical narratives that are *better grounded* or *more reliable* than others. Failure to make this differentiation, or an indifference to it, would mean that the historian could not regard his activity, in any significant sense, as different from that of a fiction writer or novelist who employed historical characters.

Second, in every historical account some events enter which are of a kind, regarded as relevant by the historian, that do not require reference to acts of intuition or insight to make them credible or plausible. For example, the consequences of the invention of the cotton-gin on the history of American economy and more particularly, the Civil War, can be explained or understood without empathetic self-identification with anyone or anything. Or a claim will be made for the existence of certain historical regularities which can be accepted or denied without reference to any inner experience on the part of the historian: for example, the claim made by Teggart that for the period from 58 B.C. to A.D. 107 "every uprising on the European borders of the Roman Empire had been preceded by the outbreak of war either on the eastern frontiers of the empire or in the western regions of the Chinese."

Third, only where individuals are directly involved, as distinct from the operation of the conditions of their activity, is the historian called upon to make an essay in understanding which at first blush seems to differentiate it from scientific explanation of the type found in the natural sciences. And here only insofar as the *motives* of action are concerned, not the fact of their activity. *That* an individual, it is sometimes said, did such and such can be established scientifically as well as the consequences of his action, but *why* he did it cannot be explained but only understood by an intuition. Thus, in criticizing the historian's technique of sifting evidence by the canons of scientific explanation, Hocking writes:

> The only difficulty with this procedure, from the standpoint of living history, is *that the important facts are never verified for they take place in the mind!* They have to do with the passions and motives of men which no one ever sees. The real historical events are decisions, not the consequent movements of arms and legs; but the historian can verify only the leg-motion. The decision itself, and its preceding tempest of inner debate, remain invisible and inaccessible. Caesar crossed the Rubicon, that was his leg-motion or other verifiable procedure in the world of space and 'fact.' But why did he do it? What were his thoughts, his anxieties, his hopes, his plans: there lies the true history. [Italics in the original.]

The suppressed premises of the whole argument, particularly of the italicized sentence, is that what takes place in the mind is never verifiable, that the mind is something not organically related to the behavior of the body in space—time—society, and therefore must be understood in a unique sense. Insofar as the conflict between the two schools of historical thought, distinguished above, reduces itself to the question of whether motives and decisions can be scientifically explained, this becomes a philosophical question just as relevant to the understanding of the present as of the past, of human behavior that is nonhistorical as of human behavior that is historical.

Fourth, whatever his ultimate philosophical position may be on this question, the working historian, who writes about motives, decisions and ideals, must deny the suppressed premise of the passage quoted, viz., that what takes place in the mind is never verifiable. For the historian's own state of mind is not the state of mind of his historical subject nor evidence of it, and what he offers as evidence of the historical subject's *state of mind* does not differ in kind from the evidence that he offers for the *physical behavior* of the historical subject. The reason that Hocking gives for believing that it is impossible to verify Caesar's decision would make it impossible to verify even Caesar's leg-motion, for no living historian has seen it. Both are objects of inquiry. We verify statements about Caesar's crossing the Rubicon as well as about his purposes in doing so by the same method, viz., by inference from present observable data of various kinds, and from certain general laws of personal and social behavior which are themselves verifiable. If the historian could understand the personalities he wrote about only by an imaginative act of self-identification, it would be a little hard on him when discussing Nero, Caligula and Messalina.

Fifth, insofar as the issue reduces itself to the question of the nature of evidence, the practicing historian proceeds on the basis of the postulate of *contemporaneity of evidence*. That is to say, the present is the point of departure for the definition of his terms. The historian must be able to indicate the kind of behavior whose presence will justify him in attributing a character to an object, say "religious," or a motive to a person, say "ambition." Further, when he asserts a connection between events of a certain character and motives of persons in order to justify the consequential order by which he relates specific events and specific persons, he asserts the relative invariance of the connection and hence its *present* observability on the basis of which he makes his extrapolation to the past. Since the postulate of the contemporaneity of evidence holds for *all* fields of scientific inquiry, no special faculty of *historical* understanding need be introduced to account for it.

CHAPTER V

PROPOSITIONS

IN ORDER to promote clarity and understanding, the committee has deemed it wise to define the meaning it has attached to certain basic terms frequently used in the Propositions.

The word *history* is used in at least five overlapping senses: (1) the systematic study of, or a treatise dealing with, natural phenomena—as in "natural history" or "life history"; (2) the past of mankind (or any part thereof)—as in "history as actuality" or "the totality of history"; (3) the survivals and records (whether primary or secondary) of the past of mankind (or any part thereof)—as in "recorded history," "a history book," or "a case history"; (4) the study, representation, and explanation of the past of mankind (or any part thereof) from the survivals and records—as in "written or spoken history"; and (5) the branch of knowledge that records, studies, represents, and explains the past of mankind (or any parts thereof)—as in "department of history" or "school of history."

Historical method is used in two senses. (1) Applied to branches of knowledge other than history, it designates a method of investigation by which the past developments or experiences of the object under consideration are studied and generalizations derived therefrom. (2) Applied to the study of history, it means the process by which the historian gathers, examines, selects, verifies, and presents historical facts and interpretations in an orderly context or edits historical sources. Historical method in sense 2 includes *analysis*—i.e., the testing of historical sources for authenticity and the selection of particulars from the authentic materials—and *synthesis*—i.e., the putting together of particulars into a narrative or exposition that will stand the tests of critical methods.

Historical literature is the body of written history, whether primary or secondary, authentic or inauthentic, credible or incredible, as opposed to purely imaginative fiction and legend. It furnishes some of the source material for *history* and *historiography*, for both of which words it is often loosely used as a synonym.

Historiography is used in three senses: (1) primarily as the intellectual processes, critical and constructive, by which history is written (in which sense it is often treated as equivalent to *synthesis in historical work*); (2) the results of those processes (in which sense it is largely equivalent to *secondary historical literature*); and (3) the study and criticism of the sources and development of history (in which sense it is largely equivalent to *the history and critique of history*).

The *scientific spirit in history* is characterized by (1) awareness of the existence and nature of problems that may be treated historically; (2) recognition of the functions and the limitations of the historical method in the treatment of historical problems; (3) readiness to collect and to submit to careful selection, in accordance with the established rules of historical method, the available evidence necessary to support the statements made in any piece of written history and to sustain the context of the historical construct; (4) willingness to give proper weight to the various pieces of the evidence thus selected; (5) acknowledgment of one's own socio-economic and other biases and the effort to eliminate their effects; and (6) determination to make only such conclusions or inferences as are justified by the evidence.

PROPOSITIONS
Basic Premises

I

The historian is one of the guardians of the cultural heritage of mankind. He is also an interpreter of the development of mankind. In carrying on these functions he aims to compose accurate accounts and analyses of selected portions of the past. From these accounts and analyses, or from the original sources themselves, he endeavors to reach generalizations that appear to be valid. On the basis of his knowledge he also seeks to provide credible explanations of the development of contemporary events, thoughts, manners, and institutions.

II

The utmost understanding of history attainable to the human mind is to be acquired by extending historical research and thought as far as possible in the direction of comprehensiveness and synthesis as well as by inquiring more deeply into the particular and the unique.

III

Historiography has a necessary relevance to all the social sciences, to the humanities, and to the formulation of public and private policies, because (1) all the data used in the social sciences, in the humanities, and in the formulation of public and private policies are drawn from records of, experience in, or writing about the past; because (2) all policies respecting human affairs, public or private, and all generalizations of a nonstatistical character in the social sciences and in the humanities involve interpretations of or assumptions about the past; and because (3) all workers in the social sciences and in the humanities are personalities of given times, places, and experiences whose thinking is consequently in some measure conditioned and determined by the historical circumstances of their lives and experiences.

IV

Any selection of data from historical records in the interest of a particular interpretation of history, such as political, military, economic, or cultural, comes within the proper scope of historiography if the selection and treatment conform to the rules of critical scholarship and if it is made evident by the author that the work in which it appears is in fact an interpretation or emphasis and is to be regarded as limited by the very nature of the interpretation or emphasis.

V

In a scientific methodology clear distinctions must be maintained between the unrecoverable totality of the past, the records of the past, and written or spoken history.[1]

VI

Every written history, particularly that covering any considerable area of time and space, is a selection of facts[2] made by some person or persons and is ordered or organized under the influence of some scheme of reference, interest, or emphasis—avowed or unavowed—in the thought of the author or authors. Historiography should set forth this proposition to all workers in history and should indicate to them the many schemes of reference, interest, or emphasis which have influenced written or spoken history.

VII

Written or spoken history is to be best understood not only by analysis of its structure and documentation, but also by a study of the possible attitudes arising from the life and circumstances of the author.

VIII

Since every written-history represents a selection of facts and an emphasis, it follows that the writing of such a history involves acts of thinking and purpose. Therefore the clarification of thought and purpose

---

[1] Inasmuch as most students receive a large part of their historical information in lecture form we must include spoken history.

[2] See above, 123-125.

is a necessary preliminary for all historians who desire to emancipate themselves from bondage to the subconscious, the routine, and the surreptitious and to seek the utmost impartiality possible to the human mind.

Important Sources of Methodological Error

IX

Those who work in historiography in the scientific spirit cannot embrace any of the absolutes put forth by theologians or philosophers of any school as furnishing mandates by which the data of the past must be selected and organized or shaped to fit the institutional requirements of those who espouse such absolutes. Historians should seek to place absolute systems of thought in their appropriate settings of time and place.

X

The concept of causality has entered into narrative to such an extent that the writing of history might become mere cataloguing or chronology without it. Historians should be aware, however, that investigation of "cause" in history must be posited on two arbitrary limitations: (1) of the extent of past time in which antecedent interrelations will be sought, and (2) of the number of impinging factors that will be assumed to remain constant and therefore will not be examined. In terms of these limitations the moot question of First or Single Cause is a metaphysical and not a historical problem.[3]

---

[3] The undersigned are of the opinion that the terms "cause" and "causality" should never be used in written-history. They hold that the use of the word "cause," if permissible in conversations and in the consideration of small practical affairs (as, "the cause of that train wreck was a broken rail") is unnecessary to the making of true statements concerning history-as-actuality, and owing to the ambiguity and connotations of its meanings, is more likely to be misleading than correctly informing to the reader. Many grounds could be presented in support of this dissenting position but only a few will be given here. The word "cause," as Mr. Hook says in the Illustrations (110ff.), is "an ambiguous and difficult term of varied and complex meaning." It involves fundamental theories concerning the nature of our universe which theologians and philosophers have long debated without arriving at any general consensus of conviction; such as, "Is God the first cause of all things? Does the first cause operate in or outside our universe? Were all things determined from the beginning, thus eliminating particular causes?" Any definition of a complicated aggregation of events, conditions, and personalities in history-as-actuality, such as the French Revolution or the American Revolution, is an arbitrary delimitation in time and space—an isolation of the "data" in the mind or the imagination, not outside the mind or the imagination (as in chemistry, for example); and the assignment of cause or causes to anything that cannot be accurately defined and isolated in fact is at best a highly dubious intellectual operation. In any case, if Event A is assigned as the cause of Event B, the act is wholly arbitrary

XI

The term "cause," as used by historians, must therefore be regarded as a convenient figure of speech, describing motives, influences, forces, and other antecedent interrelations not fully understood. It may be defined as any preceding event in what is assumed to be a consequential and interrelated complex. It follows from this definition that a "cause" never operates except as part of a complex or series. Consequently the phrase "the cause" while justifiable when used to indicate a precipitating event or phenomenon, should be avoided in favor of its plural, "the causes," which likewise should be used only with great circumspection. The assumption that one knows the "cause" or "causes" has sometimes resulted in the formulation of superficial "remedies" which add to the fanaticism that accompanies controversies.

XII

The so-called "constants" or "repetitions" derived from the study of history—such as war, tyranny, revolution, dictatorship and democracy—may be used as furnishing analogous situations. They are valuable as serving analytical, comparative and descriptive purposes and as supplying guidance in the search for approximate historical patterns and for future probabilities, a search capable of much social usefulness. However, they are not exact repetitions nor do they afford proof of "laws" in history. Action based on such an assumption is likely to prove erroneous.

XIII

The word "understanding" is frequently loosely used by historians. What is called an "understanding" of history or of historical events is often merely the feeling of satisfaction which comes over us when a new impression or treatment of history falls easily into one or another of the categories already accepted and established in our minds. Although his-

---

as far as time is concerned, and any person who does not arbitrarily stop at Event A will ask: "What is the cause of Event A and so on backward into the darkness of prehistory?" Where historians are concerned, as they should be, with consequential and coexisting relations between events and personalities and interests, which are intimate in nature and have the appearance of necessity, they can describe such relations in terms more precise than those of causality; without using the word "cause" or "causes"—"ambiguous and difficult" terms, "of varied and complex meaning." As to cause in natural science and grounds for discarding it there, see E. W. Hobson, *The Domain of Natural Science*, 78ff. In general as regards history, see Raymond Aron, *Introduction à la Philosophie de l'Histoire* (Paris, 1938), 159ff., "Le determinisme historique et la pensée causale."

CHARLES A. BEARD
ALFRED VAGTS

torians working in the scientific spirit will not pretend to have an "understanding" of history, they may approach understanding of history by discovering and accurately describing relationships among occurrences in history and seeking greater comprehensiveness in studying and writing history.

XIV

There are limiting, conditioning, and determining features in a history such as the psychological, cultural, economic, biological, and physical; for instance, the use of the English language in American courts of law is determined by circumstances beyond the control of legislators and judges. But the precise nature, limits, and influences of such features constitute problems of knowledge and thought not easily resolved by historians. A search for such features is a valid and appropriate operation in historiography.

Desirable Principles and Techniques

XV

The ideal which controls the historian in search of the utmost knowledge of the past is to achieve the most informed understanding of occurrences and personalities that available sources and discriminating imagination will permit, so as to write history with the highest possible degree of credibility.

XVI

Historians may formulate generalizations of limited validity which are useful in the interpretation of the past until their modification is called for by new evidence. This is indeed essential if historical work is to rise above a merely empirical level and if it is to serve any purpose other than propaganda or literary effect. In forming generalizations, historians may profit by using the methods of modern science, such as measurement, insofar as these prove applicable to historical data.

Attempts to discover "laws" as exact as those now employed in the physical sciences have failed, however, for a number of reasons. Among these are (1) the apparent impossibility of using certain modern scientific methods, notably experimentation and the use of instruments to aid the senses; (2) the greater complexity of social data as compared to physical: as seen in the circumstance that history presents unique personalities who seem to affect the course of history (or events) and from time to time emergent phenomena not apparently explicable by preexisting phenomena; (3) the paucity in the social and psychological sciences of adequate generalizations which might be applied in historical studies; (4) the changing character of social phenomena from one age to the next, in comparison with the relatively constant character of the data of the physical sciences; and (5) the circumstance that many potentially pertinent data are lost beyond recall. Whether these difficulties can ever be so overcome as to render historical studies as exact as physics is open to question. Since at least some of the difficulties noted above may be overcome to some degree in the future, the important point in practice is to make historical work as exact as possible.

XVII

For the advancement of historical knowledge the exercise of the power to distinguish between questions which can and questions which cannot be answered by historical research is necessary to economy of effort and is an indispensable adjunct to effective and valid work. But there should be no institutional attempt to delimit the exercise of this power.

XVIII

Many large questions of public interest cannot be answered conclusively out of historical knowledge, and historians true to the scientific spirit will avoid encouraging the pretensions that they can be so answered. In certain and limited cases, however, by the use of historical knowledge and analogies, the historian may, in respect of given situations, indicate various contingencies, one or more of which may be anticipated with a high degree of probability.

History and Related Disciplines

XIX

Since the writing of history involves acts of thinking, as well as the use of knowledge, training in thought about history is no less necessary to the advancement of historiography than training in related and auxiliary subjects and in various technical operations. This applies not only to historians but also to all who make historical investigations in any field.

XX

In view of recent specialization in historical work and the parallel rise of the social sciences, significant advances in making the most comprehensive historical generalizations will require the close and constant co-operation of specialists in historical work with specialists in the social sciences and humanities. To some extent, coordination of the work of historians with that done in the physical and biological sciences is also indicated.[4]

XXI

Inasmuch as the utmost precision in the use of terms is necessary to the advancement of any science, in all efforts to advance historiography a careful consideration of the meaning of the terms employed is of the utmost importance to such operations. Where no precise definition is generally accepted, the shades of meaning attached to the term in various usages should be taken into account and the resulting passage phrased in such a way as to minimize ambiguity.

[4] By "generalization" above, is meant a statement of relationships—one not possessing the exactness of "laws" in the physical sciences but still having tentative validity and meaningfulness. One may, for example, generalize that the wasteful methods of early American farmers were due to a poor agricultural tradition rather than to their geographical or social environment. Such a generalization, if supported by the evidence, is helpful in interpreting the long-run history of American agriculture. In reaching it, however, historians should do what has often been neglected—i.e., consult the pertinent findings of geologists, botanists, and social scientists.

CHAPTER VI

SELECTIVE READING LIST
ON HISTORIOGRAPHY AND
PHILOSOPHY OF HISTORY

By RONALD THOMPSON

SELECTIVE READING LIST

I. THE PROFESSION OF HISTORIAN
1. HISTORICAL METHOD
2. HISTORY OF HISTORY
3. HISTORY AND THE SOCIAL SCIENCES

II. THE PHILOSOPHICAL APPROACH
4. EARLY SYNTHESES
5. PERSISTENT PROBLEMS
6. CURRENT TRENDS

III. CONTENDING SCHOOLS
7. THE ECONOMIC INTERPRETATION
8. THE SPIRITUAL INTERPRETATION

IV. NATIONAL DEVELOPMENTS
9. GERMANY
10. OTHER PARTS OF EUROPE
11. THE UNITED STATES

V. NEW INTERPRETATIONS
12. GENERAL
13. THE SOCIAL INTERPRETATION
14. THE CYCLICAL INTERPRETATION
15. HISTORICAL SOCIOLOGY

I. THE PROFESSION OF HISTORIAN

1. *Historical Method*

BERNHEIM, ERNST. *Lehrbuch der historischen Methode und der Geschichtsphilosophie.* Leipzig, 1903.

BERR, HENRI, and LUCIEN FEBVRE. "History," *Encyclopaedia of the Social Sciences,* 1932.

BRADLEY, F. H. "The Presuppositions of Critical History," *Collected Essays,* vol. 1. Oxford, 1935.

COCHRANE, C. N. *Thucydides and the Science of History.* London, 1929.

CRUMP, C. G. *History and Historical Research.* London, 1928.

DROYSEN, J. G. *Outline of the Principles of History.* Boston, 1893. Tr. from *Grundriss der Historik,* 1858.

FLING, F. M. *The Writing of History.* New Haven, 1920.

GEORGE, H. B. *Historical Evidence.* Oxford, 1909.

GOTTSCHALK, LOUIS. "The Evaluation of Historical Writings," L. R. Wilson, ed. *The Practice of Book Selection.* Chicago, 1940.

GREENLAW, E. A. *The Province of Literary History.* Baltimore, 1931.

HALDANE, R. B. *The Meaning of Truth in History* (Creighton lecture). London, 1914.

HARSIN, PAUL. *Comment on écrit l'histoire.* Paris, 1933. (English adaptation, *The Writing of History* by Louis O'Brien, Berkeley, 1935.)

HAYEK, F. A. VON. "Scientism and the Study of Society," *Economica,* IX (1942), 267-291; X (1943), 34-63; XI (1944), 27-39.

HOCKETT, H. C. *Introduction to Research in American History.* New York, 1931.

JOHNSON, ALLEN. *The Historian and Historical Evidence.* New York, 1926.

JUSSERAND, J. J., W. C. ABBOTT, C. W. COLBY, and J. S. BASSETT. *The Writing of History.* New York, 1926.

KENT, SHERMAN. *Writing History.* New York, 1941.

LAMBERT, SIR HENRY. *The Nature of History.* London, 1933.

LANGLOIS, C. V., and C. SEIGNOBOS. *Introduction to the Study of History.* New York, 1898. Tr. from *Introduction aux études historiques,* 1898.

LUCIAN. "The Way to Write History," and "The True History," H. W. and

SELECTIVE READING LIST 145

F. G. Fowler, eds. *The Works of Lucian*, vol. 2. Oxford, 1905. Tr. from the Greek, c. 165 A.D.
MEADOWS, PAUL. "The Scientific Use of Historical Data," *Philosophy of Science*, XI (1944), 53-58.
MEYER, EDUARD. *Zur Theorie und Methodik der Geschichte*. Halle, 1902.
NEVINS, ALLAN. *The Gateway to History*. Boston, 1938.
OMAN, SIR CHARLES. *On the Writing of History*. New York, 1939.
RANKE, LEOPOLD VON. *Zur Kritik neuerer Geschichtschreiber*. Leipzig, 1874. (*Sämmtliche Werke*, vol. 34.)
REIS, LINCOLN, and P. O. KRISTELLER. "Some Remarks on the Method of History," *Journal of Philosophy*, XL (1943), 225-245.
RHODES, JAMES F. "History," and "The Profession of Historian," *Historical Essays*. New York, 1909.
SALMON, LUCY M. *Historical Material*. New York, 1933.
———. *Why Is History Rewritten?* New York, 1929.
SCHLESINGER, A. M. "History," W. Gee, ed. *Research in the Social Sciences*. New York, 1929.
SELLAR, W. C., and R. J. YEATMAN. *1066 and All That*. London, 1930.
SHOTWELL, JAMES T. "History," *Encyclopaedia Britannica*, 1941.
TAYLOR, A. M. "The Historical Novel as a Source in History," *Sewanee Review*, XLVI (1938), 459-479.
TAYLOR, HUGH. *History as a Science*. London, 1933.
TREVELYAN, G. M. "History and Literature," *Yale Review*, XIV (1924), 109-125.
TURBERVILLE, A. S. "History Objective and Subjective," *History*, XVII (1933), 289-302.
VINCENT, JOHN M. *Aids to Historical Research*. New York, 1934.
WILLIAMS, CHARLES H. *The Modern Historian*. London, 1938.
YOUNG, LOUISE M. *Thomas Carlyle and the Art of History*. Philadelphia, 1939.

2. *History of History*

BARNES, HARRY E. *A History of Historical Writing*. Norman, Oklahoma, 1937.
BARNES, HARRY E., and HOWARD BECKER. *Social Thought from Lore to Science*, 2 vol. Boston, 1938.
BASSETT, J. S. *The Middle Group of American Historians*. New York, 1917.
BLACK, J. B. *The Art of History: A Study of Four Great Historians of the Eighteenth Century*. London, 1926.
BREYSIG, KURT. *Die Meister der entwickelnden Geschichtsforschung*. Breslau, 1936.
BURY, JOHN B. *The Ancient Greek Historians*. New York, 1909.
BUTTERFIELD, HERBERT. *The Englishman and His History*. Cambridge, England, 1944.
———. *The Whig Interpretation of History*. London, 1931.
DAVIES, W. W. *How to Read History*. New York, 1924.
DAWSON, CHRISTOPHER. "Edward Gibbon," *British Academy Proceedings*, XX (1934), 159-180.
DUTCHER, G. M., et al. eds. *A Guide to Historical Literature*. New York, 1931.
FARMER, PAUL. *France Reviews Its Revolutionary Origins*. New York, 1944.

FUETER, EDUARD. *Histoire de l'historiographie moderne.* Paris, 1914. Tr. from *Geschichte der neueren Historiographie,* 1911.
GARDNER, CHARLES S. *Chinese Traditional Historiography.* Cambridge, Massachusetts, 1938.
GOOCH, G. P. *History and Historians in the Nineteenth Century.* London, 1913.
——, "Some Conceptions of History," *Sociological Review,* XXXI (1939), 233-247.
GUILLAND, ANTOINE. *Modern Germany and Her Historians.* London, 1915. *Histoire et historiens depuis cinquante ans,* 2 vol. Paris 1927-28.
HOLT, W. STULL, ed. *Historical Scholarship in the United States, 1876-1901.* Baltimore, 1938.
HUTCHINSON, W. T., ed. *The Marcus W. Jernegan Essays in American Historiography.* Chicago, 1937.
KRAUS, MICHAEL. *A History of American History.* New York, 1937.
MAZOUR, A. G. *An Outline of Modern Russian Historiography.* Berkeley, 1939.
PEARDON, T. P. *The Transition in English Historical Writing, 1760-1830.* New York, 1933.
RITTER, MORIZ. *Die Entwicklung der Geschichtswissenschaft.* Munich, 1919.
SCHMITT, B. E., ed. *Some Historians of Modern Europe.* Chicago, 1942.
SHOTWELL, JAMES T. *The History of History,* vol. 1. New York, 1939.
THOMPSON, J. W. *A History of Historical Writing,* 2 vol. New York, 1942.
VOLGIN, V. P., E. V. TARLE and A. M. PANKRATOVA, eds. *Dvadtsat' pyat' let istoricheskoï nauki v SSSR* (Twenty-five Years of Historical Studies in the USSR). Moscow, 1942.
WANG YU-CHUAN. "The Development of Modern Social Science in China," *Pacific Affairs,* XI (1938), 345-362.

3. History and the Social Sciences

AUBREY, E. E. "Social Psychology as Liaison between History and Sociology," *American Historical Review,* XXXIII (1928), 257-277.
BARNES, HARRY E. *The New History and the Social Studies.* New York, 1925.
BEARD, CHARLES A. *A Charter for the Social Sciences in the Schools.* New York, 1932.
———. *The Nature of the Social Sciences.* New York, 1934.
BOAS, FRANZ. *Anthropology and Modern Life.* New York, 1932.
BRISTOL, L. M. *Social Adaptation.* Cambridge, Massachusetts, 1915.
BURGESS, E. W. *The Function of Socialization in Social Evolution.* Chicago, 1916.
DAVIS, M. M. *Psychological Interpretations of Society.* New York, 1909.
ELIOT, T. D. "The Use of History for Research in Theoretical Sociology," *American Journal of Sociology,* XXVII (1922), 628-636.
FEBVRE, LUCIEN, and LIONEL BATAILLON. *A Geographical Introduction to History.* London, 1925. Tr. from *La terre et l'évolution humaine,* 1922.
FORDE, C. D. "Human Geography, History and Sociology," *Scottish Geographical Magazine,* LV (1939), 217-235.
GOLDENWEISER, ALEXANDER. *History, Psychology, and Culture.* New York, 1933.

———."A New Approach to History," *American Anthropologist*, XXII (1920), 26-47.
GOTTSCHALK, LOUIS, CLYDE KLUCKHOHN, and ROBERT ANGELL, *The Use of Personal Documents in History, Anthropology, and Sociology.* New York, 1945.
HANKINS, F. H. *The Racial Basis of Civilization.* New York, 1931.
HULME, E. M. *History and Its Neighbors.* New York, 1942.
HUNTINGTON, ELLSWORTH. *Civilization and Climate.* New Haven, 1933.
KROEBER, A. L. "History and Science in Anthropology," *American Anthropologist*, XXXVII (1935), 539-569.
MCLAUGHLIN, I. C. "History and Sociology: A Comparison of Their Methods," *American Journal of Sociology*, XXXII (1926), 379-395.
MILLER, HERBERT A. *Races, Nations and Classes.* Philadelphia, 1924.
NASMYTH, GEORGE. *Social Progress and the Darwinian Theory.* New York, 1916.
OGBURN, W. F. "The Historical Method in the Analysis of Social Phenomena," *American Sociological Society Publications*, XVI (1921), 70-83.
OGBURN, W. F., and A. GOLDENWEISER, eds. *The Social Sciences and Their Interrelations.* Boston, 1927.
POSTAN, M. M. *The Historical Method in Social Science: An Inaugural Lecture.* Cambridge, England, 1939.
RATNER, S. "The Historian's Approach to Psychology," *Journal of the History of Ideas*, II (1941), 95-109.
RICE, STUART A., ed. *Methods in Social Science.* Chicago, 1931.
RIVERS, W. H. R. "History and Ethnology," *History*, V (1920), 65-80.
SALVEMINI, GAETANO. *Historian and Scientist.* Cambridge, Massachusetts, 1939.
SEIGNOBOS, CHARLES. *La méthode historique appliquée aux sciences sociales.* Paris, 1901.
SEMPLE, ELLEN C. *Influences of Geographic Environment on the Basis of Ratzel's System of Anthropogeography.* New York, 1911.
SUMNER, W. G. *Folkways.* Boston, 1906.
SWAIN, J. W. "History and the Science of Society," D. S. Muzzey, *et al. Essays in Intellectual History, Dedicated to James Harvey Robinson.* New York, 1929.
TEGGART, F. J. "Anthropology and History," *Journal of Philosophy*, XVI (1919), 691-696.
THOMAS, FRANKLIN. *The Environmental Basis of Society.* New York, 1925.
TODD, ARTHUR J. *Theories of Social Progress.* New York, 1934.
VAYSON DE PRADENNE, A. *Prehistory.* London, 1940. Tr. from *La préhistoire*, 1938.

II. THE PHILOSOPHICAL APPROACH

4. *Early Syntheses*

ADAMS, HENRY P. *The Life and Writings of Giambattista Vico.* London, 1935.
BAGEHOT, WALTER. *Physics and Politics.* New York, 1873.
BECKER, CARL L. *The Heavenly City of the Eighteenth Century Philosophers.* New Haven, 1932.
BODIN, JEAN. *Method for the Easy Comprehension of History.* New York,

1945. Tr. from *Methodus ad facilem historiarum cognitionem*. 1566.
BOSSENBROOK, W. J. "Justus Möser's Approach to History," J. L. Cate and E. N. Anderson, eds. *Medieval and Historiographical Essays in Honor of James Westfall Thompson*. Chicago, 1938.
BUCKLE, HENRY T. *History of Civilization in England*, 2 vol. London, 1857-61.
CARLYLE, THOMAS. *On Heroes, Hero-Worship, and the Heroic in History*. London, 1840.
COMTE, AUGUSTE. *The Positive Philosophy*, 2 vol. New York, 1853. Tr. from *Cours de philosophie positive*, 1830-42.
CONDORCET, M. JEAN, MARQUIS DE. *Outlines of an Historical View of the Progress of the Human Mind*. London, 1795. Tr. from *Esquisse d'un tableau historique des progrès de l'esprit humain*, 1795.
ELLWOOD, C. A. *The Story of Social Philosophy*. New York, 1938.
FERGUSON, ADAM. *An Essay on the History of Civil Society*. London, 1768.
FISKE, JOHN. *Outlines of Cosmic Philosophy*, 2 vol. Boston, 1874.
FLINT, ROBERT. *Historical Philosophy in France and French Belgium and Switzerland*. New York, 1894.
―――. *The Philosophy of History in France and Germany*. Edinburgh, 1874.
HEGEL, GEORG W. F. *The Philosophy of History*. London, 1902. Tr. from *Vorlesungen über die Philosophie der Geschichte*, 1837.
HERDER, JOHANN G. VON. *Outlines of a Philosophy of the History of Man*. London, 1800. Tr. from *Ideen zur Philosophie der Geschichte der Menschheit*, 1784-91.
IBN KHALDŪN. *A Selection from the Prolegomena of Ibn Khaldūn*. Leiden, 1905. Tr. from *Kitab al-Ibar*, c. 1380.
LIN MOU-SHENG. *Men and Ideas: An Informal History of Chinese Political Thought*. New York, 1942.
LOVEJOY, ARTHUR O. *The Great Chain of Being*. Cambridge, Massachusetts, 1936.
LUCRETIUS. *Of the Nature of Things*. London, 1921. Tr. from *De rerum natura*, c. 60 B.C.
MARCUSE, HERBERT. *Reason and Revolution: Hegel and the Rise of Social Theory*. London, 1941.
MARVIN, F. S. *Comte: The Founder of Sociology*. London, 1936.
MORRIS, G. S. *Hegel's Philosophy of the State and of History*. Chicago, 1892.
NIETZSCHE, FRIEDRICH. "The Use and Abuse of History," *Thoughts Out of Season*, vol. 2. New York, 1924. Tr. from *Vom Nutzen und Nachtheil der Historie*, 1874.
NORBORG, C. SVERRE. *From Plato to Hitler: Interpretations of History*. Minneapolis, 1940.
ROBERTSON, JOHN M. *Buckle and His Critics*. London, 1895.
SCHELLING, FRIEDRICH VON. *The Ages of the World*. New York, 1942. Tr. from *Die Weltalter*, 1854.
SHINE, HILL. *Carlyle and the Saint-Simonians*. Baltimore, 1941.
SPENCER, HERBERT. *The Study of Sociology*. New York, 1877.
TOLSTOY, LEO. "Second Epilogue," *War and Peace*. New York, 1942. Tr. from *Voina i mir*, 1865-69.

Vico, Giovanni B. *Principes de la philosophie de l'histoire.* Paris, 1827. Tr. from *Principi di una scienza nuova,* 1725.
Voltaire, François de. *Essay on Universal History,* 4 vol. Dublin, 1759. Tr. from *Essai sur l'histoire générale et sur les moeurs,* 1756.

5. Persistent Problems

Benjamin, A. C. "The Scientific Status of Value Judgments," *Ethics,* LIII (1943), 212-218.
Buchan, John. *The Causal and the Casual in History* (Rede lecture). Cambridge, England, 1929.
Burke, Kenneth. *Permanence and Change.* New York, 1935.
Carr, H. W. "'Time' and 'History' in Contemporary Philosophy," *British Academy Proceedings,* VIII (1917-18), 331-349.
Cleugh, Mary F. *Time and Its Importance in Modern Thought.* London, 1937.
Cohen, M. R. "Causation and Its Application to History," *Journal of the History of Ideas,* III (1942), 12-29.
Cohen, M. R., and Ernest Nagel. *An Introduction to Logic and Scientific Method.* New York, 1934.
Creegan, R. F. "The Actual Occasion and Actual History," *Journal of Philosophy,* XXXIX (1942), 268-273.
Dewey, John. *Logic: The Theory of Inquiry.* New York, 1938.
Eck, Samuel. "Geschichtsphilosophie," *Die Religion in Geschichte und Gegenwart,* 2 vols. Tübingen, 1908-10.
Field, G. C. "Some Problems of the Philosophy of History," *British Academy Proceedings,* XXIV (1938), 55-83.
Goldenweiser, Alexander. "The Concept of Causality in the Physical and Social Sciences," *American Sociological Review,* III (1938), 624-636.
Hempel, C. G. "The Function of General Laws in History," *Journal of Philosophy,* XXXIX (1942), 35-48.
Hocking, W. E. "On the Law of History," *University of California Publications in Philosophy,* II (1909), 45-65.
Hook, Sidney. "Determinism" and "Materialism," *Encyclopaedia of the Social Sciences,* 1932.
———. "A Pragmatic Critique of the Historico-Genetic Method," *Essays in Honor of John Dewey.* New York, 1929.
Klibansky, Raymond, and H. J. Paton, eds. *Philosophy and History.* Oxford, 1936.
Lamprecht, S. P. "Causality," *Essays in Honor of John Dewey.* New York, 1929.
Lewis, Wyndham. *Time and Western Man.* New York, 1928.
Mandelbaum, Maurice. "Can There Be a Philosophy of History?" *American Scholar,* IX (1939-40), 74-84.
———. "Causal Analysis in History," *Journal of the History of Ideas,* III (1942), 30-50.
———. *The Problem of Historical Knowledge.* New York, 1938.
McKeon, Richard. "Plato and Aristotle as Historians: A Study of Method in the History of Ideas," *Ethics,* LI (1940), 66-101.

MEAD, GEORGE H. *The Philosophy of the Present.* Chicago, 1932.
MILLER, HUGH. *History and Science.* Berkeley, 1939.
OAKELEY, HILDA D. "How Is History Possible?" *Aristotelian Society Proceedings,* XLI (1940), i-xviii.
OAKELEY, H. D., K. CORNFORTH, and M. GINSBERG. "Symposium: Explanation in History," *Aristotelian Society Proceedings,* sup. vol. XIV (1935), 113-153.
OGDEN, C. K., and I. A. RICHARDS. *The Meaning of Meaning.* New York, 1936.
PARKER, D. H. "The Metaphysics of Historical Knowledge," *University of California Publications in Philosophy,* II (1913), 103-186.
PIERCE, DONALD J. *An Introduction to the Logic of the Philosophy of History.* Toronto, 1939.
SOROKIN, P. A., and R. K. MERTON. "Social Time: A Methodological and Functional Analysis," *American Journal of Sociology,* XLII (1937), 615-629.
TAYLOR, A. M. "A Vitalistic Philosophy of History," *Journal of Social Philosophy,* VI (1941), 137-150.
TEGGART, F. J. "Causation in Historical Events," *Journal of the History of Ideas,* III (1942), 3-11.
VAIHINGER, H. *The Philosophy of 'As if.'* New York, 1924. Tr. from *Die Philosophie des Als Ob,* 1911.
WIDGERY, A. G. "Philosophy of History and the Particularity of Values," *Philosophical Review,* XLIV (1935), 567-576.
WIENER, P. P. "On Methodology in the Philosophy of History," *Journal of Philosophy,* XXXVIII (1941), 309-324.
ZILSEL, EDGAR. "Physics and the Problem of Historico-sociological Laws," *Philosophy of Science,* VIII (1941), 567-579.

6. Current Trends

ACTON, H. B. "The Philosophy of History," *Aristotelian Society Proceedings,* XL (1940), 75-88.
ADAMS, JAMES L. "The Changing Reputation of Human Nature," *Journal of Liberal Religion,* IV (1942-43), 59-79; 137-160.
BOAS, GEORGE. "Prophecy and History," *American Scholar,* V (1936), 431-440.
BOODIN, J. E. "Philosophy of History," D. D. Runes, ed. *Twentieth Century Philosophy.* New York, 1943.
COLE, C. W. "The Relativity of History," *Political Science Quarterly,* XLVIII (1933), 161-171.
COLLINGWOOD, R. G. "Human Nature and Human History," *British Academy Proceedings,* XXII (1936), 97-127.
———. *The Philosophy of History* (Historical Association Leaflet No. 79). London, 1930.
COULBORN, RUSHTON. "Historian's Consolation in Philosophy," *Southern Review,* VII (1941), 40-51.
DE BURGH, W. G. "Philosophy and History," *Hibbert Journal,* XXXV (1936), 40-52.
DURANT, WILL. "Philosophy of History," *The Mansions of Philosophy* (Part VI). Garden City, New York, 1929.

FLECHTHEIM, O. K. "History and Theodicy," *Phylon*, II (1941), 238-249; III (1942), 46-65.
FRIESS, H. L. "On the History of the Philosophy of History in Western Culture," *Journal of Philosophy*, XXXIV (1937), 5-18.
HAUSHEER, H. "Plato's Conception of the Future as Opposed to Spengler's," *Monist*, XXXIX (1929), 204-224.
JORDAN, H. P. "Some Philosophical Implications of Max Weber's Methodology," *International Journal of Ethics*, XLVIII (1938), 221-231.
LAMPRECHT, S. P. "Historiography of Philosophy," *Journal of Philosophy*, XXXVI (1939), 449-460.
———. "Philosophy of History," *Journal of Philosophy*, XXXIII (1936), 197-204.
LEIGHTON, J. A. "History as the Struggle for Social Values," *Philosophical Review*, XLVIII (1939), 118-154.
LOVEJOY, ARTHUR O. "The Historiography of Ideas," *American Philosophical Society Proceedings*, LXXVIII (1938), 529-543.
———. "Present Standpoints and Past History," *Journal of Philosophy*, XXXVI (1939), 477-489.
———. "Reflections on the History of Ideas," *Journal of the History of Ideas*, I (1940), 3-23.
MANASSE, E. M. "Moral Principles and Alternatives in Max Weber and John Dewey," *Journal of Philosophy*, XLI (1944), 29-48; 57-68.
NICHOLS, ROY F. "The Dynamic Interpretation of History," *New England Quarterly*, VIII (1935), 163-178.
ROSENSTOCK-HÜSSY, E. "The Predicament of History," *Journal of Philosophy*, XXXII (1935), 93-100.
SETH PRINGLE-PATTISON, A. "The Philosophy of History," *British Academy Proceedings*, X (1921-23), 513-529.
SWAIN, J. W. "What Is History?" *Journal of Philosophy*, XX (1923), 281-289; 312-327; 337-349.
URBAN, W. M. "Progress or Regress: The Philosophy of History," *Rice Institute Pamphlet*, XXX (1943), 115-138.
WILTSE, C. M. "History as Social Philosophy," *International Journal of Ethics*, XLVI (1935), 49-63.

III. CONTENDING SCHOOLS

7. *The Economic Interpretation*

ADLER, MAX. *Lehrbuch der materialistischen Geschichtsauffassung*, 2 vol. Berlin, 1930-32.
BOBER, M. M. *Karl Marx's Interpretation of History*. Cambridge, Massachusetts, 1927.
BUKHARIN, N. *Historical Materialism: A System of Sociology*. New York, 1925. Tr. from *Teoriya istoricheskogo materialisma*, 1922.
CROCE, BENEDETTO. *Historical Materialism and the Economics of Karl Marx*. New York, 1914. Tr. from *Materialismo storico ed economia marxistica*, 1907.
CUNOW, HEINRICH. *Die Marxsche Geschichts-, Gesellschafts- und Staatstheorie*, 2 vol. Berlin, 1920-21.

ENGELS, FRIEDRICH. *Herr Eugen Dühring's Revolution in Science*. New York, 1935. Tr. from *Herrn Eugen Dühring's Umwälzung der Wissenschaft*, 1886.
———. *The Origin of the Family, Private Property and the State*. New York, 1942. Tr. from *Der Ursprung der Familie*, 1884.
FEDERN, KARL. *The Materialist Conception of History*. London, 1939.
HARPER, SAMUEL N. "A Communist View of Historical Studies," *Journal of Modern History*, I (1929), 77-84.
HECKER, J. F. *Russian Sociology*. London, 1934.
HOOK, SIDNEY. *From Hegel to Marx*. New York, 1936.
———. *Towards the Understanding of Karl Marx*. New York, 1933.
HYNDMAN, H. M. *The Evolution of Revolution*. New York, 1921.
KAUTSKY, KARL. *Ethics and the Materialist Conception of History*. Chicago, 1907. Tr. from *Ethik und materialistische Geschichtsauffassung*, 1906.
———. *Die materialistische Geschichtsauffassung*, 2 vol. Berlin, 1927.
KNIGHT, FRANK H. "Ethics and the Economic Interpretation," *Quarterly Journal of Economics*, XXXVI (1922), 454-481.
KORSCH, KARL. *Karl Marx*. London, 1938.
LABRIOLA, ANTONIO. *Essays on the Materialistic Conception of History*. Chicago, 1904. Tr. from *La concezione materialistica della storia*, 1896.
MARX, KARL. *A Contribution to the Critique of Political Economy*. Chicago, 1904. Tr. from *Zur Kritik der politischen Oekonomie*, 1859.
———. *Selected Works* (V. Adoratsky, ed.) 2 vol. London, 1942-43.
MARX, KARL, and FRIEDRICH ENGELS. *The German Ideology*. New York, 1939. Tr. from *Die Deutsche Ideologie*, 1845-46.
———. "Ideology in General," *Labour Monthly*, XV (1933), 182-188.
———. *Über historischen Materialismus: ein Quellenbuch* (H. Duncker, ed.). Berlin, 1930-31.
MIRSKY, D. S. "Bourgeois History and Historical Materialism," *Labour Monthly*, XIII (1931), 453-459.
NEARING, SCOTT, ed. *The Law of Social Revolution*. New York, 1926.
PLEKHANOV, G. V. *Art and Society*. New York, 1937. Tr. from the Russian.
———. *Essays in Historical Materialism*. New York, 1940. Tr. from the Russian, 1897-98.
———. *Fundamental Problems of Marxism*. London, 1929. Tr. from *Osnovnyye voprosy marksizma*, 1928.
POKROVSKI, M. N. *Istoricheskaya nauka i borba klassov* (Historical Science and the Class Struggle), 2 vol. Moscow, 1933.
———. *Pages d'histoire: la méthode du matérialisme historique*. Paris, 1929.
ROGERS, J. E. THOROLD. *The Economic Interpretation of History*. New York, 1888.
SÉE, HENRI. *The Economic Interpretation of History*. New York, 1929. Tr. from *Matérialisme historique et interprétation économique de l'histoire*, 1927.
SELIGMAN, E. R. A. *The Economic Interpretation of History*. New York, 1917.
SOMERVILLE, JOHN M. *Methodology in Social Science: A Critique of Marx and Engels*. New York, 1938.
TIUMENIEV, A. I. "Marxism and Bourgeois Historical Science," N. Bukharin

et al. Marxism and Modern Thought. New York, 1935. Tr. from the Russian.
TOMPKINS, S. R. "Trends in Communist Historical Thought," *Slavonic Review*, XIII (1935), 294-319.
WILSON, EDMUND. *To the Finland Station: A Study in the Writing and Acting of History.* New York, 1940.

8. The Spiritual Interpretation

ALBRIGHT, W. F. *From the Stone Age to Christianity: Monotheism and the Historical Process.* Baltimore, 1940.
AUGUSTINE, SAINT AURELIUS. *The City of God.* London, 1931. Tr. from *De Civitate Dei*, c. 413-426.
BERDYAEV, NICOLAS. *The End of Our Time.* London, 1933.
――――. *The Meaning of History.* London, 1936. Tr. from *Smyslistorii*, 1923.
BRABANT, F. H. *Time and Eternity in Christian Thought.* London, 1937.
CASE, S. J. *The Christian Philosophy of History.* Chicago, 1943.
COHEN, MORRIS R. "Philosophies of Jewish History," *Jewish Social Studies*, I (1939), 39-72.
DAWSON, CHRISTOPHER H. *Progress and Religion.* London, 1929.
DODD, C. H. "Hellenism and Christianity," *Independence, Convergence, and Borrowing. Harvard Tercentenary Publications*, 1937.
FULLERTON, KEMPER. "Calvinism and Capitalism," *Harvard Theological Review*, XXI (1928), 163-195.
GORDON WALKER, P. C. "Capitalism and the Reformation," *Economic History Review*, VIII (1937), 1-19.
GRAY, L. H., *et al.* "Ages of the World," *Encyclopaedia of Religion and Ethics*, 1922.
GUILDAY, PETER, ed. *The Catholic Philosophy of History.* New York, 1936.
HOFFMAN, ROSS J. S. "Catholicism and Historismus," *Catholic Historical Review*, XXIV (1939), 401-412.
MACMURRAY, JOHN. *The Clue to History.* New York, 1939.
MATHEWS, SHAILER. *The Spiritual Interpretation of History.* Cambridge, Massachusetts, 1916.
MCLAUGHLIN, R. W. *The Spiritual Element in History.* New York, 1926.
MILLAR, M.F.X. *Unpopular Essays in the Philosophy of History.* New York, 1928.
NIEBUHR, REINHOLD. *Reflections on the End of an Era.* New York, 1934.
PHYTHIAN-ADAMS, W. J. "The Thought and Significance of N. Berdyaev," *Church Quarterly Review*, CXXVI (1938), 245-268.
POWICKE, F. M. *History, Freedom and Religion.* London, 1938.
SCHLATTER, R. B. "The Problem of Historical Causation in Some Recent Studies of the English Revolution," *Journal of the History of Ideas*, IV (1943), 349-367.
SHANLEY, A. J. *Catholicism and the Writing of History.* Washington, 1941.
TAWNEY, R. H. *Religion and the Rise of Capitalism.* New York, 1926.
TILLICH, PAUL. "History as the Problem of Our Period," *Review of Religion*, III (1939), 255-264.
――――. *The Interpretation of History.* New York, 1936.

———. "Kairos," *Tat*, XIV (1922), 330-350.
———. "The Meaning of Our Present Historical Existence," *Hazen Conference on Student Guidance*, 1938.
TOYNBEE, ARNOLD J. *Christianity and Civilization* (Burge memorial lecture). London, 1940.
TROELTSCH, ERNST. *Protestantism and Progress*. London, 1912. Tr. from *Die Bedeutung des Protestantismus*, 1911.
WEBER, MAX. *The Protestant Ethic and the Spirit of Capitalism*. London, 1930. Tr. from *Die protestantische Ethik und der Geist des Kapitalismus*, 1920.
WOOD, HERBERT G. *Christianity and the Nature of History*. Cambridge, England, 1934.
WOOD, HERBERT G., et al. *The Kingdom of God and History*. London, 1938.

IV. NATIONAL DEVELOPMENTS

9. Germany

ANDERSON, E. N. "Meinecke's *Ideengeschichte* and the Crisis in Historical Thinking," J. L. Cate and E. N. Anderson, eds. *Medieval and Historiographical Essays in Honor of James Westfall Thompson*. Chicago, 1938.
ARON, RAYMOND. *Essai sur la théorie de l'histoire dans l'Allemagne contemporaine*. Paris, 1938.
BARTH, PAUL. *Die Philosophie der Geschichte als Soziologie*. Leipzig, 1915.
BELOW, GEORG VON. *Die deutsche Geschichtschreibung*. Munich, 1924.
BREYSIG, KURT. *Vom geschichtlichen Werden*, 3 vol. Stuttgart, 1925-28.
BROCK, WERNER. *An Introduction to Contemporary German Philosophy*. Cambridge, England, 1935.
BURCKHARDT, JACOB. *Force and Freedom: Reflection on History* (J. H. Nichols, ed.). New York, 1943. Tr. from *Weltgeschichtliche Betrachtungen*, 1905.
CHAMBERLAIN, H. S. *The Foundations of the Nineteenth Century*, 2 vol. London, 1911. Tr. from *Die Grundlagen des neuzehnten Jahrhunderts*, 1899.
DEWEY, JOHN. "The Germanic Philosophy of History," *German Philosophy and Politics*. New York, 1942.
DILTHEY, WILHELM. *Einleitung in die Geisteswissenschaften. Gesammelte Schriften*, bd. 1. Leipzig, 1922.
DODD, WILLIAM E. "Karl Lamprecht and Kulturgeschichte," *Popular Science Monthly*, LXIII (1903), 418-424.
GOBINEAU, J. A., COMTE DE. *The Inequality of Human Races*. New York, 1915. Tr. from *Essai sur l'inégalité des races humaines*, 1853-55.
GURVITCH, G. "La théorie des valeurs de Heinrich Rickert," *Revue philosophique*, CXXIV (1937), 80-88.
HAERING, T. L. *Hauptprobleme der Geschichtsphilosophie*. Karlsruhe, 1925.
HENDERSON, K. T. "Ethics and the Control of History: A Study of Troeltsch," *Church Quarterly Review*, XCIX (1924), 116-144.
HEUSSI, KARL. *Die Krisis des Historismus*. Tübingen, 1932.
KAUFMANN, FRITZ. *Geschichtsphilosophie der Gegenwart*. Berlin, 1931.
LAMPRECHT, KARL. *What Is History?* New York. 1905. Tr. from *Moderne Geschichtswissenschaft*, 1904.
LESSING, THEODOR. *Geschichte als Sinngebung des Sinnlosen*. Munich, 1921.

LYMAN, E. W. "Ernst Troeltsch's Philosophy of History," *Philosophical Review*, XLI (1932), 443-465.
MAIER, HEINRICH. *Das geschichtliche Erkennen*. Göttingen, 1914.
MANNHEIM, KARL. "German Sociology (1918-1933)," *Politica*, I (1934), 12-33.
MEHLIS, GEORG. *Lehrbuch der Geschichtsphilosophie*. Berlin, 1915.
MEINECKE, FRIEDRICH. *Die Entstehung des Historismus*, 2 vol. Munich, 1936.
———. "Klassizismus, Romantizismus und historisches Denken im 18. Jahrhundert," *Authority and the Individual*. Harvard Tercentenary Publications, 1937.
PARSONS, TALCOTT. "'Capitalism' in Recent German Literature: Sombart and Weber," *Journal of Political Economy*, XXXVI (1928), 641-661; XXXVII (1929), 31-51.
RICKERT, HEINRICH. *Die Grenzen der naturwissenschaftliche Begriffsbildung*. Tübingen, 1929.
———. *Die Probleme der Geschichtsphilosophie*. Heidelberg, 1924.
RIESS, LUDWIG. *Historik: Ein Organon geschichtlichen Denkens und Forschens*, bd. 1. Berlin, 1912.
RIEZLER, KURT. "Idee und Interesse in der politischen Geschichte," *Dioskuren*, III (1924), 1-13.
SCHAUMKELL, ERNST. *Geschichte der deutschen Kulturgeschichtschreibung*. Leipzig, 1905.
SCHNEIDER, HERMANN. *Philosophie der Geschichte*, 2 vol. Breslau, 1923.
SELL, F. C. "Intellectual Liberalism in Germany about 1900," *Journal of Modern History*, XV (1943), 227-236.
SIMMEL, GEORG. *Die Probleme der Geschichtsphilosophie*. Leipzig, 1907.
SMALL, ALBION W. *Origins of Sociology*. Chicago, 1924.
THYSSEN, JOHANNES. *Die Einmaligkeit der Geschichte*. Bonn, 1924.
TROELTSCH, E. "Contingency," and "Historiography," *Encyclopaedia of Religion and Ethics*, 1922.
———. *Der Historismus und seine Probleme*. Tübingen, 1922.
WACH, JOACHIM. *Das Verstehen*, bd. 3. *Das Verstehen in der Historik*. Tübingen, 1933.
WIRTH, OTTO. *William Scherer, Josef Nadler, and Wilhelm Dilthey as Literary Historians*. Chicago, 1937.

10. *Other Parts of Europe*

ACTON, J. D. A., 1st baron. *Historical Essays and Studies*. London, 1926.
———. *A Lecture on the Study of History*. London, 1911.
ARON, RAYMOND. *Introduction à la philosophie de l'histoire*. Paris, 1938.
BECKER, CARL. "Mr. Wells and the New History," *American Historical Review*, XXVI (1921), 641-656.
BERR, HENRI. *L'histoire traditionnelle et la synthèse historique*. Paris, 1935.
———. *La synthèse en histoire*. Paris, 1911.
BRYCE, JAMES. "World History," *British Academy Proceedings*, IX (1919-20), 187-211.
BURY, JOHN B. "The Science of History" and "Darwinism and History," *Selected Essays*. Cambridge, England, 1930.

BUTTERFIELD, HERBERT. *The Study of Modern History: An Inaugural Lecture.* London, 1944.
CARR, H. W. *The Philosophy of Benedetto Croce.* London, 1917.
COLLINGWOOD, R. G. "Croce's Philosophy of History," *Hibbert Journal*, XIX (1921), 263-278.
———. *The Historical Imagination: An Inaugural Lecture.* Oxford, 1935.
COURNOT, A. A. *Traité de l'enchaînement des idées fondamentales dans les sciences et dans l'histoire*, 2 vol. Paris, 1861.
CROCE, BENEDETTO. *History: Its Theory and Practice.* New York, 1921. Tr. from *Teoria e storia della storiografia*, 1919.
GINSBERG, M. "The Sociology of Pareto," *Sociological Review*, XXVIII (1936), 221-245.
HARRISON, FREDERIC. *The Meaning of History and Other Historical Pieces.* New York, 1908.
KELLETT, E. E. *Aspects of History.* London, 1938.
LACOMBE, PAUL. *De l'histoire considérée comme science*, 2 vol. Paris, 1894-98.
LALLY, F. E. *As Lord Acton Says.* Newport, Rhode Island, 1942.
LE BON, GUSTAVE. *Bases scientifiques d'une philosophie de l'histoire.* Paris, 1931.
LECKY, WILLIAM E. H. *The Political Value of History.* London, 1892.
MCDOUGALL, W., C. MURCHISON, J. H. TUFTS, and F. N. HOUSE. "A Symposium on Pareto's Significance for Social Theory," *Journal of Social Philosophy*, I (1935), 36-89.
PIRENNE, HENRI. "De la méthode comparative en histoire," *Compte rendu du Ve. congrès international des sciences historiques. Brussels, 1923*, pp. 19-32.
———. "What Are Historians Trying to Do?" S. A. Rice, ed. *Methods in Social Science.* Chicago, 1931.
RENARD, GEORGES. *La méthode scientifique de l'histoire littéraire.* Paris, 1900.
ROWSE, A. L. *Science and History.* New York, 1928.
SCOTT, ERNEST. *History and Historical Problems.* London, 1925.
SÉE, HENRI. *Science et philosophie de l'histoire.* Paris, 1928.
TARN, W. W. "Alexander the Great and the Unity of Mankind," *British Academy Proceedings*, XIX (1933), 123-166.
TEGGART, F. J. Review of *History: Its Theory and Practice*, by B. Croce, *American Historical Review*, XXVIII (1923), 288-290.
TREVELYAN, G. M. *Clio, a Muse and Other Essays.* London, 1913.
———. *The Present Position of History: An Inaugural Lecture.* London, 1927.
WELLS, H. G. "The Poison Called History," *Nineteenth Century*, CXXIII (1938), 521-534.
XENOPOL, A. D. *Les principes fondamentaux de l'histoire.* Paris, 1899.

11. The United States

ADAMS, GEORGE B. "History and the Philosophy of History," *American Historical Review*, XIV (1909), 221-236.
BARNES, HARRY E. *History and Social Intelligence.* New York, 1926.
———. "James Harvey Robinson," H. W. Odum, ed. *American Masters of Social Science.* New York, 1927.

SELECTIVE READING LIST

BARNES, H. E., H. and F. B. BECKER, eds. *Contemporary Social Theory.* New York, 1940.
BEAN, W. E. "Revolt Among Historians," *Sewanee Review,* XLVII (1939), 330-341.
BEARD, CHARLES A. *The Discussion of Human Affairs.* New York, 1936.
———. "That Noble Dream," *American Historical Review,* XLI (1935), 74-87.
———. "Written History as an Act of Faith," *American Historical Review,* XXXIX (1934), 219-229.
BEARD, C. A., and A. VAGTS. "Currents of Thought in Historiography," *American Historical Review,* XLII (1937), 460-483.
BECKER, CARL. *Everyman His Own Historian.* New York, 1935.
———. "Some Aspects of the Influence of Social Problems and Ideas upon the Study and Writing of History," *American Sociological Society Publications,* VII (1912), 73-107.
———. "What Is Historiography," *American Historical Review,* XLIV (1938), 20-28.
BLINKOFF, MAURICE. *The Influence of Charles A. Beard upon American History.* Buffalo, 1936.
BRINTON, CRANE. "The 'New History' and 'Past Everything'," *American Scholar,* VIII (1939), 144-157.
———. "The New History: Twenty-five Years After," *Journal of Social Philosophy,* I (1936), 134-147.
CATE, J. L., and E. N. ANDERSON, eds. *Medieval and Historiographical Essays in Honor of James Westfall Thompson.* Chicago, 1938.
CHEYNEY, EDWARD P. *Law in History, and Other Essays.* New York, 1927.
CURTI, MERLE. *The Growth of American Thought.* New York, 1943.
DUNNING, W. A. *Truth in History and Other Essays.* New York, 1937.
GIDDINGS, FRANKLIN H. "A Theory of Social Causation," and Discussion, *American Economic Association Publications,* 3rd series, V-2 (1904), 139-199.
GOLDMAN, ERIC F., ed. *Historiography and Urbanization.* Baltimore, 1941.
GOTTSCHALK, LOUIS. "The Scope and Subject Matter of History," *University* [of Kansas City] *Review,* VIII (1941), 75-83.
HOLCOMBE, A. N. "The Political Interpretation of History," *American Political Science Review,* XXXI (1937), 1-11.
HOLT, W. STULL. "The Idea of Scientific History in America," *Journal of the History of Ideas,* I (1940), 352-362.
HUIZINGA, J. "History Changing Form," *Journal of the History of Ideas,* IV (1943), 217-223.
MUZZEY, D. S., *et al. Essays in Intellectual History, Dedicated to James Harvey Robinson.* New York, 1929.
NICHOLS, ROY F. "Confusions in Historical Thinking," *Journal of Social Philosophy,* VII (1942), 334-343.
ROBINSON, JAMES H. *The Human Comedy.* New York. 1937.
———. *The New History.* New York, 1912.
———. "The Newer Ways of Historians," *American Historical Review,* XXXV (1930), 245-255.
SCHLESINGER, A. M. *New Viewpoints in American History.* New York, 1928.
SCHLESINGER, A. M., *et al. Historical Scholarship in America.* New York, 1932.

SCHUYLER, R. L. "The Usefulness of Useless History," *Political Science Quarterly*, LVI (1941), 23-37.
SHOTWELL, JAMES T. "The Interpretation of History," *American Historical Review*, XVIII (1913), 692-709.
SHRYOCK, R. H. "American Historiography: A Critical Analysis and a Program," *American Philosophical Society Proceedings*, LXXXVII (1943), 35-46.
TAYLOR, HENRY O. "Continuities in History," *American Historical Review*, XLIV (1938), 1-19.
———. *A Historian's Creed*. Cambridge, Massachusetts, 1939.
TEGGART, F. J. *The Processes of History*. New Haven, 1918.
———. *Prolegomena to History*. Berkeley, 1916.
———. "World History," *Scientia*, LXIX (1941), 30-35.
WARE, CAROLINE, ed. *The Cultural Approach to History*. New York, 1940.
WOODBRIDGE, F. J. E. *The Purpose of History*. New York, 1916.
WRIGHT, ESMOND. "History: the 'New' and the Newer," *Sewanee Review*, XLIX (1941), 479-491.
ZUCKER, MORRIS. *The Philosophy of American History*, 2 vol. New York, 1945.

V. NEW INTERPRETATIONS
12. *General*

ADAMS, HENRY. *The Degradation of the Democratic Dogma*. New York, 1919.
BEARD, CHARLES A., ed. *Toward Civilization*. New York, 1930.
———. *Whither Mankind*. New York, 1934.
BELL, CLIVE. *Civilization: An Essay*. New York, 1928.
BURKE, KENNETH. *Attitudes toward History*. 2 vol. New York, 1937.
BURY, JOHN B. *The Idea of Progress*. London, 1920.
CHASE, STUART. *The Economy of Abundance*. New York, 1934.
COULBORN, RUSHTON. "The Individual and the Growth of Civilizations," *Phylon*, I (1940), 69-89; 136-148; 243-264.
COWAN, A. R. *Master-Clues in World-History*. London, 1914.
CROCE, BENEDETTO. *History as the Story of Liberty*. London, 1941. Tr. from *La storia come pensiero e come azione*, 1938.
DRUCKER, PETER F. *The End of Economic Man*. New York, 1939.
FAŸ, BERNARD. *L'homme, mésure de l'histoire*. Paris, 1939.
FLEWELLING, R. T. *The Survival of Western Culture*. New York, 1943.
GIDDINGS, F. H. *Studies in the Theory of Human Society*. New York, 1922.
———. "A Theory of History," *Political Science Quarterly*, XXXV (1920), 493-521.
HEARD, GERALD. *The Source of Civilization*. London, 1935.
HOOK, SIDNEY. *The Hero in History: A Study in Limitation and Possibility*. New York, 1943.
———. *Reason, Social Myths and Democracy*. New York, 1940.
KAHLER, ERICH. *Man the Measure: A New Approach to History*. New York, 1943.
KIDD, BENJAMIN. *Social Evolution*. New York, 1898.
LASKI, HAROLD J. *Faith, Reason and Civilisation: An Essay in Historical Analysis*. London, 1944.

SELECTIVE READING LIST

MACKINDER, H. J. *Democratic Ideals and Reality.* London, 1919.
———. "The Geographical Pivot of History," *Geographical Journal,* XXIII (1904), 421-437.
MARVIN, F. S., ed. *Progress and History.* London, 1916.
MÜLLER-LYER, FRANZ. *The History of Social Development.* London, 1920. Tr. from *Die Entwicklungsstufen der Menschheit,* bd. 2. *Phasen der Kultur,* 1908.
MUMFORD, LEWIS. *The Condition of Man.* New York, 1944.
———. *The Culture of Cities.* New York, 1938.
———. *Technics and Civilization.* New York, 1934.
NEF, JOHN U. *The United States and Civilization.* Chicago, 1942.
NORDAU, MAX. *The Interpretation of History.* London, 1910. Tr. from *Der Sinn der Geschichte,* 1909.
OAKELEY, HILDA D. *History and the Self.* London, 1934.
ORTEGA Y GASSET, JOSÉ. *The Revolt of the Masses.* New York, 1932. Tr. from *La rebelión de las masas,* 1929.
———. *Toward a Philosophy of History.* New York, 1941.
PARETO, VILFREDO. *The Mind and Society,* 4 vol. New York, 1935. Tr. from *Trattato di sociologia generale,* 1923.
POLANYI, KARL. *The Great Transformation.* New York, 1944.
RANDALL, JOHN H., JR. *Our Changing Civilization.* New York, 1929.
ROBINSON, JAMES H. *The Mind in the Making.* New York, 1921.
ROSENSTOCK-HUESSY, E. *Out of Revolution: Autobiography of Western Man.* New York, 1938.
RUSSELL, BERTRAND. *Freedom versus Organization, 1814-1914.* New York, 1934.
SARKAR, BENOY. *The Futurism of Young Asia.* Berlin, 1922.
———. *The Sociology of Races, Cultures and Human Progress.* Calcutta, 1939.
SCHWARTZ, EMIL. *A Philosophy of History.* Boston, 1940.
SIMKHOVITCH, V. G. "Approaches to History," *Political Science Quarterly,* XLIV (1929), 481-497; XLV (1930), 481-526; XLVII (1932), 410-439; XLVIII (1933), 23-61; XLIX (1934), 44-83; LI (1936), 117-151.
SPENGLER, OSWALD. *Man and Technics.* New York, 1932. Tr. from *Der Mensch und die Technik,* 1931.
STACE, W. T. *The Destiny of Western Man.* New York, 1942.
STRAYER, J. R., ed. *The Interpretation of History.* Princeton, 1943.
TAYLOR, HENRY O. *Freedom of the Mind in History.* London, 1923.
WALLAS, GRAHAM. *The Great Society.* New York, 1914.
WALLIS, W. D. *Culture and Progress.* New York, 1930.
WELLS, H. G. *The Fate of Man.* New York, 1939.
WHITEHEAD, ALFRED N. *Adventures of Ideas.* New York, 1933.
WISSLER, CLARK. *Man and Culture.* New York, 1923.

13. The Social Interpretation

AKADEMIYA NAUK, INSTITUT ISTORII (Academy of Sciences, Institute of History). *Protiv istoricheskoi kontseptsii M. N. Pokrovskogo* (Against the Historical Conceptions of M. N. Pokrovski), 2 vol. Leningrad, 1939-40.
BEARD, CHARLES A. *An Economic Interpretation of the Constitution of the United States.* New York, 1913; with a new introduction, 1935.

CAUDWELL, CHRISTOPHER [pseud.]. *Illusion and Reality*. London, 1937.
CLARK, G. N. "Social and Economic Aspects of Science," *Science and Social Welfare in the Age of Newton*. Oxford, 1937.
CHOUKAS, M. "The Concept of Cultural Lag Re-examined," *American Sociological Review*, I (1936), 752-760.
FEUER, L. S. "The Economic Factor in History," *Science and Society*, IV-2 (1940), 168-192.
———. "Ethical Theories and Historical Materialism," *Science and Society*, VI (1942), 242-272.
FLORES, ANGEL, ed. *Literature and Marxism: A Controversy by Soviet Critics*. New York, 1938. Tr. from the Russian.
GITTLER, J. B. "Possibilities of a Sociology of Science," *Social Forces*, XVIII (1940), 350-359.
GUTHRIE, E. F. "Historical Materialism and Its Sociological Critics," *Social Forces*, XX (1941), 172-184.
HESSEN, B. "The Social and Economic Roots of Newton's *Principia*," N. Bukharin, *et al. Science at the Crossroads*. London, 1932.
HINSHAW, V. G., JR. "The Epistemological Relevance of Mannheim's Sociology of Knowledge," *Journal of Philosophy*, XL (1943), 57-72.
JACKSON, THOMAS A. *Dialectics: The Logic of Marxism*. London, 1936.
KAZAKÉVICH, V. D. "Social Sciences in the Soviet Union," *American Sociological Review*, IX (1944), 312-318.
KNIGHT, FRANK H. "Some Notes on the Economic Interpretation of History," American Council of Learned Societies Conference of Secretaries, *Studies in the History of Culture*. Menasha, Wisconsin, 1942.
LALO, CHARLES. *L'art et la vie sociale*. Paris, 1921.
LUKÁCS, GEORG. *Geschichte und Klassenbewusstsein*. Berlin, 1923.
MANNHEIM, KARL. "The Crisis of Culture in the Era of Mass-Democracies and Autarchies," *Sociological Review*, XXVI (1934), 105-129.
———. *Diagnosis of Our Time*. London, 1943.
———. *Ideology and Utopia*. New York, 1936. Parts II-IV tr. from *Ideologie und Utopie*, 1929.
———. *Man and Society in an Age of Reconstruction*. London, 1940. Based on *Mensch und Gesellschaft im Zeitalter des Umbaus*, 1935.
MERTON, R. K. "Karl Mannheim and the Sociology of Knowledge," *Journal of Liberal Religion*, II (1941), 125-147.
———. "The Sociology of Knowledge," *Isis*, XXVII (1937), 493-503.
MILLS, C. WRIGHT. "Language, Logic, and Culture," *American Sociological Review*, IV (1939), 670-680.
OGBURN, WILLIAM F. *Social Change*. New York, 1928.
PANNEKOEK, A. "Society and Mind in Marxian Philosophy," *Science and Society*, I (1937), 445-453.
RANDALL, JOHN H., JR. Review of *Man and Society in an Age of Reconstruction* by Karl Mannheim, *Journal of the History of Ideas*. II (1941), 372-381.
ROSENTHAL, MARK, *et al*. "Relative vs. Absolute Criteria in Art," *Dialectics*, VIII, 15-24; IX, 24-32.
SCHELTING, A. VON. Review of *Ideologie und Utopie* by Karl Mannheim, *American Sociological Review*, I (1936), 664-674.

SPEIER, HANS. Review of *Ideology and Utopia* by Karl Mannheim, *American Journal of Sociology*, XLIII (1937), 155-166.
———. "The Social Determination of Ideas," *Social Research*, V (1938), 182-205.
SUMNER, B. H. "Soviet History," *Slavonic Review*, XVI (1938), 601-615; XVII (1938), 151-161.
VEBLEN, THORSTEIN. *The Theory of the Leisure Class: An Economic Study of Institutions.* New York, 1918.
WHITE, H. B. "Materialists and the Sociology of American Literature," *Social Research*, VII (1940), 184-200.
WILLIAM, MAURICE. *The Social Interpretation of History: A Refutation of the Marxian Economic Interpretation of History.* Long Island City, 1921.
WIRTH, LOUIS. "Ideological Aspects of Social Disorganization," *American Sociological Review*, V (1940), 472-482.
WOODARD, JAMES W. "Critical Notes on the Culture Lag Concept," *Social Forces*, XII (1934), 388-398.

14. *The Cyclical Interpretation*

ADAMS, BROOKS. *The Law of Civilization and Decay.* New York, 1895; with an introduction by C. A. Beard, 1943.
BRINTON, CRANE. "Socio-astrology" [a review of *Social and Cultural Dynamics* by P. A. Sorokin], *Southern Review*, III (1937), 243-266.
CHAMBERS, F. P. *Cycles of Taste.* Cambridge, Massachusetts, 1928.
COLLINGWOOD, R. G. "Oswald Spengler and the Theory of Historical Cycles," "The Theory of Historical Cycles II: Cycles and Progress," *Antiquity*, I (1927), 311-325; 435-446.
COULBORN, RUSHTON. "Cyclic Revolution," *Southwest Review*, XXVII (1941), 97-112.
COULBORN, RUSHTON, and W. E. B. DU BOIS. "Mr. Sorokin's Systems," *Journal of Modern History*, XIV (1942), 500-521.
CRAWFORD, O. G. S. "Historical Cycles," *Smithsonian Institution Annual Report, 1932*, 445-459.
FEBVRE, LUCIEN. "De Spengler à Toynbee: Quelques philosophies opportunistes de l'histoire," *Revue de métaphysique et de morale*, XLIII (1936), 573-602.
GAY, E. F. "The Rhythm of History," *Harvard Graduates' Magazine*, XXXII (1923), 1-16.
GODDARD, E. H., and P. A. GIBBONS. *Civilisation or Civilisations: An Essay in the Spenglerian Philosophy of History.* London, 1926.
GOUGH, A. B. "An Alleged Periodic Factor in History," *Sociological Review*, XXVIII (1936), 361-388.
HAMMOND, J. L. "The Fate of Western Civilization" [a review of *A Study of History* by Arnold J. Toynbee], *Political Quarterly*, X (1939), 545-561.
HOYLAND, JOHN S. *History as Direction.* London, 1930.
JERROLD, DOUGLAS. "Oswald Spengler and the Meaning of History," *English Review*, XLVIII (1929), 394-407.
LEE, J. S. "The Periodic Recurrence of Internecine Wars in China," *China Journal*, XIV (1931), 111-115; 159-163.

OAKELEY, HILDA D. "Philosophic History and Prophecy: Professor Arnold Toynbee's Outlook," *Philosophy*, XI (1936), 186-194.
PETRIE, W. M. F. *The Revolutions of Civilisation*. London, 1911.
SHOTWELL, JAMES T. "Spengler," *Essays in Intellectual History, Dedicated to James Harvey Robinson*. New York, 1929.
SOROKIN, P. A. "Arnold J. Toynbee's Philosophy of History," *Journal of Modern History*, XII (1940), 374-387.
———. *Social and Cultural Dynamics*, 4 vol. New York, 1937-41.
———. "A Survey of the Cyclical Conceptions of Social and Historical Process," *Social Forces*, VI (1927), 28-40.
SPENGLER, OSWALD. *The Decline of the West*, 2 vol. New York, 1926-28. Tr. from *Der Untergang des Abendlandes*, 1921-22.
———. "The Downfall of Western Civilization," *Dial*, LXXVII (1924), 361-378; 482-504; LXXVIII (1925), 9-26.
TAWNEY, R. H. "Dr. Toynbee's Study of History," *International Affairs*, XVIII (1939), 798-806.
TIBBS, A. E. "Book Reviews of 'Social and Cultural Dynamics': A Study in Wissenssoziologie," *Social Forces*, XXI (1943), 473-480.
TOYNBEE, ARNOLD J. "Historical Parallels to Current International Problems," *International Affairs*, X (1931), 477-488.
———. *A Study of History*, 6 vol. London, 1934-39.
WEIGERT, H. W. "Oswald Spengler, Twenty-five Years After," *Foreign Affairs*, XXI (1942), 120-131.

15. Historical Sociology

BECKER, HOWARD. "Culture Case Study and Ideal-Typical Method," *Social Forces*, XII (1934), 399-405.
———. "Historical Sociology," H. E. Barnes, H. and F. B. Becker, eds. *Contemporary Social Theory*. New York, 1940.
BROWN, J. F. "Towards a Theory of Social Dynamics," *Journal of Social Psychology*, VI (1935), 182-213.
CASE, C. M. "Method in the Social Sciences," *Journal of Applied Sociology*, XI (1927), 255-265.
CHENG CHE-YU. *Oriental and Occidental Cultures Contrasted: An Introduction to "Culturology."* Berkeley, 1943.
EDWARDS, LYFORD P. *The Natural History of Revolution*. Chicago, 1927.
FALK, W. "Democracy and Capitalism in Max Weber's Sociology," *Sociological Review*, XXVII (1935), 373-393.
FREYER, HANS. *Soziologie als Wirklichkeitswissenschaft*. Leipzig, 1930.
GINSBERG, M. "The Conception of Stages in Social Evolution," *Man*, XXXII (1932), 87-91.
GOTTSCHALK, LOUIS. "Causes of Revolution," *American Journal of Sociology*, L (1944), 1-8.
HERTZLER, J. O. "The Sociological Uses of History," *American Journal of Sociology*, XXXI (1925), 173-198.
———. "Sources and Methods of Historical Sociology," L. L. Bernard, ed. *The Fields and Methods of Sociology*. New York, 1934.

SELECTIVE READING LIST

LÖWITH KARL. "Max Weber und Karl Marx," *Archiv für Sozialwissenschaft und Sozialpolitik*, LXVII (1932), 53-99; 175-214.
MACIVER, R. M. "Civilization versus Culture," *University of Toronto Quarterly*, I (1932), 316-332.
——. "The Historical Pattern of Social Change," *Authority and the Individual*. Harvard Tercentenary Publications, 1937.
——. "History and Social Causation," *Journal of Economic History Supplement* (1943), 135-145.
——. *Social Causation*. Boston, 1942.
MAYER, J. P. "Sociology of Politics: An Interpretation of Max Weber's Political Philosophy," *Dublin Review*, CCVII (1940), 188-196.
MERTON, R. K. "Civilization and Culture," *Sociology and Social Research*, XXI (1936), 103-113.
PARSONS, TALCOTT. "H. M. Robertson on Max Weber and His School," *Journal of Political Economy*, XLIII (1935), 688-696.
——. *The Structure of Social Action*. New York, 1937.
RATNER, SIDNEY. "Patterns of Culture in History," *Philosophy of Science*, VI (1939), 88-97.
ROBERTSON, H. M. *Aspects of the Rise of Economic Individualism: A Criticism of Max Weber and His School*. Cambridge, England, 1933.
ROSE, H. J. *Concerning Parallels* (Frazer lecture). Oxford, 1934.
SALOMON, ALBERT. "Max Weber's Methodology," "Max Weber's Sociology," "Max Weber's Political Ideas," *Social Research*, I (1934), 147-168; II (1935), 60-73; 368-384.
——. "The Place of Alfred Weber's *Kultursoziologie* in Social Thought," *Social Research*, III (1936), 494-500.
SCHELTING, A. VON. *Max Webers Wissenschaftslehre*. Tübingen, 1934.
SIMS, NEWELL L. *The Problem of Social Change*. New York, 1939.
STERN, B. J. "Concerning the Distinction between the Social and the Cultural," *Social Forces*, VIII (1929), 264-271.
TEGGART, F. J. "Notes on 'Timeless' Sociology," *Social Forces*, VII (1929), 362-365.
——. *Rome and China: A Study of Correlations in Historical Events*. Berkeley, 1939.
——. *Theory of History*. New Haven, 1925.
TÖNNIES, FERDINAND. *Fortschritt und soziale Entwicklung*. Karlsruhe, 1926.
WEBER, ALFRED. *Fundamentals of Culture-Sociology*. New York, 1939. Tr. from "Prinzipielles zur Kultursoziologie," *Archiv für Sozialwissenschaft und Sozialpolitik*, XLVII (1920-21), 1-49.
——. *Kulturgeschichte als Kultursoziologie*. Leiden, 1935.
WEBER, MAX. *General Economic History*. New York, 1927. Tr. from *Wirtschaftsgeschichte*, 1924.
——. *Gesammelte Aufsätze zur Wissenschaftslehre*. Tübingen, 1922.
WEINREICH, MARCEL. *Max Weber, l'homme et le savant*. Paris, 1938.
WOODARD, JAMES W. *Intellectual Realism and Culture Change*. Hanover, New Hampshire, 1935.
——. "A New Classification of Culture and a Restatement of the Culture Lag Theory," *American Sociological Review*, I (1936), 89-102.

INDEX OF NAMES

Abbott, W. C., 144
Acton, H. B., 150
Acton, J. D. A., 155
Adams, B., 13, 30, 161
Adams, C. F., 109
Adams, G. B., 32-35, 124, 156
Adams, Henry, 13, 28, 30, 37n, 89, 93, 125, 158
Adams, Henry P., 147
Adams, Herbert B., 19, 23-24, 32, 34, 36-38, 40-41, 44, 108
Adams, J., 79
Adams, J. L., 150
Adams, J. Q., 58-59, 74
Adams, J. T., 79, 93
Adler, M., 151
Adoratsky, V., 152
Albright, W. F., 153
Allen, J. S., 72-73, 93
Allen, W. F., 37, 45
Anderson, E. N., 148, 154, 157
Anderson, R., 82
Andrews, C. M., 37-39, 41-43, 51, 117
Angell, R., 147
Aptheker, H., 66, 72, 93
Arnett, A. M., 66, 93, 98
Arnold, B., 60
Arnold, T., 37
Aron, R., 137n, 154-155
Atchison, D. R., 59
Aubrey, E. E., 146
Auchampaugh, P. G., 76, 93
Augustine, St., 153

Bacon, F., 19, 31
Bagehot, W., 147
Bagley, W. C., 94, 99
Ballagh, J. C., 98
Bancroft, G., 19, 23-24, 29
Baringer, W. E., 76, 93
Barnes, G. H., 63-64, 88, 93-95
Barnes, H. E., 19, 145-146, 156-157, 162
Barth, P., 154

Barzun, J., 22
Bassett, J. S., 144-145
Bataillon, L., 146
Beale, H K., viii
Bean, W. E., 157
Beard, C. A., vii-ix, 13n, 26-27, 36, 43-44, 47-48, 50-51, 55, 63, 68-72, 85, 87, 89, 94, 99, 119, 137n, 146, 157-159, 161
Beard, M. R., 63, 68-71, 87, 94
Becker, C., 26-27, 30n, 36, 47, 50-51, 147, 155, 157
Becker F. B., 157, 162
Becker, H., 145, 157, 162
Bell, C., 158
Below, G. von, 154
Benjamin, A. C., 149
Bentley, A. F., 123
Berdyaev, N., 153
Bernard, L. L., 162-163
Bernheim, E., 144
Berr, H., 144, 155
Black, J. B., 145
Blaine, J. G., 60, 63, 71, 89, 94
Blinkoff, M., 157
Bluntschli, J. K., 35, 41
Boas, F., 146
Boas, G., 150
Bober, M. M., 151
Bodin, J., 147-148
Boodin, J. E., 150
Bossenbrook, W. J., 148
Brabant, F. H., 153
Bradley, F. H., 144
Breysig, K., 145, 154
Brinkman, C., 119
Brinton, C., vii, 157, 161
Bristol, L. M., 146
Brock, W., 154
Brooks, P. S., 59, 75
Brown, G. W., 74, 94
Brown, J., 58, 83
Brown, J. F., 162
Browning, O. H., 82, 94

165

Bryant, W. C., 80, 94, 96
Bryce, J., 155
Buchan, J., 149
Buchanan, J., 59-60, 64, 67, 75-76, 81
Buck, P. H., 117
Buckle, H. T. 30, 46, 148
Buford, J. 59
Bukharin, N., 151-152, 160
Burckhardt, J., 154
Burgess, E. W., 146
Burgess, J. W., 23-24, 28, 32, 34-37, 39, 41, 44, 62, 68, 76, 83, 86, 94
Burke, K., 149, 158
Burr, G. L., 50
Bury, J. B., 145, 155, 158
Butterfield, H., 145, 156

Caesar, Julius, 11, 124-125, 129-130
Calhoun, J. C., 59, 64-65, 68-69, 74
Calvin, J., 119
Carlyle, T., 148
Carman, H. J., 66, 71, 94
Carpenter, J. T., 66, 94
Carr, H. W., 149, 156
Case, C. M., 162
Case, S. J., 153
Cate, J. L., 148, 154, 157
Caudwell, C., 160
Chamberlain, H. S., 154
Chambers, F. P., 161
Chandler, Z., 75
Channing, E., 66, 71, 76, 81-83, 89-90, 94
Chase, S., 158
Chase, S. P., 58, 64, 75
Cheng Che-yu, 162
Cheyney, E. P., 116, 157
Choukas, M., 160
Churchill, W., 20
Clark, G. N., 160
Cleugh, M. F., 149
Cochran, T. C., ix, 65, 94
Cochrane, C. N., 144
Cohen, M. R., 149, 153
Colby, C. W., 144
Cole, A. C., 57, 71, 79, 94
Cole, C. W., 150
Collingwood, R. G., 150, 156, 161

Columbus, C., 113
Commager, H. S., 66, 73, 79, 94-95, 99
Comte, A., 30, 148
Condorcet, M. J., 148
Corey, L., 19
Cornforth, K., 150
Cotterill, R. S., 66-67, 71, 79, 95
Coulborn, R., 150, 158, 161
Coulter, E. M., 99
Cournot, A. A., 156
Cowan, A. R., 158
Craven, A. O., 63, 68, 71, 75-76, 81-85, 89-90, 95, 102
Crawford, O. G. S., 161
Crawford, S. W., 81, 95
Creegan, R. F., 149
Croce, B., 9, 151, 156, 158
Cromwell, O., 11
Crump, C. G., 144
Cunow, H., 151
Curtis, M., vii, 28n, 36, 46n 157
Curtis, E. N., 116
Curtis, G. T., 75-76, 95

Darwin, C., 46
Davies, W. W., 145
Davis, J., 59-62, 64-65, 68-69, 75, 95
Davis, M. M., 146
Dawson, C. H., 145, 153
De Burgh, W. G., 150
Dewey, J., 47, 149, 154
Dilthey, W., 154
Dodd, C. H., 153
Dodd, W. E., 68, 80, 83, 90, 95, 154
Douglas, S. A., 59, 64, 67, 75-77, 80
Douglass, F., 73, 95
Draper, J. W., 28, 30, 56, 63, 95
Droysen, J. G., 144
Drucker, P. F., 158
Du Bois, W. E. B., 72, 95, 161
Dubois-Reymond, E., 12
Dumond, D. L., 57, 63, 83, 88, 93-95
Dumouriez, C. F., 116
Duncker, H., 152
Dunning, W. A., 60, 157

INDEX OF NAMES

Durant, W., 150
Dutcher, G. M., 145

Eck, S., 149
Eckenrode, H. J., 78-80, 95
Edmonds, J. E., 69, 95, 102
Edwards, E. E., 101
Edwards, L. P., 162
Eichhorn, K. F., 38
Einstein, A., 115
Eliot, T. D., 146
Ellis, H., 9
Ellwood, C. A., 148
Elson, H. W., 63, 69, 95-96
Engels, F., 152
Enmale, R., 72-73
Erdmannsdoerffer, O. H., 37
Evans, C. A., 81, 96-97

Falk, W., 162
Farmer, P., 145
Farrand, M., 83, 96
Fay, S. B., 89
Faÿ, B., 158
Febvre, L., 144, 146, 161
Federn, K., 152
Ferguson, A., 148
Ferguson, Mrs. W. K., ix, 107
Feuer, L. S., 160
Field, G. C., 149
Fish, C. R., 81-82, 96
Fiske, J., 28-30, 34, 42-43, 76, 96, 98, 148
Fite, E. D., 69, 96
Fitzhugh, G., 66, 78, 96
Flechtheim, O. K., 151
Flewelling, R. T., 158
Fling, F. M., 144
Flint, R., 148
Flores, A., 160
Ford, G. S., 99
Forde, C. D., 146
Fowler, F. G. and H. W., 144-145
Fox, D. R., 27, 36n, 41n, 42n, 45n, 94, 96
Freeman, E. A., 35, 38
Freyer, H., 162
Friess, H. L., 151

Fueter, E., 146
Fullerton, K., 153
Fustel de Coulanges, N. D., 37, 39

Gabriel, R. H., 36
Galileo, 115
Gardner, C. S., 146
Garrison, W. L., 63
Gates, P. W., vii
Gay, E. F., 161
Gay, S. H., 80, 94, 96
Gayda, V., 61
Gee, W., 145
George, H. B., 144
Gibbons, P. A., 161
Giddings, F. H., 157-158
Giddings, J., 58, 63, 96
Gilman, D. C., 35
Ginsberg, M., 150, 156, 162
Gittler, J. B., 160
Gobineau, J. A., 154
Goddard, E. H., 161
Goebbels, P., 61
Goldenweiser, A., 118, 146-147, 149
Goldman, E. F., 157
Gooch, G. P., 89, 146
Gordon Walker, P. C., 153
Gottschalk, L., vii, ix, 144, 147, 157, 162
Gough, A. B., 161
Grant, U. S., 28
Gray, L. H., 153
Greeley, H., 60, 63, 96
Green, B. E., 73, 96
Green, J. R., 38
Greenlaw, E. A., 144
Greg, P., 81, 83, 88, 96-97
Grimm, J. L. K., 38
Guilday, P., 153
Guilland, A., 146
Gurvitch, G., 154
Guthrie, E. F., 160

Hacker, L. M., 36, 71-72, 87, 97
Haering, T. L., 154
Haines, G., IV, viii
Haldane, R. B., 144
Hall, G. S., 32n, 41n

Hamilton, A., 45
Hamilton, J. G. de R., 57, 97
Hammond, J. L., 161
Handlin, W. W., 79, 97
Hankins, F, H., 147
Harper, S. N., 152
Harrell, J. M., 69, 97
Harrison, F., 156
Harsin, P., 144
Hart, A. B., 40-41, 63, 97
Hausheer, H., 151
Hayek, F. A. von, 144
Heard, G., 158
Hecker, J. F., 152
Heeren, A. H. L., 24
Hegel, G. W. F., 29, 120-122, 148
Hegel, K., 20, 37
Helper, H. R., 58, 78, 97
Hempel, C. G., 149
Henderson, K. T., 154
Herder, J. G. von, 148
Hertzler, J. O., 162-163
Hessen, B., 160
Heussi, K., 154
Hicks, J. D., 71, 83, 97
Hildreth, R., 29
Hinshaw, V. G., Jr., 160
Hitler, A., 78
Hoar, E. R., 59
Hobson, E. W., 137n
Hockett, H. C., 144
Hocking, W. E., 129-130, 149
Hodder, F. H., 76, 97
Hoffman, R. J. S., 153
Hofstadter, R., 28n
Hohenzollerns, 31
Holcombe, A. N., 157
Holst, H. E. von, 62-63, 79, 88, 97
Holt, W. S., 24n, 146, 157
Hook, S., ix, 107-108, 136n, 149, 152, 158
Hoover, H., 22
Horton, R. G., 60-61, 79, 86, 97-98
House, F. N., 156
Howard, G. E., 40
Hoyland, J. S., 161
Huizinga, J., 157
Hulme, E. M., 147

Humboldt, W. von, 106
Huntington, E., 147
Hutchinson, W. T., 146
Hyndman, H. M., 152

Ibn Khaldūn, 148
Ingle, E., 79, 98

Jackson, A., 29
Jackson, T. A., 160
Jameson, J. F., 24
Jefferson, T., 29, 45
Jerrold, D., 161
Johnson, A., 95, 101, 144
Johnston, A., 63, 69, 98
Jordan, H. P., 151
Julian, G. W., 75
Jusserand, J. J., 144

Kahler, E., 158
Kammerer, O., 126
Kaufmann, F., 154
Kautsky, K., 152
Kazakévich, V. D., 160
Kellett, E. E., 156
Kemble, J. M., 38
Kendrick, B. B., 66, 72, 93, 98
Kent, S., 144
Kidd, B., 158
Kimmel, W. G., 94
King, H., 75-76, 98
Kingsley, C., 38
Klibansky, R., 149
Klingberg, F. W., 76, 98
Kluckhohn, C., 147
Knight, F. H., 152, 160
Knox, C. E., 73-74, 98
Korsch, K., 152
Kraus, M., 23n, 146
Kristeller, P. O., 145
Kroeber, A. L., 147
Krout, J. A., vii

Labriola, A., 152
Lacombe, P., 156
La Follette, R., 89
Lally, F. E., 156
Lalo, C., 160
Lambert, H., 144

INDEX OF NAMES

Lamprecht, K., 50, 154
Lamprecht, S. P., 149, 151
Langlois, C. V., 31-32, 144
Laski, H. J., 158
Latané, J. H., 69, 98
Lea, H. C., 28
Le Bon, G., 156
Lecky, W. E. H., 156
Lee, J. S., 161
Lee, R. E., 61
Leighton, J. A., 151
Lenin, N., 113-114
Lessing, T., 154
Lewis, W., 149
Lieber, F., 24
Lin Mousheng, 148
Lincoln, A., 57-58, 60-61, 64-65, 67-68, 74-77, 79-83, 87, 89, 123
Lloyd, A. Y., 57, 98
Lloyd George, D., 89
Löwith, K., 163
Logan, J. A., 60, 69, 98
Lovejoy, A. O., 148, 151
Lucian, 144-145
Lucretius, 148
Lukács, G., 160
Luther, M., 31
Lyman, E. W., 155

MacIver, R. M., 163
Mackinder, H. J., 159
Macmurray, J., 153
Madison, J., 69
Maier, H., 155
Maine, H. J. S., 35, 37-38, 41
Maitland, F. W., 35, 41
Malinowski, B., 118
Manasse, E. M., 151
Mandelbaum, M., 149
Mannheim, K., 155, 160-161
Marcuse, H., 148
Marvin, F. S., 148, 159
Marx, K., 19, 26-27, 30, 44, 49, 56, 69, 72-73, 88, 119, 121, 152
Masters, E. L., 81-82, 98.
Mather, C., 4, 28
Mather, I., 28
Mathews, S., 153

Maurer, G. L. Von, 37-38
Mayer, J. P., 163
Mazour, A. G., 146
McDougall, W., 156
McKee, S., Jr., 94
McKeon, R., 149
McLaughlin, A. C., 73, 98
McLaughlin, I. C., 147
McLaughlin, R. W., 153
McMaster, J. B., 31, 55, 60, 76, 96, 98
Mead, G. H., 50, 150
Meadows, P., 145
Mehlis, G., 155
Meinecke, F., 155
Merriam, G. S., 69, 98
Merton, R. K., 150, 160, 163
Meyer, E., 145
Mill, J. S., 19, 31, 34
Millar, M. F. X., 153
Miller, H., 150
Miller, H. A., 147
Miller, W., 94
Mills, C. W., 160
Milton, G. F., 76, 81-83, 98-99
Mirsky, D. S., 152
Montesquieu, Baron de, 38
Mood, F., 46n
Moore, J. B., 75-76, 99
Morgan, L. H., 118
Morison, S. E., 66, 73, 79, 94-95, 99
Morris, G. S., 148
Morse, J. T., Jr., 97-98, 100
Müller-Lyer, F., 159
Mumford, L., 159
Murchison, C., 156
Mussolini, B., 78
Muzzey, D. S., 147, 157
Myers, G., 19, 50

Nagel, E., 115, 149
Napoleon I, 7, 11
Nasmyth, G., 147
Nearing, S., 152
Nef, J. U., 159
Nettels, C., 43
Nevins, A., 94, 145
Newton, I., 115
Nichols, J. H., 154

Nichols, J. P., 99
Nichols, R. F., vii, 76, 94, 99, 151, 157
Niebuhr, R., 153
Nietzsche, F., 148
Norborg, C. S., 148
Nordau, M., 159

Oakeley, H. D., 150, 159, 162
O'Brien, L., 144
Odum, H. W., 156
Ogburn, W. F., 147, 160
Ogden, C. K., 150
Oman, C., 145
Ortega y Gasset, J., 159
Osgood, H. L., 36, 38, 41-43
Otto of Freising, 37
Owsley, F. L., 61, 63, 65, 99

Palfrey, J. G., 37
Palgrave, F., 38
Pankratova, A. M., 146
Pannekoek, A., 160
Pareto, V., 159
Parker, D. H., 150
Parrington, V. L., 26-27, 36
Parsons, T., 155, 163
Pasteur, L., 126
Paton, H. J., 149
Peardon, T. P., 146
Pease, T. C., 94
Peirce, C., 125
Perry, R. B., 36
Petrie, W. M. F., 162
Phillips, U. B., 66, 71, 79, 99
Phythian-Adams, W. J., 153
Pierce, D. J., 150
Pierson, G. W., 45n
Pirenne, H., 156
Plekhanov, G. V., 152
Pokrovski, M. N., 152, 159
Polanyi, K., 159
Pollard, E. A., 60, 66, 69, 79, 81, 89, 99-100
Postan, M. M., 147
Potter, D. M., 76, 82-83, 89, 100
Powicke, F. M., 153

Quételet, L. A. J., 30

Ramsdell, C. W., 63, 68, 82-3, 89-90, 100
Randall, J. G., 73, 76, 82-85, 87, 89-90, 94, 100
Randall, J. H., Jr., viii, 159-160
Ranke, L. von, 30-31, 33, 145
Ratner, S., 147, 163
Ratzel, F., 46
Reis, L., 145
Renard, G., 156
Rhett, R. B., 59
Rhodes, J. F., 60, 63, 74, 76, 100, 109, 145
Rice, S. A., 46n, 147, 156
Richards, I. A., 150
Rickert, H., 155
Riess, L., 155
Riezler, K. 155
Riley, F. L., 97, 99
Ritter, M., 146
Rivers, W. H. R., 147
Robertson, H. M., 163
Robertson, J. M., 148
Robespierre, M., 116
Robinson, J. H., 19, 26, 28, 50, 127, 157, 159
Rogers, J. E. T., 152
Roosevelt, F. D., 89
Roosevelt, T., 60, 89, 100
Rose, H. J., 163
Rosenstock-Hüssey, E., 151, 159
Rosenthal, M., 160
Rowse, A. L., 156
Royce, J., 46
Ruffin, E., 59
Runes, D. D., 150
Russel, R. R., 71, 83, 100
Russell, B., 159

Salmon, L. M., 145
Salomon, A., 163
Salvemini, G., 147
Santayana, G., 17
Sarkar, B., 159
Saveth, E. N., 38n
Savigny, F., 38, 127
Schaumkell, E., 155
Schelling, F. von, 148
Schelting, A. von, 160, 163

INDEX OF NAMES

Schlatter, R. B., 153
Schlesinger, A. M., vii, 27, 94, 96, 145, 157
Schmitt, B. E., 146
Schmoller, G., 42
Schneider, H., 155
Schneider, H. W., 28n
Schnittkind, H. T., 83, 100
Schouler, J., 60, 63, 81, 100
Schuyler, R. L., 158
Schwartz, E., 159
Scott, E., 156
Scrugham, M., 76, 81, 100
Sée, H., 152, 156
Seebohm, F., 39
Seignobos, C., 31-32, 144, 147
Seligman, E. R. A., 122, 152
Sell, F. C., 155
Sellar, W. C., 145
Semple, E. C., 77-78, 100, 147
Seth Pringle-Pattison, A., 151
Seward, W. H., 58, 64, 76, 82
Shanks, H. T., 66, 71, 100
Shanley, A. J., 153
Shine, H., 148
Shotwell, J. T., 145-146, 158, 162
Shryock, R. H., vii, 23n, 31n, 45n, 47n, 158
Shugg, R. W., 64, 68, 73, 100
Simkhovitch, V. G., 159
Simmel, G., 155
Simms, H. H., 73, 81-82, 88, 101
Simons, A. M., 19, 50, 69, 72, 101
Sims, N. L., 163
Sitterson, J. C., 71, 101
Small, A. W., 37n, 46, 155
Smith, A., 8-11
Snyder, A. E., 79, 101
Somerville, J. M., 152
Sorokin, P. A., 150, 161-162
Speier, H., 161
Spence, J., 69, 101
Spencer, H., 28, 30, 38, 46-47, 148
Spengler, O., 108, 119, 121, 159, 162
Stace W. T., 159
Stalin, J., 61, 114
Stephens, A. H., 61-62, 101
Stephenson, N. W., 66, 68, 73, 101

Stern, B. J., 163
Stevens, T., 75
Strayer, J. R., 159
Stubbs, W., 35, 38, 41
Sumner, B. H., 161
Sumner, C., 58-59, 64, 75, 84
Sumner, W. G., 115, 147
Swain, J. W., 147, 151

Taney, R. B., 64
Tarle, E. V., 146
Tarn, W. W., 156
Tawney, R. H., 153, 162
Taylor, A. M., 145, 150
Taylor, G. R., 97
Taylor, H., 145
Taylor, H. O., 158-159
Taylor, W., 77, 101
Teggart, F. J., 30, 129, 147, 150, 156, 158, 163
Thomas, F., 147
Thompson, J. W., 146
Thompson, R., ix
Thorndike, L., 26-27, 50
Thyssen, J., 155
Tibbs, A. E., 162
Tillich, P., 153-154
Tiumeniev, A. I., 152-153
Todd, A. J., 147
Tönnies, F., 163
Tolstoy, L., 148
Tompkins, S. R., 153
Torrey, H., 24
Toynbee, A. J., 154, 161-162
Trevelyan, G. M., 145, 156
Troeltsch, E., 154-155
Tufts, J. H., 156
Turberville, A. S., 145
Turner, F. J., 26, 37, 41, 43-50, 61, 65, 77-78, 101
Tyler, M. C., 36, 38
Tylor, E. B., 30, 38, 47, 118

Urban II, Pope, 115
Urban, W. M., 151

Vagts, A., 137n, 157
Vaihinger, H., 8n, 150

Van Deusen, J. G., 71, 101
Van Tyne, C. H., 98
Vannest, C. G., 93
Vayson de Pradenne, A., 147
Veblen, T., 161
Vico, G. B., 149
Vincent, J. M., 35n, 145
Vinogradoff, P., 39
Volgin, V. P., 146
Voltaire, F. de, 149

Wach, J., 155
Wade, B. F., 75
Wagner, A., 42
Walker, M. G., 94
Wallas, G., 159
Wallis, W. D., 159
Wang Yu-chuan, 146
Ware, C., 158
Webb, W. P., 65, 72, 101
Weber, A., 163
Weber, M., 154, 163
Webster, D., 65, 75
Weigert, H. W., 162
Weinreich, M., 163
Wells, H. G., 156, 159
Wesley, C., 72-74, 101
White, A. D., 24, 28
White, H. B., 161

White, L. A., 75, 102
Whitehead, A. N., 159
Widgery, A. G., 150
Wiener, P. P., 150
William, M., 161
Williams, C. H., 145
Williams, G. W., 73, 102
Wilson, E., 153
Wilson, H., 60, 63, 102
Wilson, L. R., 144
Wilson, W., 45, 48, 89
Wiltse, C. M., 151
Wirth, L., 161
Wirth, O., 155
Wish, H., 66, 78, 102
Wissler, C., 159
Wood, H. G., 154
Wood, W. B., 69, 95, 102
Woodard, J. W., 161, 163
Woodbridge, F. J. E., 158
Wright, E., 158

Xenopol, A. D., 156

Yancey, W. L., 59
Yeatman, R. J., 145
Young, L. M., 145

Zilsel, E., 150
Zucker, M., 158

INDEX OF SUBJECTS

Abolition, 58, 60-61, 63, 69-70, 73, 75, 78, 80, 84
Absolute principles, 136
Abstraction, 7-12, 84-85
Accident, definition of, 108, 115-116
Actuality, history as, 5-13, 18-20, 111, 122, 133, 136n
Aggression, 20, 79-80, 88, 90
Agrarianism, 44-45, 48, 69-70, 87-88
Agriculture, Southern, 71-72, 78
American Historical Association, 48, 50
Analogy, 10, 12, 35, 37-41, 91-92, 108-110, 113, 120-121, 125, 137, 139
Anthropology, 38-39, 46, 118
Anticipation, 40, 139
Apologia, 86
Appeal, to history, 3-5, 30-31, 139
Aristocracy, vs. democracy, 66, 68, 73, 87
Arrangement, see Organization
Association, 107, 109-110
Assumptions: about history, 6-9, 105, 111-112, 135; controlling, 17-52, 57, 84, 91, 137
Atlantic Monthly, 50
Attitude, 28, 30, 58, 61, 83, 87, 91, 135
Authenticity, 14, 127, 133

Behavior, human, 8-9, 19, 109, 117, 122, 125, 128-130
Bias, 25, 29-32, 42-43, 55, 60, 74, 80, 86-89, 91, 126, 134
Biological science, 38, 46, 91, 108-109, 128, 139-140
Blunders, human, 89-90
Business, 70-72, 89

California, 64
Capitalism, 44, 49, 70, 72-73
Causation, viii, 18-20, 23, 32, 38-39, 55-92, 110-115, 136-137
Cause, definition of, 110-115, 136-137
Census, see United States Census

Centralization, of government, 62
Chance, definition of, 115-116
Change, definition of, 116-117
Chronology, 32, 56, 85, 136
Civil liberties, 77
Civil War, in the United States, viii, 14, 35, 55-93, 113, 115, 123, 129
Civilization, see Culture
Class, social, 30, 42-44, 48, 66, 69-70, 72-73, 108
Clermont, Council of, 115
Collection, of data, 32-33, 56, 105, 124
Colonial history, 37, 41-44
Colorado, 68
Columbia University, 19, 23-24, 40
Common sense, 9, 105
Communication, 84
Comparison, see Analogy
Compromise of 1850, 64, 75
Congress, see United States Congress
Conspiracy, as cause of Civil War, 58-61, 65, 68, 73-74, 88
Constitution: English, 38; United States, 29-30, 40-41, 58-60, 62-63, 88
Constitutional history, 34-38, 40, 61-62
Constructs, 7-9, 14, 124, 127, 134
Context, importance of, 23, 110, 117-118, 125, 134
Contingency, definition of, 115-116
Control: group, 21-22; scientific, 91, 110, 112-113; see also Assumptions
Cornell University, 23
Credibility, 128-129, 138
Crisis, in Western world, 5-6
Criticism, historical, 27
Crusades, 115
Culture, 38-39, 44, 46, 50, 65, 75, 118-122, 128

Dakota, 68
Deduction, 109
Definitions, 5n, 107-130, 133-134
Democratic Party, 59-60, 67, 70-71
Depression, economic, 36, 49

173

Destiny, definition of, 119-120
Determinism, 116, 120; economic, 26, 88-89; geographical, 26, 47, 55-56, *see also* Sectionalism
Development, definition of, 116-117
Dialectic, definition of, 120-122
Dictatorship, 11
Dictionaries, 106
District of Columbia, 58
Documents, 5n, 10, 14, 30
Dred Scott Decision, 58-59, 64
Dualism, in history, 6

Economic, definition of, 122-123
Economic determinism, *see* Determinism, Interpretation
"Economic man," 8-9
Education, 80, 87-88
Emancipation, 66, 69
Emotion, 84-85, 88-89
Empathy, 128-130
Emphasis, 7-10, 17, 20, 22, 34, 36, 41-42, 49, 56, 59, 63, 65, 69, 87-90, 135
Environment, 41, 46-47, 86, 90, 121
Error, methodological, 136-138
Evidence, contemporaneity of, 130
Evolution, 28-30, 35, 38-41, 46-47, 117
Experiment, scientific, 91, 112-113, 138
Extrapolation, 130

Fact, definition of, 123-125
Fascism, 19, 78
Fate, definition of, 119-120
Federalist, 9, 11, 69
Fiction, *see* Constructs
Force, definition of, 125
Frame of reference, 14, 17, 27, 55, 125-127, 135
Free will, 90
Free-Soil Party, 58
Freeport Doctrine, 64
Frontier hypothesis, 26, 43-48, 65
Fugitive Slave Act, 58-59
Functional conception of history, 47-51

Generalization, 5, 30-31, 85, 109, 115, 122, 127-128, 130, 133-135, 137-140

Geographical determinism, *see* Determinism, Interpretation
German scholarship, 24, 28-31, 35-37
Goals: as factor in understanding, 22; of history, 121-122
Göttingen, University of, 24, 29
Graduate training, 23-24, 33
Guidance, from history, 3-4, 43, 92

Habit, 47, 59
Harvard University, 23-24, 28
Heidelberg, University of, 35, 37
Heredity, 47
Historicization, 4
Historiography, definition of, 134
Humanistic sciences, related to history, 7-13, 106, 134-135, 139-140
Humanitarianism, 79, 88
Hypothesis, role of, viii, 19, 25-26, 31-32, 35, 40, 44, 47, 50, 112-113, 124

Identity, 108
Ideology, 22, 36, 49, 78, 85
Illiteracy, 80
Illustration, from history, 5, 8-9
Imagination, 10, 14, 128, 130, 138
Immigration, 79
Indian, American, 116
Induction, 31-32, 34, 47
Industrialism, Northern, 70, 78
Industrialization, 48-49, 70, 78
Inference, 14, 114, 130, 134
Influence: of history, 4; on history, 17-52, 85-87, 135
Insight, 18, 89, 128-129
Institutional history, 34-41, 45
Institutionalization, of history, 25-27, 45
Intellectual history, 21, 36
Interest, of historians, 17, 26-28, 33, 37
Interpretation, of history, viii, 6, 10, 23, 30-33, 44-52, 55-57, 63-64, 79, 85, 87-89, 92, 128, 135, 138; economic, 26, 34, 36, 41-44, 47-50, 63-64, 69-73, 75, 78, 83, 88-89; geographical, 26, 34, 46, 77-79; nationalistic, 29-31; political, *see*

# INDEX OF SUBJECTS

Political history; psychological, 73, 83-84, 89-90; sociological, 34; spiritual, 8, 19, 29-30, 77
Intuition, 121, 128-129

Johns Hopkins University, 19, 23, 35, 40, 45, 78
Judgment, of history, 10-11

Kansas, 58-59, 64, 67-68
Kansas-Nebraska Act, 59, 64, 76, 83

Labor, 48, 64, 72-73
Laissez faire, 21
Land policy, 70
Language, 106-107, 138
Law: governmental, 8n, 36, 42-43, 47; "of history," 28, 30, 32-34; natural, 30-31; scientific, see Generalization
Leadership, 42, 68, 74, 82, 89-90
League of Nations, 19
Lecompton Constitution, 58-59
Liberator, 58
Literature, historical, 133-134
Local history, 23, 46
Logic, 10, 31, 39, 108, 119-120, 122, 128
Louisiana, 64, 68, 73, 79

Maladjustment, economic, 5
Manners, 77, 79-80
Marxist Quarterly, 72, 87
Materialism, Northern, 77
Meaning, problems of, 18, 20, 105, 140, see also Significance
Memorials, 5n, 10
Memory, 10
Mercantilism, 43, 73
Metaphysics, 119-120, 122, 136
Method: dialectic, 121-122; historical, 23-26, 30-35, 37-42, 44, 50-51, 55, 90-91, 106, 113, 128-129, 133-134, 136-139; scientific, 24-25, 30-34, 47, 51, 91, 112, 120, 124-126, 129, 135, 138
Mexican War, 58-59
Michigan, University of, 23-24
Minorities, 74

Missouri, 64
Missouri Compromise, 59, 64
Morality, 8, 61-64, 73, 84-85, 88, 90
Mores, 87
Motivation, 55, 62-63, 69, 71, 75, 78, 81, 86-87, 89, 91-92, 122-125, 129-130
Municipal history, 36-37

Nation, 37
Nationalism, 29-31, 38, 44-45, 49, 62, 65-66, 74
Natural science, 8n, 11-12, 25, 51, 115, 129, 137n, see also Biological science, Physical science
Nature, human and physical, 6
Nazism, 19
Negroes, free, 59, 66, 73, 87
Nevada, 68
New England Emigrant Aid Society, 58
New Mexico, 64
Normal times, concept of, 6-7

Objectivity, 22-23, 25, 30-31, 34, 42-43, 50, 55, 86-87, 91, 124-126
Observation, 5n, 8, 10, 90-91, 130
Occasion vs. cause, 115
Opinion, public, 4, 40, 74, 82, 86-87
Oregon, 59
Organization: of data, 14, 17, 71, 105, 135-136; international, 19; social, 66, 80-81

Panic of 1857, 71
Particulars, 123, 127, 133-134
Pearl Harbor, attack on, 20
Pennsylvania, University of, 23
Periodicity, 120
Personal factors, influence of, 86-87, 91, 125-127, 135
Philology, 38
Physical science, 10, 105-106, 108-109, 128, 138-140, see also Natural science
Pickens, Fort, 82
Polemics, 8-9
Policy, formation and validation of, 3-6, 8, 11, 134-135

Political history, 26, 28, 33-42, 45, 47, 51
"Political man," 8-9
Politics: domestic, 29, 35-36, 67-68, 70, 76, 88; power, 20
Popular Science Monthly, 50
Populists, 44
Practical affairs, conduct of, 3-7
Predestination, definition of, 119-120
Prediction, 8, 13, 20-21, 30, 110, 113-114, 116, 119
Prejudice, see Bias
Prestige, 31
Probability, 112-114, 119-120
Production, 122-123
Professionalization, of history, 24-27, 30-32, 35-36, 40, 62
Progress, definition of, 116-117
Progressivism, 44, 47-48, 89
Proof, history as, 3-4
Propaganda, 20, 61, 63, 138
Property, 79-80, 87
Propositions: as basis of knowledge, viii-ix, 10-11, 14, 107, 133-136; classes of, 124
Prosperity, 81, 88
Publishers, see Textbooks
Puritanism, 29

Racism, 38, 56, 78-79
Railroads, 70, 76
Reason, 89, 121
Reconstruction, 14, 72, 88
Record, history as, 5n, 133, 135
Regionalism, see Sectionalism
"Relativism," 22-23
Relativity, historical, 128
Reliability, 109, 111, 128-129
Religion, 28-29, 63-64, 84
Repetition, of history, 6-7, 11, 137
Republican Party, 58, 62, 67-68, 70, 72, 74-76, 79-80, 82-83
Revolution: American, 30, 41-42, 109-110; Civil War as, 69, 71, 73-74; French, 30, 109; Russian, 19, 109-110, 113-114
Rise of American Civilization, 18
Romanticism, 22, 77

Sarajevo, 115
Science: nature of, 19, 25; and religion, 28; spirit of, 127, 134, 136-139; see also Method, Natural science, Social science
"Scientific historians," 19, 23, 25-27, 30-34, 36-37, 40-41, 43, 45, 47, 50-52, 111, 115
Secession, 57-60, 62-64, 67-70, 72-75, 80-83, 85, 87
Sectionalism, 26, 44, 46, 48, 57, 61-65, 68, 78-79, 83-87, 89
Selection, 14, 17-23, 25-28, 34, 36-37, 41, 44, 50-51, 56, 71, 87, 111-113, 125-126, 133, 135-136
Significance, of the past, 18-21; see also Interpretation, Meaning
Slavery, 55-68, 70, 72-80, 82-85, 87-88, 90
Slogans, 84-85
Snell's law, 115
Social change, 10, 120-121
Social science, related to history, vii, 7-13, 19, 25, 28, 33-34, 47, 50, 105, 107, 134-135, 138-140
Sources, 32, 133-134
South Carolina, 82
Stages, of history, 6
State rights, 62-63, 65
Style, ix, 9, 108
Subjectivity, 22, 87, 91
Sumter, Fort, 58, 60, 77, 81-82, 89, 113
Supreme Court, see United States Supreme Court

Tariff, 70-72, 84
Technology, 21
Terminology, ix, 5n, 14, 105-130, 133-134, 140
Territories, of the United States, 59, 64, 67-68, 74, 77, 80-82, 84, 87
Testing: of hypotheses, 31, 123-124, 126; see also Verification
Teutonic "origins," 19, 25, 34-41, 46
Texas, annexation of, 58-59, 64
Textbooks, 87, 89
Theology, 28-29

INDEX OF SUBJECTS

Time, as factor in understanding, 18-21, 83
Totality, 7, 111-112, 122, 133, 135
Traditionalists, among historians, 26-27, 33, 50
Truth, 9-10, 12, 43, 90, 107, 111-112, 120, 123-124, 128, *see also* Verification

Uncle Tom's Cabin, 58, 63
Underground Railway, 58
Understanding, 5, 13, 18-22, 25, 43-44, 47-52, 56, 74, 107, 113, 120-122, 127-130, 134, 137-138
Unique case, 9, 11, 113, 128-129, 134, 138
United States Census, 70
United States Congress, 58-59, 67, 73-74, 84

United States Supreme Court, 59, 86

Validity, 4, 10-12, 108-109, 113, 124, 126, 128, 138, 140n
Valuation, 128
Values, 55, 77, 109, 117-119, 126-127
Verification, 10-12, 91, 112, 117, 121, 124, 127-130
Vicksburg, 115
Virginia, 82

Wilmot Proviso, 58, 67-68, 84
Wisconsin, University of, 23, 37
World War I, 19-20, 89, 115
World War II, 20-21, 89
Written history, 5n, 7, 12, 17-18, 85-86, 106, 133-135, 136n